P9-DDT-031

More Praise for the Second Edition of *Mergers & Acquisitions from A to Z*

"Sherman and Hart have done a terrific job assembling and synthesizing the basic, yet critical, issues to be aware of before/during/after the deal. A well-rounded, up-to-date primer filled with pragmatic information that will serve as an excellent reference regardless of the reader's M&A experience."

—Edward J. Hayes, Jr.
Executive Vice President and Chief Financial Officer
Quantum Corporation

"After reading Andrew's book, it became clear that his insight and processes assist entrepreneurs looking to expand their businesses. Andrew's book offers guidance for non–U.S.-based businesses considering mergers and acquisitions in the United States."

—Nancye Miller, CEO, EO
The Entrepreneurs' Organization

MERGERS & ACQUISITIONS FROM A TO Z

SECOND EDITION

Andrew J. Sherman
and Milledge A. Hart

AMACOM
American Management Association
New York • Atlanta • Brussels • Chicago • Mexico City • San Francisco
Shanghai • Tokyo • Toronto • Washington, D.C.

*Special discounts on bulk quantities of AMACOM books are available to corporations, professional associations, and other organizations. For details, contact Special Sales Department, AMACOM, a division of American Management Association, 1601 Broadway, New York, NY 10019.
Tel.: 212-903-8316. Fax: 212-903-8083.
Web site: www.amacombooks.org*

Library of Congress Cataloging-in-Publication Data

Sherman, Andrew J.
Mergers & acquisitions from A to Z / Andrew J. Sherman and Milledge A. Hart.— 2nd ed.
p. cm.
Includes bibliographical references and index.
ISBN 0-8144-0880-X
1. Consolidation and merger of corporations. 2. Small business—Mergers. I. Hart, Milledge A. II. Title.

HD58.8.S484 2006
658.1'62—dc22

2005016449

Printing number

10 9 8 7 6 5 4 3 2 1

THIS BOOK IS DEDICATED TO
MAX AND SUSIE JOFFE
AND
TO THE MEMORIES OF
BERNIE AND HELEN HUNTER AND
M. GARY GOLDMAN.
I THANK THEM FOR THEIR NEVER-ENDING SUPPORT.
—Andrew J. Sherman

THIS BOOK IS DEDICATED TO MY WIFE, PATTI,
WITH LOVE AND GRATITUDE.
—Milledge A. Hart

Contents

List of Exhibits

List of Boxed Material

Acknowledgments

The authors would like to thank the team at AMACOM—namely Jacqueline Flynn, Mike Sivilli, and Niels Buessem—for all of their hard work on the editing and organization of the manuscript.

Andrew would like to thank his partners at Dickstein Shapiro Morin & Oshinsky for their support and encouragement, especially Mike Nannes, Fred Lowther, and Jim Kelly. Chapter 6 would not have been possible without the excellent input from Myron Mintz (tax and benefits), Milton Marquis (antitrust), Andrew Cooper (environmental), and Steve Walter (HSR). As always, Jo Lynch was a key player in pulling everything together and helping to produce an organized manuscript. And for the fourteenth time I gratefully acknowledge my wife Judy, son Matthew, and daughter Jennifer for tolerating my writing at the dining room table when we should have all been together having fun.

Milledge would like to thank the entire team at Pagemill Partners for their encouragement and support, especially the tremendous help provided by Christian Bennett and Karl Rinderknecht, who were instrumental in this endeavor.

MERGERS & ACQUISITIONS FROM A TO Z

SECOND EDITION

Introduction

In business there is one simple rule: grow or die. Companies on a growth path will take away market share from competitors, create economic profits, and provide returns to shareholders. Those that do not grow tend to stagnate, lose customers and market share, and destroy shareholder value. Mergers and acquisitions (M&A) play a critical role in both sides of this cycle—enabling strong companies to grow faster than competition and providing entrepreneurs rewards for their efforts, and ensuring weaker companies are more quickly swallowed, or worse, made irrelevant through exclusion and ongoing share erosion.

Mergers and acquisitions are a vital part of any healthy economy and importantly, the primary way that companies are able to provide returns to owners and investors. This fact, combined with the potential for large returns, make acquisition a highly attractive way for entrepreneurs and owners to capitalize on the value created in a company. Exhibit I-1 illustrates this point from the perspective of the venture-backed company. In the past five years, 92 percent of liquidity events from venture capital funded firms were realized via merger and acquisitions, with only 8 percent of these companies achieving liquidity through an initial public offering (IPO).

Starting a company and selling it can be the fastest way to create substantive wealth. While it is difficult to start a successful company, the economic rewards are tremendous. The authors of this book have enabled transactions that created enormous value for shareholders. In one case, a two-year-old technology company had only $150,000 of invested capital and zero revenue, yet was able to obtain a $13 million sale price. Another transaction involved a 30-year-old, second-generation, family-run business that provided nearly $30 million to the family shareholders. A merger or acquisi-

Exhibit I-1. Mergers and acquisitions vs. IPOs: 1995–2004.

Year	Venture Backed IPO	Venture Backed M&A
2004	67	376
2003	22	332
2002	20	379
2001	22	402
2000	202	459
1999	250	304
1998	68	253
1997	120	232
1996	216	199
1995	143	160

0% 20% 40% 60% 80% 100%

■ Venture Backed IPO □ Venture Backed M&A

SOURCE: *VentureOne.*

tion is frequently the happy ending to the tales written by productive and fortunate entrepreneurs.

Mergers and acquisitions have played a variety of roles in corporate history, ranging from the "greed is good" corporate raiders buying companies in a hostile manner and breaking them apart, to today's trend to use mergers and acquisitions for external growth and industry consolidation.

During the 1980s, nearly half of all U.S. companies were restructured, over 80,000 were acquired or merged, and over 700,000 sought bankruptcy protection in order to reorganize and continue operations. The 1980s featured swashbucklers and aggressive tactics to gain control over targets. The 1990s were equally dynamic in terms of companies evolving through upsizing and growth, downsizing, roll-ups, divestitures, and consolidation, but with a different focus on operational synergies, scale efficiencies, increases in customer bases, strategic alliances, market share, and access to new technologies. This period, however, came to a crashing end with the bursting of the tech bubble and the global recession that followed.

The more recent wave of M&A activity seen since mid-2004 has been driven by the more general macroeconomic recovery and several key trends. First, many companies have exhausted cost cutting and operational efficiencies as a means to increase profitability, and are looking to top-line growth as a primary enabler of shareholder return. The increased pressure to grow highlights the opportunity to achieve growth through acquisition. Second, the M&A market has been supported by the return of corporate profits and with it, improved stock price valuation. The improved valuations have enabled corporations to leverage their internal currencies to acquire target companies who are willing to swap their illiquid private stock for valuable public company shares. Third, interest rates have hovered at historical lows, enabling firms to cost-effectively utilize debt to finance acquisition-based growth.

In 2004, 31,233 deals transactions were announced worldwide, a 9 percent increase over the 28,702 announcements in 2003. These transactions were valued at $1.9 trillion, a 39 percent increase over the $1.4 trillion worth of transactions in 2003 (see Exhibit I-2). The U.S. marketplace saw 8,504 of these 28,702 transactions, valued at $841 billion.

In addition to the aforementioned macroeconomic forces, many large industries have seen strong consolidation trends, with energy and power, financial services, and telecommunications leading the way by deal value, and high technology leading in terms of the total number of deals (see Exhibit I-3).

Exhibit I-2. Worldwide transactions: May 2002–May 2005.

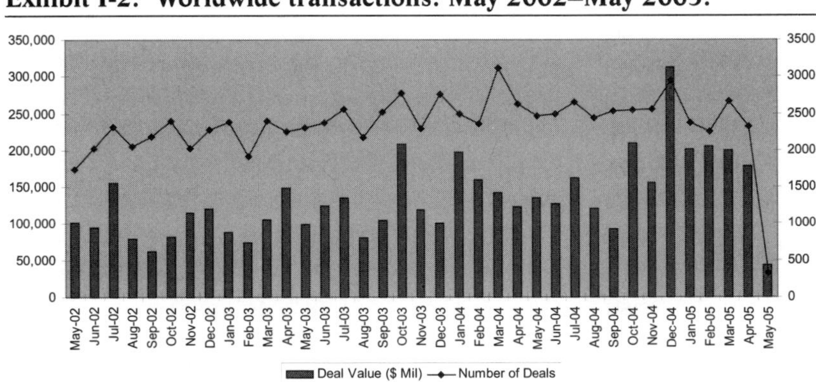

SOURCE: Thomson Financial.

Exhibit I-3. Last twelve-months' deal activity by industry sector (as of May 2005).

Target Macro Industry	Deal Value ($ Mil)	Mkt. Share	Number of Deals	Average Deal Size ($ Mil)
Energy and Power	327,947	15.6	2188	$150
Financials	305,841	14.6	3835	$80
Telecommunications	209,831	10.0	957	$219
Real Estate	178,132	8.5	1382	$129
Media and Entertainment	165,446	7.9	2363	$70
Industrials	157,365	7.5	3892	$40
Materials	145,673	6.9	3131	$47
Healthcare	141,880	6.8	1699	$84
Retail	128,631	6.1	1467	$88
High Technology	123,727	5.9	4348	$28
Consumer Products and Services	123,163	5.9	2930	$42
Consumer Staples	92,676	4.4	2022	$46
Government and Agencies	903	0.0	34	$27
Industry Total	2,101,215	100.0	30,250	$69

SOURCE: Thomson Financial.

The telecommunications industry, in particular, has been transformed by merger activity in the last 18 months. After nearly $100 billion in deal making, Verizon Communications and SBC Communications have emerged as two giants set to dominate the industry. These two companies control end-to-end connections from copper to the home to mobile telephony—a power position not seen since the days before the 1982 Justice Department ordered the breakup of AT&T. With Verizon's acquisition of MCI in response to SBC's purchase of AT&T, these telephony giants will own nearly 87 percent of the business market for telephony and data communications. Companies like BellSouth and Qwest were left out of the merger frenzy, and as such, are in substantially inferior competitive positions.

Finally, this decade is decidedly marked by the return of the mega-deal. It seems that nearly every week a large, industry redefining transaction is announced. Whether it is the oil and gas industry continuing to consolidate or the telecommunications sector returning to the structure before AT&T's breakup, today's headlines are riddled with news about massive structural change. Listed in Exhibit I-4 are the largest ten deals announced in the six months prior to May 2005.

Exhibit I-4. Ten largest deals: October 2004–April 2005.

Date Announced	Target Name	Acquirer Name	Value ($mil)
10/28/2004	Shell Transport & Trading Co	Royal Dutch Petroleum Co	80,088.37
1/28/2005	Gillette Co	Procter & Gamble Co	57,226.81
12/15/2004	Nextel Communications Inc	Sprint Corp	46,513.70
2/18/2005	UFJ Holdings Inc	Mitsubishi Tokyo Financial Grp	41,431.03
12/7/2004	Telecom Italia Mobile SpA	Telecom Italia SpA	28,820.69
12/20/2004	Public Svc Enterprise Grp Inc	Exelon Corp	27,356.59
12/15/2004	Guidant Corp	Johnson & Johnson Inc	25,020.48
1/31/2005	AT&T Corp	SBC Communications Inc	22,076.11
12/23/2004	Almanij NV	KBC Bank & Insurance Holding	20,891.21
4/4/2005	Unocal Corp	ChevronTexaco Corp	18,919.22

SOURCE: Thomson Financial.

In addition to the substantial activity from large industry players, financial buyers have increased the scale, scope, and visibility of their transactions. While these companies no longer employ the junk-debt style leveraged buyouts that were popular in the 1980s, they now compete for large deals via large buyout funds and consortium behavior. The Carlyle Group, a premier private equity firm run by former IBM CEO Louis Gerstner, illustrates this scale phenomenon precisely. In 2004, The Carlyle Group returned $5.3 billion to investors, invested $2.7 billion, and raised another $7.8 billion in capital for acquisition purposes. In addition, many of these large private equity firms are starting to collectively compete for large deals. In March of 2005, a consortium of financial buyers took Sungard Data Systems private in a transaction valued at $11.3 billion dollars. Leading private equity firms Silver Lake Partners, Bain Capital, The Blackstone Group, Goldman Sachs Capital Partners, Kohlberg Kravis Roberts & Co. L.P., Providence Equity Partners and Texas Pacific Group worked collaboratively to complete the buyout. This transaction is particularly noteworthy in that it is the largest leveraged buyout since KKR bought RJR Nabisco for $25 billion in 1988, and it is the largest buyout of a technology company.

Yet with so many dollars changing hands, there remains a very limited number of readily available resources for business executives and professional advisors to turn to for strategic and legal guidance. This book is intended to be such a resource.

There is no more complicated transaction than a merger or acquisition. The various issues raised are broad and complex, from valuation and deal structure, to tax and securities laws. The industries affected by this rapid activity are also diverse, from banking and computer software companies, to retailers and healthcare organizations. It seems that virtually every executive of every major industry faces a buy or sell decision at some point during his or her tenure as leader of the company. In fact, it is estimated that some executives spend as much as one third of their time considering merger and acquisition opportunities and other structural business decisions. As we will see in the chapters to follow, the strategic reasons for considering such transactions are also numerous, from achieving economies of scale, to mitigating cash flow risk via diversification, to satisfying shareholder hunger for steady growth and dividends.

The federal government's degree of intervention in these transactions varies from administration to administration, depending on the issues and concerns of the day. During the Reagan-Bush years, the government took a passive role, generally allowing market forces to determine whether a given transaction would have an anti-competitive effect. During the Clinton years, regulatory bodies took a more proactive approach, with more intervention by the U.S. Department of Justice and the Federal Trade Commission, such as a refusal to provide the necessary approval for the proposed merger of Staples and Office Depot in mid-1997. The current Bush administration, however, has taken a more laissez-faire approach only to have the European Union take a more aggressive role in preventing potentially anti-competitive mergers. The European Competition Commission's landmark rejection of GE's 2001 proposed acquisition of Honeywell signified a shift in the role that the EU played in the global M&A marketplace.

This book will *not* focus on the mechanics of the mega-mergers of recent years, such as the private equity consortium purchase of Sungard for $11.3 billion, the Shell Transport & Trading Co acquisition by Royal Dutch Petroleum Co valued at $80 billion, or the

$46 billion Nextel-Sprint merger. Nor will it address the recent trend by overseas companies to buy in to the U.S. market via acquisitions in the banking, computer, and telecommunications industries. When the value of a transaction is $1 billion or more, there is a team of skilled investment bankers and professional advisors quarterbacking the transaction, and in such cases the importance of this book will be less.

But what about the thousands and thousands of transactions each year that range from $1 million at the low end to $100 million at the high end? Where do these small- and middle-market company executives turn for guidance? For many of these executives, mergers and acquisitions represent a digestible and manageable strategy for business growth. Buying an additional $2.5 million, or even $25 million, in sales or profits may be easier, faster, and more profitable than building it from scratch.

Recent years have seen a significant increase in merger and acquisition activity within industries that are growing rapidly and evolving overall, such as in health care, information technology, communications, and software development, as well as in traditional industries such as manufacturing, consumer products, and food services. Many developments reflect an increase in strategic buyers and a decrease in the amount of leverage, implying that these deals were being done because they made sense for both parties, which is different from the highly leveraged, financially driven deals of the late 1980s.

The middle-market transaction is the clear focus of this book. Fortunately for that audience, middle-market transactions continue to attract compelling valuations. In the twelve-month period ending in April 2005, deals in the $25 million to $100 million transaction value had an 8.5 × EBITDA multiple (EBITDA, also known as earnings before interest tax depreciation and amortization, is considered a decent approximation of pre-tax cash flow). See Exhibit I-5.

Companies in this segment need to understand the key drivers of valuation since they are often able to focus their operating goals in order to maximize the potential valuation range. Therefore it is important to know that the multiple a company achieves for its business directly correlates with the following seven characteristics:

1. Strong revenue growth
2. Significant market share or strong niche position

3. A market with barriers to entry by competitors
4. A strong management team
5. Strong, stable cash flow
6. No significant concentration in customers, products, suppliers, or geographic markets
7. Low risk of technological obsolescence or product substitution

Exhibit I-5. Last twelve-months' transaction multiples (as of April 27, 2005).

By Size ($ in millions)	EBIT	EBITDA
Less than $25	5.9×	4.7×
$25 to $100	11.7×	8.5×
$100 to $250	11.8×	8.4×
$250 to $1,000	16.7×	10.8×
Over $1,000	16.3×	12.7×

SOURCE: Thomson Financial Securities Data Corporation. Based on multiples between 0× and 25×d; excluding media and telecom.

Successful mergers and acquisitions are neither an art nor a science but a *process.* In fact, regression analysis demonstrates that the number one determinant of deal multiples is the growth rate of the business. The higher the growth rate, the higher the multiple of cash flow the business is worth.

A study of deals that close with both buyer and seller satisfied show that the deal followed a sequence, a pattern, a series of steps that have been tried and tested. This book focuses on conveying this process to the reader, as we learn to understand the objectives of both buyer and seller in Chapters 2 and 3, through the process of negotiations and closing in Chapters 4 through 10, to closing and beyond in Chapters 11, 12, and 13.

For example, when a deal is improperly valued, one side wins big while the other loses big. By definition, a transaction is a failure if it does not create value for shareholders and the easiest way to fail, therefore, is to pay too high a price. To be successful, a transaction must be fair and balanced, reflecting the economic needs of both buyer and seller, and convey real and durable value to the shareholders of both companies. Achieving this involves a review and analysis of financial statements, a genuine understanding of how the proposed transaction meets the economic objectives of each party, and a recognition of the tax, accounting, and legal implications of the deal.

A transaction as complex as a merger or acquisition is fraught with potential problems and pitfalls. Many of these problems arise either in the preliminary stages, such as forcing a deal that shouldn't really be done (i.e., some couples were just never meant to be married); as a result of mistakes, errors, or omissions owing to inadequate, rushed, or misleading due diligence; in not properly allocating risks during the negotiation of definitive documents; or because it became a nightmare to integrate the companies after closing. These pitfalls can lead to expensive and protracted litigation unless an alternative method of dispute resolution is negotiated and included in the definitive documents. This book is designed to share the pitfalls of such transactions, with the hope that buyers and sellers and their advisors can avoid these problems in their future transactions.

Finally, with merger and acquisition activity continuing to grow at rapid rates, entrepreneurs and venture capitalists continuing to form new entities and pursue new market opportunities, it is critical to have a firm grasp on the key drivers and inhibitors of any potential deal. With so much money on the line, it is essential to understand how to maximize price and valuation goals while ensuring the transaction is successfully consummated.

CHAPTER 1

The Basics of Mergers and Acquisitions

Over the past decade, we have seen countless examples of companies, such as General Electric, Citigroup and Cisco, that have grown dramatically and built revenues through an aggressive acquisition program. After a pause in the early part of the twenty-first century, the wave of consolidations, mergers, and acquisitions is once again moving to record heights in the United States and is sweeping through the small- and middle-market company sector of our economy. After several years of downsizing, cost cutting, and slow growth, seasoned executives and entrepreneurs are searching for efficient and profitable ways to increase revenues and win market share. The growth options are as follows: organic, inorganic, or by external means. Examples of *organic* growth are hiring additional salespeople, developing new products, or expanding geographically. The best example of *inorganic* growth is an acquisition of another firm, often done to gain access to a new product line, customer segment, or geography. Finally, *external* revenue growth opportunities are franchising, licensing, joint ventures, strategic alliances, and the appointment of overseas distributors, which are available to growing companies as an alternative to mergers and acquisitions as a growth engine. This book focuses primarily on mergers and acquisitions as a means to grow, although toward the end of the book we explore certain external opportunities as well.

Understanding Key Terms

The terms *merger* and *acquisition* are often confused or used interchangeably. It is important to understand the difference between the two. A technical definition of the words from David L. Scott in *Wall Street Words: An A to Z Guide to Investment Terms for Today's Investor* follows:

- *Merger:* A combination of two or more companies in which the assets and liabilities of the selling firm(s) are absorbed by the buying firm. Although the buying firm may be a considerably different organization after the merger, it retains its original identity. The merger of equals between Sprint and Nextel is an example.
- *Acquisition:* The purchase of an asset such as a plant, a division, or even an entire company. For example, Procter & Gamble made a major acquisition in 2005 when it purchased The Gillette Company, Inc., in order to extend its reach in the consumer products industry.

On the surface, the distinction in meaning may not really matter, since the net result is often the same: two companies (or more) that had separate ownership are now operating under the same roof, usually to obtain some strategic or financial objective. Yet the strategic, financial, tax, and even cultural impact of a deal may be very different, depending on the type of transaction. A *merger* typically refers to two companies joining together (usually through the exchange of shares) as peers to become one. An *acquisition* typically has one company—the *buyer*—that purchases the assets or shares of the *seller,* with the form of payment being cash, the securities of the buyer, or other assets of value to the seller. In a *stock purchase* transaction, the seller's shares are not necessarily combined with the buyer's existing company, but often kept separate as a new subsidiary or operating division. In an *asset purchase* transaction, the assets conveyed by the seller to the buyer become additional assets of the buyer's company, with the hope and expectation that the value of the assets purchased will exceed the price paid over time, thereby enhancing shareholder value as a result of the strategic or financial benefits of the transaction.

M&A Basics: Buy vs. Build

At the heart of all decisions regarding mergers and acquisitions is a fundamental question: Are we better off *buying* a new capability, market entry, customer base, earnings opportunity, etc. or attempting to *build* it ourselves? The dedication of financial and human resources to organize growth must be based on long-term, sustainable value creation to the company's stakeholders, but may require more patience to achieve these objectives and may result in some lost opportunities. The allocation of resources to M&A will tend to expedite the achievement of growth objectives, but also increase the *level of risk* if deals are not structured and negotiated properly. What variables should a growing company consider in striking the right balance between organic growth (*build*) vs. mergers and acquisitions (*buy*)? These include:

- The competitiveness, fragmentation and pace of your marketplace and industry
- The access to and cost of capital
- The specific capabilities of your management and advisory teams
- The strength and growth potential of your current core competencies
- The volatility and loyalty of your distributions channels and customer base
- The degree to which speed to market and scale are critical in your business (including typical customer acquisition costs and timeframes)
- The degree to which your company operates in a regulated industry

What's All the Fuss About?

What factors have fueled the current resurgence of merger and acquisition activity? There is no one explanation, and the full impact on the economy is complex and remains to be seen, but there are certain themes and trends that have emerged. The ten key reasons deals are getting done today are:

1. Mergers can be the most effective and efficient way to enter a new market, add a new product line, or increase distribution reach.

2. Mergers and acquisitions are more strategically motivated than in the past. One key trend in M&A is to acquire a company to access today's "knowledge worker" and to obtain the intellectual property. Many technology companies—such as Cisco, Google and Yahoo!—pursue acquisitions as a means to get the employees in addition to the products and intellectual property.

3. The financing behind the deal is more sound and secure than ever before. Companies continue to use their stock as currency giving the seller potential upside in the combined entity. This motivates both parties to work together on a post-closing basis to truly *enhance* shareholder value. In addition, third-party financing is more readily available. The number of financing sources has continued to grow giving middle market companies more access to capital than in the past.

4. Mergers and acquisitions are being driven in many cases by a key trend within a given industry, such as:

   a. Rapidly changing technology, which is driving many of the deals in high technology.
   b. Fierce competition, which is driving many of the deals in the telecommunications and banking industries.
   c. Changing consumer preferences, which is driving many of the deals in the food and beverage industry.
   d. The pressure to control costs, which is driving many of the deals in the healthcare industry.
   e. A reduction in demand, such as the shrinking federal defense budget, which is driving the consolidation in the aerospace and defense contractor industries.

5. Some deals are motivated by the need to transform corporate identity. In 2003, videogame company Infogrames, for example, gained instant worldwide recognition by acquiring and adopting the old but famous Atari brand. Similarly, First Union adopted the

brand of acquisition target Wachovia in hopes of benefiting from Wachovia's reputation of quality and customer service.

6. Many deals are fueled by the need to spread the risk and cost of:
   a. Developing new technologies, such as in the communications and aerospace industries.
   b. Research into new medical discoveries, such as in the medical device and pharmaceutical industries.
   c. Gaining access to new sources of energy, such as in the oil and gas exploration and drilling industries.

7. The global village has forced many companies to explore mergers and acquisitions as a means to develop an international presence and expanded market share. This market penetration strategy is often more cost-effective than trying to build an overseas operation from scratch.

8. Many recent mergers and acquisitions come about with the recognition that a complete product or service line may be necessary to remain competitive or to balance seasonal or cyclical market trends. Transactions in the retail, hospitality, food and beverage, entertainment, and financial services industries have been in response to consumer demand for "one-stop shopping."

9. Many deals are driven by the premise that it is less expensive to buy brand loyalty and customer relationships than it is to build them. Buyers are paying a premium for this intangible asset on the balance sheet, which is often referred to as goodwill. In today's economy, goodwill represents an asset that is very important but which is not adequately reflected on the seller's balance sheet. Veteran buyers know that long-standing customer and other strategic relationships that will be conveyed with the deal have far greater value than machinery and inventory.

10. Some acquisitions happen out of competitive necessity. If an owner of a business decides to sell a business, every potential buyer realizes that their competitors may buy the target, and in so doing, must evaluate whether they would prefer to be the owner of the business for sale.

The motivation for the deal, and the underlying goals and objectives for the transaction on a post-closing basis, often affects the structure of the transaction, pricing and valuation issues, and the ability to obtain necessary third-party or governmental approvals.

Why Bad Deals Happen to Good People

Nobody ever plans to enter into a bad deal. But many well-intentioned entrepreneurs and business executives enter into mergers and acquisitions that they later regret. Classic mistakes include a lack of adequate planning, an overly aggressive timetable to closing, a failure to really look at possible post-closing integration problems, or, worst of all, the projected synergies that were intended to be achieved turn out to be illusory.

As evident in the ten key reasons for today's deals, the underlying theme is the goal of post-closing synergy. What is synergy and how can you be sure to get some? The key premise to *synergy* is that the "whole will be greater than the sum of its parts." But the quest for synergy can be deceptive, especially if there is inadequate communication between buyer and seller, a situation that usually leads to a misunderstanding regarding what the buyer is really buying and the seller is really selling. Every company says that it wants synergy when doing a deal, but few take the time to develop a transactional team, draw up a joint mission statement of the objectives of the deal, or solve post-closing operating or financial problems on a timely basis.

Why Do Buyers Buy, and Why Do Sellers Sell?

In Chapters 2 and 3, we'll look at the basic reasons why a buyer buys and a seller sells in the context of a merger or acquisition. The goal here is twofold: (1) to educate you as a prospective buyer or seller on how to define your own goals and objectives; and (2) to provide some insight into the motivations of the other party to the transaction, which will usually facilitate a more successful and mutually rewarding transaction.

The Cyclical Nature of Mergers and Acquisitions

The mergers and acquisitions activity is often driven by cycles—both at a macro level in the overall marketplace driven by such factors as the availability of capital and state of the economy, and at a micro level based upon where this *particular* buyer or seller stands in their growth plans or life cycle. Some acquiring companies are early on in the cycle and may be looking for their first major deal as a platform for additional acquisitions, while others may be nearing the end of their cycle and are only looking for smaller "tuck-in" transactions. Other buyers may now appear to be more like sellers, since they are now in the phase of the cycle where they have digested what they have purchased and are ready to divest themselves of assets which have not been a strong fit or which have failed to meet their strategic objectives. The M&A strategic cycle in some ways mimics the human digestive cycle:

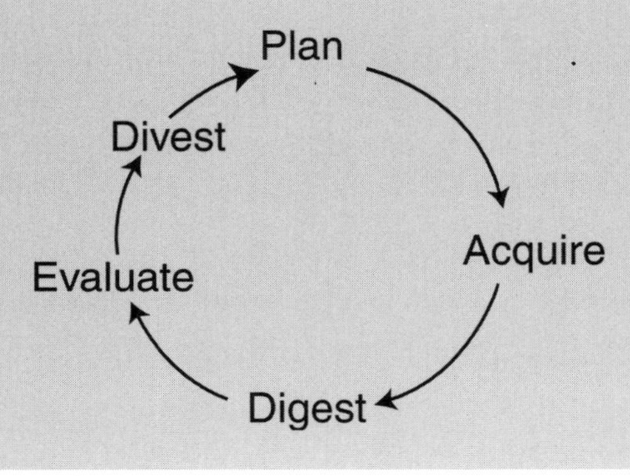

Motivations in an Acquisition

For the seller, the key "motivators" in an acquisition (which will be discussed in more detail in Chapter 2) usually include one or more of the following:

- Ownership nearing retirement or ready for an exit
- Inability to compete as an independent concern
- The need or desire to obtain cost savings through economies of scale
- Access to the greater resources of the acquiring company

For the buyer, the key "motivators" in an acquisition (which will be discussed in more detail in Chapter 3) usually include one or more of the following:

- Revenue enhancement
- Cost reduction
- Vertical and/or horizontal operational synergies or economies of scale
- Growth pressures from investors
- Underutilized resources
- A desire to reduce the number of competitors (increase market share and reduce price competition)
- A need to gain a foothold in a new geographic market (especially if the current market is saturated)
- A desire to diversify into new products and services

Motivations in a Merger

It is important to note that a merger is a different animal from an acquisition and thus a different set of objectives typically emerges for either party:

- To restructure the industry value chain
- To respond to competitive cost pressures through economies of scale and scope (e.g., HP/Compaq)
- To improve process engineering and technology
- To increase the scale of production in existing product lines
- To find additional uses for existing management talent
- To redeploy excess capital in more profitable or complementary uses
- To obtain tax benefits

In a classic merger, there is no buyer or seller, though one party may be quarterbacking the transaction or have initiated the discussion. Therefore, the culture and spirit of the negotiations are different from those for an acquisition. In a merger, data gathering and due diligence are two-way and mutual, with each party positioning its contribution to the post-merger entity to justify its respective equity share, management, and control of the new company.

Common Seller and Buyer Motivations

Common Seller Motivations	*Common Buyer Motivations*
The desire to retire	The desire to grow
Lack of successors	Opportunity to increase profits
Business adversities	Desire to diversify
Inability to compete	Value-driven acquisition strategy
Lack of capital to grow	Buying up competitors
Inadequate distribution system	Using excess capital
To eliminate personal guarantees or other personal obligations	Achieving new distribution channels or efficiencies
No ability to diversify	Diversify into new products or geographic markets
Age and health concerns	Particular people, existing business or assets are needed
Particular amount of money is needed for estate planning	Access to new or emerging technologies
Irreconcilable conflict among owners	Need to efficiently deploy key people or resources
Losing key people or key customers	Strategic fit between buyer and seller's current operations

Before turning to the details of structuring and negotiating these complex transactions, let's take a look at the individual perspective of both buyer and seller in Chapters 2 and 3. An understanding of each party's goals and objectives is critical to understanding the overall dynamics of the transaction.

Preparing for the Dance

The Seller's Perspective

Two houses in my neighborhood recently went up for sale. The sellers took very different approaches to preparing for the transaction. One couple, who were nearing retirement, began the process almost two years ago. Every weekend they would work on a different part of the house or garden, taking steps to increase the value and hence raise the ultimate selling price. The proceeds represented the bulk of their retirement nest egg, and every dollar of value was critical. Naturally, there were certain items that could not be specifically addressed, such as new wallpaper and paint, because they did not know the needs and wants of the possible buyer. In such cases, steps were taken to make the rooms more generic, so as to appeal to the varying tastes of prospective buyers.

The other couple, in their mid-thirties with three young children, seemed as if they started preparing about one week before the first prospective buyer arrived. They were on their way to their next home, and although selling price mattered, it really only affected the size of their next mortgage. In fact, with three wild and destructive kids, it seemed that they were taking steps to decrease the value of the house on a weekly basis! Clearly, their approach to the buyer was, "Take it as is and perhaps it will meet your needs." Prospective buyers came into the transaction knowing that a lot of time, care, and attention would need to go into the house after closing.

In many ways, these two approaches mirror the attitudes of sellers of businesses. Some companies become available for sale only after years of planning and preparation, with the sellers laying the groundwork for maximizing value. These sellers take the time to anticipate the needs and wants of different types of buyers, yet they realize that some items must be kept "plain vanilla" because each buyer will have different objectives and motivations. Other companies become available for sale owing to boredom of the founding entrepreneur or competitive or financial factors that may have only recently appeared.

Although each circumstance will be different, these sellers simply may not want to make the significant capital investments necessary to continue operations. Or the industry may have become less profitable, or there may be irreconcilable shareholder or management disputes driving the transaction. In these cases, the buyer is likely to be purchasing a "fixer-upper," and the price and valuation will be negotiated accordingly. In rare cases, the "hasty" decision to sell may be for positive reasons, such as an industry being perceived as hot by the financial markets, thereby creating an ability to sell at an increased price for a limited time. Or a competing business opportunity may have been presented and the company needs to diversify its assets in order to pursue that opportunity.

There are many reasons why the owners of a business may consider selling it, the most obvious of which is because businesses, like any asset, are valuable. Like many things of value, there is a market for the trade of companies—a market where people with different expectations for the future will value the same company differently, thus enabling a buyer and seller to come to a mutually agreeable "trade." Some of the common reasons companies are sold include:

- *Retirement*: The owner plans to retire.
- *Undercapitalization*: A significant infusion of cash is required to take the business to the next level.
- *Partner dispute or divorce*: A partner wants or needs to be "cashed out" due to dispute or divorce.
- *Reduce risk*: Owner wants to reduce risk from personal guarantees or liabilities.

- *Death or illness*: An owner or partner has a serious health issue.
- *Poor management*: Do not have the skills to manage the business.
- *New business idea*: Ready to move to next idea or opportunity.
- *Burnout*: Running a business full time can be overly consuming.
- *Relocation*: Some businesses are tied to specific locations and do not relocate well.
- *Serial entrepreneurship*: Some entrepreneurs are well qualified to build businesses to a certain level but then prefer to sell them and use the proceeds to build other businesses rather than take the existing company to the next level, which may require a skill set or level of patience that they are lacking.
- *Inadequate distribution system*: Channels are expensive to build; it is much easier to leverage a pre-established distribution system.
- *No ability to diversify*: The wealth of owner may be exclusively tied up in the business, creating substantial personal financial risk.
- *Estate planning*: Often with no family member as successor, a business needs to be sold for estate planning purposes.
- *Personnel*: Key people or key customers have been lost and the business needs new management to continue operations.

Selling Process and Seller's Decisional Path

Reaching the Decision to Sell

1. Understanding Your Motivations and Objectives
2. Building the Foundation for Value
3. Timing and Market Factors

Getting the House in Order

1. Assembling Your Advisory Team
2. Legal Audit and Housekeeping
3. Establishing Preliminary Valuation

4. Preparing the Offering Memorandum
5. Estate and Exit Planning

Marketing Strategy

1. Targeting Qualified Buyers
2. Use of Third Party Intermediaries
3. Narrowing the Field of Candidates

Choosing a Dance Partner

1. Selecting the Most Qualified and Synergistic Candidate (or Financial Candidate, depending on your objectives)
2. Preliminary Negotiations
3. Execution of Confidentiality Agreement
4. Preliminary Due Diligence

Fighting It Out

1. Execution of More Detailed Letter of Intent or Memorandum of Understanding
2. Extensive Negotiations and Strategic Adjustments
3. Structuring the Deal
4. Accommodating the Buyer's Team for Legal and Strategic Due Diligence
5. Doing Due Diligence on the Buyer

Preparing for the Closing

1. Preparation and Negotiation of the Definitive Legal Documents
2. Meeting Conditions to Closing
3. Obtaining Key Third Party Consents

The Closing

Post-Closing Issues

1. Monitoring Post-Closing Compensation/Earn-Outs
2. Facilitating the Post-Closing Integration Plan
3. Post-Closing Challenges (see Chapter 12)

Regardless of the seller's specific motivations or timetable, an exit strategy and plan of action is critical to protect the value of the business. There is usually a direct correlation between the amount of time a seller spends preparing for the transaction and the price ultimately paid for the business.

Preparing for the Sale of the Company

From the seller's point of view, the key to the process is *preparation,* regardless of motivation for selling. This means taking all the necessary steps to prepare the company for sale from a corporate housekeeping perspective. A seller must anticipate the questions and concerns of a prospective buyer and be prepared to provide the appropriate information for review. In addition, a seller should understand the pricing parameters for selling the business in preparation of discussing the financial terms and conditions.

We suggest that the preparation process begins with a strategy meeting of all members of the seller's team. It is the job of the team to:

- Identify the financial and structural goals of the transaction.
- Develop an action plan and timetable.
- Understand the current market dynamics and potential pricing range for the business.
- Determine who are the logical buyers of the business any why the business for sale would be a compelling asset to each of the specific the target buyers.
- Identify the potential legal and financial hurdles to a successful transaction (e.g., begin thinking about what problems may be "transactional turnoffs" to a prospective buyer), such as unregistered trademarks, illegal securities sales, or difficulties in obtaining a third-party consent.
- Outline and draft the offering memorandum.
- Develop a definitive "to do" list in connection with corporate housekeeping matters, such as preparation of board and shareholder minutes and maintenance of regulatory filings.
- Identify how and when prospective buyers will be contacted, proposed terms evaluated, and final candidates selected.

STEP 1: Selecting the Seller's Team

One of the most important steps in the preparation process is the selection of a team of advisors to orchestrate the sale of the business. The team will help the company's internal preparation and create the offering memorandum which summarizes the key aspects of the company's operations, products and services, and personnel and financial performance. In many ways, this *offering memorandum* is akin to a traditional business plan, and serves both as a road map for the seller and an informational tool for the buyer.

When selecting members for the team, a seller should choose people who:

- Understand the seller's motivation, goals, and post-closing objectives.
- Are familiar with trends in the seller's industry.
- Have access to a network of potential buyers.
- Have a track record and experience in mergers and acquisitions with emerging growth and middle-market companies.
- Have expertise with the financing issues that will face prospective buyers.
- Know tax and estate planning issues that may affect the seller both at closing and beyond.

At a minimum, the team should include the following members:

1. *Investment Banker/Financial Advisor.* An investment banker or financial advisor counsels the seller on issues relating to market dynamics, trends, potential targets, valuation, pricing, and deal structure. He or she assists the seller in understanding the market, identifying and contacting prospective buyers, and in negotiating and evaluating offers. Finally, in many cases, multiple offers may have divergent structures and economic consequences for the seller, so evaluation of each offer is conducted by the banker.

2. *Certified Public Accountant.* A certified public accountant (CPA) assists the seller in preparing the financial statements and related reports that the buyer (or buyers) inevitably request. He or she advises the seller on the tax implications of the proposed transaction. The CPA also assists in estate planning and in structuring a

compensation package that maximizes the benefits associated with the proposed transaction.

3. *Legal Counsel.* The transactional attorney is responsible for a wide variety of duties, including:

a. Assisting the seller in pre-sale corporate "housekeeping," which involves cleaning up corporate records, developing strategies for dealing with dissident shareholders, and shoring up third-party contracts.
b. Working with the investment banker in helping evaluate competing offers.
c. Assisting in the negotiation and preparation of the letter of intent and confidentiality agreements such as Exhibit 2-1, which should be signed by all potential buyers who are provided access to the seller's books and records.
d. Negotiating definitive purchase agreements with buyer's counsel.
e. Working with the seller and the CPA in connection with certain post-closing and estate and tax planning matters.

Exhibit 2-1. Sample confidentiality agreement.

THIS CONFIDENTIALITY AGREEMENT ("Agreement") is made as of this _____ day of ________, 20___ by and among Company1, Inc., a __________ corporation ("Company1") and Company2, Inc., a __________ corporation ("Company2") and each of the undersigned representatives of each of Company1 and Company2, respectively (the "Representatives"). Company1 and Company2 are collectively referred to hereinafter as the "Parties."

WHEREAS, the Representatives executing this Agreement shall include, but are not limited to, the following individuals: On behalf of Company1, ____________________, and on behalf of Company2, ____________________; provided, however, that any additional Representatives also shall execute a copy of this Agreement;

WHEREAS, Representatives of the Parties intend to meet on __________, 20___ to discuss certain transactions related to the businesses of the Parties, including a potential purchase and sale transaction between the Parties or other possible combinations of Company1 and Company2 (all of which shall be referred to hereinafter as the "Transaction");

WHEREAS, each of the Representatives, in the course of meetings and discussions relating to the Transaction, may disclose certain confidential and proprietary information regarding each Party's business plans, financial and operational data, services, products, and product development plans;

WHEREAS, each of the Parties desires to protect its proprietary rights and further desires to prevent unauthorized disclosure of any information regarding

(continues)

Exhibit 2-1. Continued.

its individual business plans, financial and operational data, products and services;

WHEREAS, the Representatives collectively desire to prevent unauthorized disclosure by any one of them of any information regarding the Transaction and the business plans, financial and operational data, products and services associated therewith;

WHEREAS, the Parties intend to have the "confidential information" as defined below treated as being confidential and/or proprietary.

NOW, THEREFORE, in consideration of the premises and the mutual covenants contained herein, the parties agree as follows:

1. Definition of Confidential Information. In connection with the Transaction being discussed among the Representatives, each of the Parties and their Representatives may disclose certain information intended to remain as proprietary and confidential, including information regarding business plans, financial data, operational data, product development plans, products and services. The information furnished by either of the Parties or any Representative is hereinafter referred to as "Confidential Information" and such Confidential Information shall belong to the Party furnishing the same (through one or more of its Representatives) and shall be treated as Confidential Information as provided herein. Confidential Information shall also include all discussions in connection with, and all information in any medium in any way related to, the Transaction.

The term "Confidential Information" shall not include information which was or becomes generally available to the public other than as a result of a disclosure by a Representative or his affiliates, agents or advisors including, without limitation, attorneys, accountants, consultants, bankers and financial advisors (collectively "Affiliates").

2. Use of Confidential Information. The Representatives of a Party shall not use any Confidential Information disclosed by the Representatives of the other Party or pertaining to the Transaction for its own use or for any purpose other than to carry out the discussions between the Parties and to further the evaluation of the Transaction and the business relationship between the Parties.

3. Permitted Disclosure. A Party or its Representatives may disclose Confidential Information if required by a governmental agency or court of competent jurisdiction, or the rules thereof; provided, however, each Party agrees to give to the other prompt notice of the receipt of the subpoena or other process requiring or requesting disclosure of Confidential Information.

4. Proprietary Right. All Confidential Information furnished by a Party or its Representatives to the other Party or its Representatives shall remain the property of the Party furnishing the same and shall be promptly returned or destroyed at the request of the Party furnishing the Confidential Information.

5. No License or Right to Reproduce. Nothing contained in this Confidentiality Agreement shall be construed as granting or conferring on any Party or its Representatives, any rights, by license or otherwise, to reproduce or use in any other matter any Confidential Information disclosed hereunder by the other Party or its Representatives or pertaining to the Transaction, except to further the Transaction and the business relationship between the Parties.

6. Non-Competition. For a period of one (1) year from the date of this Confidentiality Agreement, no Party nor any of its respective Representatives

shall, directly or indirectly, on behalf of itself or himself or any other person, use any Confidential Information disclosed by the other Party or its Representatives or pertaining to the Transaction, except in connection with the furtherance of the Transaction and the business relationship between the Parties.

7. No Further Obligation. Neither the disclosure nor receipt of Confidential Information shall obligate a Party to undertake any business relationship with the other Party in connection with the Transaction. The Parties and the Representatives understand and acknowledge that neither Party is making any representation or warranty, express, or implied, as to the accuracy or completeness of the Confidential Information, and that only those representations or warranties that are made in a definitive purchase and sale or merger agreement when, as, and if executed, and subject to such limitations and restrictions as may be specified in such definitive agreement, will have any legal effect.

8. No Waiver. Failure to enforce any provision of this Agreement shall not constitute a waiver of any other term herein and any waiver of any breach shall not be construed as a waiver of any subsequent breach. If any provision of this Agreement is held to be invalid, void or unenforceable, the remaining provisions shall continue in full force and effect without being impaired or invalidated. This Agreement shall be construed and governed in accordance with the laws of the State of ________________.

9. Termination. This Agreement shall terminate on the earlier of the execution of definitive agreement by the Parties, the unanimous agreement of the undersigned parties, or one year from the date hereof.

10. Entire Agreement. This Confidentiality Agreement embodies the entire understanding among the Parties and their respective Representatives with regard to the Transaction, the Confidential Information and all other subject matter described or contained herein. This Agreement may not be amended, changed, altered or modified in any way, except by a writing signed by the Parties. This Agreement may be executed in a number of counterparts which, when taken together, shall constitute one and the same instrument.

IN WITNESS WHEREOF, the parties hereto have executed this Confidentiality Agreement as of the day and year first above written.

COMPANY2, INC.	COMPANY1 CORPORATION
______________________________	______________________________
By:	By:
___________, Individually	___________, Individually

STEP 2: The Action Plan

An action plan is a natural outcome of the meeting with the deal team. It is important to be realistic about the time investment required and the expected amount of time required to complete a transaction. While some deals are completed within 60-90 days, it is more common for the sales process to take approximately six months. An action plan can help ensure that the process runs smoothly, and should outline the list of deal milestones and expected completion dates.

STEP 3: Market Dynamics and Valuation

When entering a sale process it is critical to understand the current market dynamics affecting the potential valuation range for the business. Market trends and merger and acquisition activity provide great insight into whether a sector is hot and will support buoyant valuations, or cool, where valuations may be somewhat depressed. Understanding industry structure, growth drivers, consolidation trends, and macroeconomic conditions (e.g., low interest rates or high oil prices) can set the stage for a more detailed valuation analysis.

Valuation is a paramount business issue for buyers and sellers alike. Valuation, however, is a not a precise science—it is based upon both objective facts and subjective beliefs and assumptions about the future performance of the business in question. The value of a business, ultimately, is based upon what a seller is willing to pay. Just as houses can be valued by skilled and analytical real estate appraisers, the house is only worth what the buyer ends up paying the seller. Fortunately for sellers of businesses and real estate, competition provides a healthy and normalizing force to ensure that sellers obtain near the maximum of what a buyer is welling to pay. EBay, an online marketplace where goods are sold by auction, provides compelling insight into how competition affects the prices paid for assets. In an eBay transaction, the price the seller receives is not typically the maximum of what the "winner" was willing to pay, but rather just a little more than the maximum the second highest bidder was willing to pay. The phenomenon of auctions plays into the sale of businesses, even in the absence of a formal auction. So long as there is perceived competition for a deal, then buyers have an incentive to increase their offer price.

While competitive market dynamics help ensure sellers obtain a good price for their businesses, many companies are sold without the presence of extensive buyer competition. But, in the absence of strong and visible competition, how can prices be "fair?" Fortunately, there are analytical tools available that help both buyers and sellers estimate what the market is willing to pay. By analyzing comparable historical transactions and comparable public-company trading multiples, and conducting net present value (discounted cash flow) analyses, buyers and sellers can quickly understand the price range for which a particular type of business will sell.

The topic of valuation is more thoroughly examined in Chapter 8.

STEP 4: The Target List

A key step in any merger or acquisition process is generating a list of the potential acquirers. The first step in generating the target list is determining the set of categories of companies that would be likely interested in the selling entity. Once all of the potential categories are determined, it is a relatively straightforward exercise to determine which companies belong in each of the categories.

After the initial target list is created the next step is applying a logical filter to reduce the set to a more focused set of buyers. Companies that clearly cannot afford to purchase the company for sale, were recently acquired themselves, or have never purchased a business before, are inferior acquirers to companies with strong balance sheets (or buoyant stock) that have a history of successfully buying and integrating companies.

STEP 5: The Legal Audit

The next step in the preparation process is to get the company ready for the buyer's analysis and due diligence investigation. A pre-sale legal audit should be conducted in order to assess the state of the company; it is critical to identify and predict the problems that will be raised by the buyer and its counsel. The legal audit should include corporate housekeeping and administrative matters, the status of the seller's intellectual property and key contracts (including issues regarding their assignability, regulatory issues, and litigation). The goal is to find the bugs before the buyer's counsel discovers them for you (which would be embarrassing as well as costly from a negotiating perspective) and to get as many of the bugs out as possible before the first buyer is considered.

For example, now may be the time to resolve any disputes with minority shareholders, complete the registration of copyrights and trademarks, deal with open issues in your stock option plan, or renew or extend your favorable commercial leases. It may also be a good time to set the stage for the prompt response of those third parties whose consent may be necessary to close the transaction, such as landlords, bankers, key customers, suppliers, or venture capitalists. In many cases, there are contractual provisions that can prevent an attempted change in control without such consent. For those bugs that can't be exterminated, don't try to hide them under the carpet. Explain the status of any remaining problems to the prospective buyers and negotiate and structure the ultimate deal accordingly.

The legal audit should include an examination of certain key financial ratios, such as debt-to-equity, turnover, and profitability. The audit should also look carefully at the company's cost controls, overhead management, and profit centers to ensure the most productive performance. The audit may also uncover certain sloppy or self-interested business practices that should be changed before you sell the company. This strategic reengineering will help build value and remove unnecessary clutter from the financial statements and operations.

Even if you don't have the time, inclination, or resources to make such improvements, it will still be helpful to identify these areas and address how the company *could* be made more profitable to the buyer. Showing the potential for better long-term performance could earn you a higher selling price, as well as assist the buyer in raising capital needed to implement the transaction.

STEP 6: Preparing the Offering Memorandum

The sixth step in the preparation process is to identify a marketing strategy to attract prospective buyers. This strategy should include developing a profile of the "ideal" buyer, identifying how and when the buyer will be identified, determining who will meet with potential buyers, and gathering a set of initial materials to be given to potential buyers and their advisors. These initial materials are often referred to as the *offering memorandum*. This offering memorandum should include the following information:

- Executive summary
- Market opportunity
- History
- Business overview
- Products, services and pricing
- Manufacturing and distribution

- Sales, marketing, and growth strategy
- Competitive landscape
- Management team and organizational overview
- Risks and litigation
- Historical financial information
- Projected financial performance
- Supplemental materials

The offering memorandum is used as a sales tool for the business. This is the key opportunity to translate the company's key attributes, the size and growth of the market and the potential profitability. However, the company must be presented accurately with a fair portrayal of the problems and challenges that the company faces.

STEP 7: Getting the House in Order

A key step before marketing the company is ensuring that the business is truly ready for sale. Once the process is started, all questions are fair game and the state of affairs will be available for full review. As such, it is necessary to develop a definitive "to do" list in connection with corporate housekeeping matters, such as preparation of board and shareholder minutes and maintenance of regulatory filings. Once the process is started, things move very quickly and there is rarely time for housekeeping matters during a transaction process.

STEP 8: The Game Plan

Once the transaction preparation is complete, the process can be managed any number of ways. A major decision at this stage is in determining how closely the process should match a formal auction. A formal auction typically is based upon sending standardized company materials to a large audience, providing the targets with specific dates of management meetings and timing for which offers are due. This formal process can lead to very positive results; however, no buyer likes an auction. An auction ensures that the "winner" values the deal more than other auction participants, and as such, some companies refuse to participate in auctions, thus closing the door to potential buyers.

A less formal approach, however, can yield similar if not better results to an auction. In this approach the investment banker coordinates more informally with identified buyers, and ensures that all of the target buyers are contacted simultaneously. In addition, each of the targets is examined more closely for strategic fit, and often the communication and marketing materials are tailored to underscore the strategic rationale of the proposed transaction.

There are multiple benefits to this approach. First, each buyer is different, and providing a tailored message may be better received. A likely buyer may review a large number of potential deals (even if few are done), and helping the evaluator come to the proper conclusion can be best accomplished in more focused communication. Second, for each pairing of buyer and seller, there are different synergies to be had. If a seller truly wants to maximize the value obtained from the buyer, then understanding the synergies available is critical and necessary. Finally, investment bankers typically have interacted with many of the target buyers in the past. As such, a less structured process allows the investment banker the opportunity to solicit more candid, direct feedback about the proposed transaction—feedback that is typically not available when the process is more structured.

The last option for running a merger and acquisition process is to the have the CEO of the company contact the targets directly. This is rarely the best option, largely due to the challenge of price negotiations. An intermediary can preserve the good working relationship between two CEOs, despite differences in price expectations. When two CEOs are working together directly, however, price can become an emotional and personal roadblock to productive discussions.

Common Preparation Mistakes

Once you have assembled your team, conducted an internal presale legal audit, and pulled together the "good, the bad, and the ugly" in a detailed offering memorandum, you are ready to start contacting potential buyers. To maximize the selling price, however, you must take certain strategic and reengineering steps in order to build value in the company and to avoid the common mistakes made by sellers, as discussed below. To properly reengineer and reposition the company for sale, hard decisions need to be made, and certain key financial ratios need to be analyzed in critical areas, such as cost management, inventory turnover, growth rates, profitability, and risk mitigation techniques. The next chapter gives some insights into the buyer's perspective, while Chapters 4 through 10 discuss the process itself. But before turning to Chapter 3, take a look at a few of the common preparation mistakes sellers make in getting ready to sell their company:

- *Being Impatient and Indecisive.* Timing is everything. If you seem too anxious to sell, buyers will take advantage of your impatience. If you sit on the sidelines too long, the window of opportunity in the market cycle to obtain a top selling price may pass you by.
- *Telling Others at the Wrong Time.* Again, timing is critical. If you tell key employees, vendors, or customers that you are considering a sale too early in the process, they may abandon your relationship in anticipation of losing their jobs, their customer or supplier, or from a general fear of the unknown. Key employees, fearful of losing their jobs, may not want to chance relying on an unknown buyer to honor their salaries or benefits. A related problem for companies that are closely-held (or if one person owns 100 percent of the shares) is how to reward and motivate key team members who may have contributed over time to the company's success and will not be participating in the proceeds of the sale at closing. It is critical that their interests are aligned with the seller and that they work hard and stay focused on getting to the closing table. A bonus plan or liquidity event participation plan can be an effective way to bridge that gap and allow them to participate in the success and share in the proceeds at closing without owning equity in the seller's company. Vendors and customers will want to protect their interests, too. Yet these key employees and strategic relationships may be items of value in the sale; the buyer may count on their being around after closing the deal. If you wait too long and disclose your news at the last minute, employees may feel resentment for

being kept out of the loop and key customers or vendors may not have time to react and evaluate the impact of the transaction on their businesses—or, where applicable, provide their approvals.

• *Retaining Third-Party Transactions with People You're Related To.* If there are relationships that will not carry over to the new owner, shed these ghost employees and family members. They should follow you out the door once the deal is secured.

• *Leaving Loose Ends.* Purchase minority shareholder interests so that the new owner won't have to contend with their demands after the sale. Very few buyers will want to own a company that still has remaining shareholders who may present legal or operational risks. It's akin to the real estate developer that needs 100 percent of all of the lots in a development to agree to sell before proceeding with its plans—a lone straggler or two can break the deal.

• *Forgetting to Look in Your Own Backyard.* In seeking out potential buyers, look for those who may have a vested interest in acquiring control of the company, such as key customers, employees, or vendors.

• *Deluding Yourself—or Your Potential Buyers—About the Risks or Weaknesses of Your Company.* Your credibility is on the line—a loss of trust by the potential buyer usually means that he will walk away from the deal.

Other Considerations for the Seller

The Importance of Recasting

Since privately owned companies often tend to keep reported profits—and thus tax obligations—as low as possible, *financial recasting* is a crucial element in understanding the real earnings history and future profit potential of your business. Since buyers are interested in the *real* earnings of a business, recasting shows how your business would look if its philosophy matched that of a public corporation, in which earnings and profits are maximized. As part of the offering memorandum, you should recast your financial statements for the preceding three years. For example, adjust the salaries and benefits to prevailing market levels, eliminate personal expenses (expensive car leases, country club dues, etc.) and exclude nonworking family members. Recasting presents the financial history of your business in a way that buyers can understand. It translates your company's past into a valuable, saleable future, and it allows sophisticated buyers the opportunity for meaningful comparisons with other investment considerations.

Selling the Pro Forma

The price that a buyer may be willing to pay depends on the quality and reasonableness of the profit projections you are able to demonstrate and substantiate. The profit and loss statement, balance sheet, cash flow, and working capital requirements are developed and projected for each year over a five-year planning period. Using these documents, plus the enhanced value of your business at the end of five years, you can calculate the discounted value of the company's future cash flow. This establishes the primary economic return to the buyer for his acquisition investment.

Prequalifying Your Buyer

It is critical to prequalify the potential buyers, especially if you contemplate a continuing business relationship after closing the deal. Thus, the buyer must demonstrate the ability to meet one or more pre-closing conditions, such as availability of financing, a viable business plan for post-closing operations (especially if the seller will be receiving part of its consideration in the form of an earn-out), or a demonstration that the post-closing efficiencies or synergies are bona fide. Take the time to understand each potential buyer's post-closing business plan, especially in a roll-up or consolidation, where the seller's upside will depend on the buyer's ability to meet its business and growth plans.

Getting Deal Terms and Structure with the Seller's Objectives, Personal Needs, and Post-Closing Plans

In addition to the information addressed in this chapter, the seller should meet with its legal and financial advisors *well before* the sale to address personal and estate planning needs. The seller's net worth, lifestyle requirements, post-closing plans, charitable goals, and estate planning objectives are all relevant to the type of offer and deal structure that it may be willing to accept. A 28-year-old seller already planning her next venture may have different goals and needs from a 46-year-old seller whose triplets are seniors in high school, or a 76-year-old seller who is finally ready for retirement and life as a philanthropist and patriarch. It is also critical that the proper estate planning techniques, trusts and other tools are recommended by the right advisors in order to maximize wealth, protect assets and minimize tax liabilities far enough ahead of the proposed transaction that adequate time is left to put these documents and structures in place in a manner which will prevent them from being set aside or disregarded down the road.

Initiating the Deal

The Buyer's Perspective

Business strategists often say that it is cheaper to buy a business than to build a business. This approach, together with the low interest rates and large pools of available capital, has created a very active market in mergers and acquisitions. Our domestic market has clearly experienced major industry consolidation via acquisitions and roll-up strategies. Notwithstanding all of the excitement, the purchase of an existing business is a complex and challenging task. Buying a company for the right price is both an art and a science. Experienced buyers and their advisors often develop a sixth sense, an instinct, a gut feel for the potential problems *and* opportunities inside a company that is for sale. They use these instincts to mitigate risk and to uncover hidden intangible assets. This chapter leads the buyer through the process, with a focus on preparation for the deal, creating an acquisition plan and preliminary negotiation tips, as we begin to understand the seller's perspective.

Assembling the Team

Every buyer needs to develop an internal working team, as well as a set of experienced external advisors, such as lawyers, accountants, investment bankers, valuation experts, and in some cases insurance or employee benefits experts. The internal work team should include representatives from the finance, sales and marketing, strategic planning, and operations departments. An effective buyer's team will not only be creative and aggressive, it also will not lose focus on the core fundamentals that drive the acquisition strategy, such as product mix, distribution, integration, and expansion of the customer base. To successfully acquire companies and enhance shareholder value, there must be cohesive thinking and constant communication among team members. For middle-market companies, the chief executive officer is typically the quarterback of the acquisition team but it can be someone appointed by the CEO. The quarterback must clearly define both the responsibilities and the authority of each team member, including who speaks on behalf of the buyer, who contacts prospective sellers, who negotiates with the selected sellers, and so forth. All parameters of operations must be clearly set.

One key decision with respect to assembling the team is whether to use an investment banker to find and evaluate targets, or whether the deal flow will be generated internally through screening, networking and industry contacts. In many cases, the sellers (or at least those who have declared their businesses eligible for sale) may have hired intermediaries. Using an investment banker can save valuable time and money and can put you at parity with the seller's representation; chasing after the wrong sellers or even trying to figure out which companies have expressed an interest in selling can be costly and time consuming. In addition, an investment bank will likely have resources and access to information unavailable to the company. Finally, an investment bank can provide invaluable counsel on valuation and negotiation. The potential of saving several million dollars (or more) through smart bargaining almost always justifies the existence of valuation and negotiation expertise.

Developing an Acquisition Plan

Mergers and acquisitions often play a key role in a company's growth. The achievement of certain corporate goals and objectives may involve the external acquisition of assets and resources needed for growth, a step that may be more efficient than internal expansion. A growing company considering an acquisition should always begin with an *acquisition plan,* which identifies the specific objectives of a transaction and the criteria to be applied in analyzing potential target companies.

The acquisition plan also identifies the value-added efficiencies and cost savings that will result from the proposed transaction and answers the fundamental question: *How will the buyer's professional management or brand equity enhance the performance or profitability of the seller's company?* The possible answers may vary, but generally they include a desire to accelerate growth in revenues and profits, strengthen the buyer's competitive position, broaden existing product lines, or break into new geographic markets or market segments as part of a diversification strategy.

The heart of the plan identifies the targeted industries and lists the criteria for evaluating candidates within these targeted industries. Why is planning a key part of any acquisition strategy? For the same reason that synergy is a key consideration in mergers and acquisition. If a buyer pays exactly what the business is worth on a stand-alone basis, then any benefit obtained from the planned changes (i.e., synergy) is profit to the buyer. Conversely, if a buyer adds no value to the seller's operations, then paying fair value does not make the buyer any better or worse off than without the transaction. This basic economic principal is the premise for why buying companies makes sense in today's economy. Simply, if a company is worth more to a buyer than a seller, then there is reason to do a deal where both parties win.

STEP 1: Identify Your Objectives

The first step in developing an effective acquisition plan is to identify key objectives. Although the reasons for considering growth through acquisition will vary from industry to industry and from company to company, certain strategic advantages provided by an acquisition should be considered. The buyer may seek to acquire another company in order to:

- Achieve certain operating synergies and economies of scale with respect to production and manufacturing, research and development, management, or marketing and distribution.

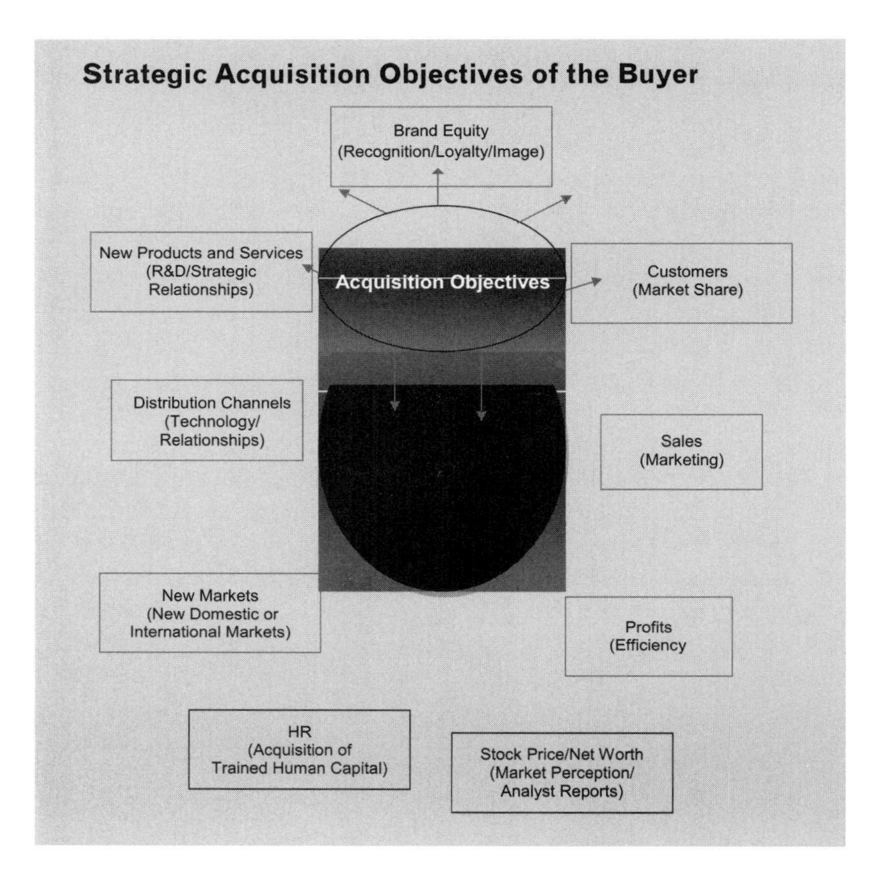

- Obtain the rights to develop products and services owned by the target company. For example, Adobe recently announced the acquisition of Macromedia, a transaction that would provide Adobe access to the mobile telephony market. Adobe sought access to mobile carriers for years. Macromedia, on the other hand, will benefit from Adobe's process discipline and strong balance sheet. Both companies benefit from the diversification that the combined product portfolios bring.
- Stabilize its earnings stream and mitigate its risk of business failure through diversification of its products and services (While many CEOs believe diversification is a good thing, shareholders often punish these companies for lack of focus. Shareholders, unlike companies, can easily diversify by buying alternative stocks—

they do not need, and in many cases, prefer that companies not diversify away from their core focus.).

• Deploy excess cash in a tax-efficient project, since both distribution of dividends and stock redemptions are generally taxable events for shareholders.

• Achieve certain production and distribution economies of scale through vertical integration, which involves the acquisition of a key supplier or customer.

• Exploit residual assets that have been undeveloped or underdeveloped by the target company's retiring or burnt-out management team. Top managers may be ready for retirement, or a key manager may have recently died, leaving the business with certain underutilized assets that can be exploited by an acquiring company.

• Strengthen key business areas, such as research and development or marketing. Sometimes it is more efficient to fill these gaps through an acquisition rather than attempt to build the departments internally.

• Penetrate new geographic markets. It may be cheaper to acquire companies already doing business in a target market than to establish market diversification from scratch.

• Acquire additional plant or production capacities, which can be utilized to achieve economies of scale.

• Take advantage of a bargain. The target company may be available at a distressed price, which tends to pique the interest of growing companies even if they are not necessarily looking for acquisition candidates. This situation often comes about because of a death or divorce affecting the company's founders.

• Acquire certain patents, copyrights, trade secrets, or other intangible assets that are available only by means of an acquisition.

In essence, the statement of the objectives should be a reality check, answering the key questions:

- Why are we doing this?
- Are we convinced that growth via acquisition makes sense as compared to other forms of growth strategies, such as internal

expansion, joint ventures, franchising, licensing, or capital formation?
- Does this improve our competitive position?
- Will this enhance shareholder value?
- If yes, have we identified and evaluated the key "value drivers" of the proposed transaction (e.g. protectable intellectual property, distribution channel efficiencies, durability of recurring revenue, loyal and dedicated customer base, etc.)?
- Are we really enhancing our shareholder value and competitive position as a result of this deal?

STEP 2: Draft the Plan

The next step is to draft the acquisition plan. The acquisition plan defines the objectives of the buyer, the relevant trends in the target's industry, the method for finding candidates and generating deal flow (especially critical when it is a seller's market and competition for deal flow is intense), the criteria to be used to evaluate candidates, the targeted budgets and timetables for accomplishing the transaction, the projected range of prices, the past acquisition track record of the company, the amount of external capital that will be required to accomplish the transaction, and related issues.

One of the key goals of the acquisition plan is to clearly define the characteristics of an ideal target. The field is initially narrowed by choosing acquisitions as a growth strategy over alternatives such as franchising or strategic alliances. It is narrowed again by targeting the industry from which a company will be chosen. And it is narrowed further by developing criteria to screen the possible candidates. This narrowing process, in most cases, will yield a small but viable field of attractive candidates that can be approached.

Other benefits to having a well-prepared acquisition plan are:

- It provides a roadmap for the company's leadership to follow.
- It is a way of informing shareholders of key company objectives.
- It reduces professional and advisory fees by clearly defining objectives.
- It serves as a screen to filter out deals that don't meet your criteria or long-term objectives.

- It mitigates the risk of doing a transaction you'll later regret by anticipating problems and clarifying objectives.
- It identifies post-closing integration challenges well in advance.
- It informs sellers of your plans for the company.

In today's marketplace and with recent trends toward consolidation strategies, it is particularly important that the seller (especially when the buyer's stock is a large component of the consideration) understand, accept, and respect the buyer's acquisition strategy and growth plans for the consolidated company. The well-prepared acquisition plan can be a valuable negotiation tool in dealing with seller's concerns with the value and continued growth of the buyer's stock.

The acquisition plan will also identify:

- The targeted *size* of the acquisition candidates.
- The *source* of acquisition financing and amount available.
- The *method* for finding candidates (e.g., internal search or use of intermediaries).
- The *desired financial returns* and/or *operating synergies* to be achieved as a result of the acquisition.
- The minimum and maximum ranges and rates of acceptable *revenue, growth, earnings,* and *net worth* of the seller.
- The *impact* of the acquisition on existing shareholders of your company.
- The likely *competing bidders* for qualified candidates.
- The members of the *acquisition team* and each of their roles.
- The nature and types of *risks* the buyer is willing to assume (versus those that are unacceptable).
- The desired *geographic location* of the target company.
- The desired *demographics* and *buying habits* of the seller's customers.
- The plans to retain or replace the *management team* of the target company, even though this policy may vary by candidate; include a section addressing at least your preliminary plans.
- Your willingness to consider *turnaround or troubled compa-*

nies. Each buyer will have a different tolerance level; some want and prefer the cost savings of buying a fixer-upper company while others prefer the company to be pretty much intact.

- Your tax and financial preferences for *asset vs. stock transactions*.
- Your openness to *full versus partial ownership* of the seller's entity, or your willingness to consider a spin-off sale, such as purchase of the assets of an operating division or the stock of a subsidiary.
- Your interest or willingness to launch an *unfriendly takeover* of a publicly held company or buy the debt from the largest creditor of a privately held company.

Applying the Criteria: How to Narrow the Field

Once all of the pertinent issues listed above have been addressed in the acquisition plan, it should be relatively easy to define the selection criteria and screen the candidates. The more typical criteria include some of the following:

- A history of stable financial and growth performance over different market cycles and under different conditions.
- A market leader in its industry niche and in its geographic region.
- A company with a recognized brand name and established market share.
- Products not susceptible to obsolescence or rapid technological change.
- A strong management team with research and development capability.
- Stable and economically favorable relationships with customers, vendors, creditors, and debtors.
- Room for growth or excess capacity in manufacturing or production.
- A minimum and maximum range of revenue (i.e., from $15 to $25 million).

- A range of cash flow or earnings before interest, taxes, depreciation and amortization (EBITDA).
- A defined range for purchase price.
- A range for purchase price consideration addressing a preferred ratio of stock, cash and earn-out.
- Geographical location.
- An existing management team that agrees to remain in place for up to _____ years.

Naturally, unless it's your birthday, you're not likely to find all of these qualifications in every candidate; if you do, there will likely be multiple bidders. Rather, the buyer must be ready to mix and match—accept compromise in some areas. But be careful not to overlook too many warts, lest you end up with a deal that you will regret later.

Again, the goal is to compare the acquisition objectives to the strengths and weaknesses of each seller. The acquisition team must have a clear idea as to *how* each targeted company will complement the buyer's strengths and/or mitigate its weaknesses. The qualitative and quantitative screening criteria suggested here will help the buying team ensure that the right candidates are selected. They are intended to filter out the wrong deals and mitigate the chances of post-closing regrets and problems.

Buyer's Acquisition Process

The buyer's planning and implementation of an acquisition program perspective typically involves the following steps:

1. Develop acquisition objectives.
2. Analyze projected economic and financial gains to be achieved by the acquisition.
3. Assemble an acquisition team (managers, attorneys, accountants, and investment bankers) and begin the search for acquisitions candidates.
4. Conduct due diligence analysis of prime candidates.
5. Conduct initial negotiations and valuation of the selected target.

6. Select the structure of the transaction.
7. Identify sources of financing for the transaction.
8. Conduct detailed bidding and negotiations.
9. Obtain all shareholder and third-party consents and approvals.
10. Structure the legal documents.
11. Prepare for the closing.
12. Hold the closing.
13. Take care of post-closing tasks and responsibilities.
14. Implement the integration of the two entities.

Approaching a Company That Is Not for Sale

As discussed earlier in this chapter, there's a definite challenge when the ideal candidate is not currently for sale. In these cases, the owner of the company must be approached subtly by a senior member of the buying team and gently informed that the target is of long-run interest to the potential buyer. Here is how that's generally done.

1. Introduce yourself and give information about your company's business, strategic direction, growth rates, financial highlights, and other high level data. Explain why the target company is a compelling fit with the buyer. This will let the prospective seller know that you are a credible buyer and that you have given serious consideration to the idea of acquiring his or her company.

2. Request a meeting in order to discuss strategic fit, and alternatives for how the two companies can establish a more formal relationship. Broach the concept of a formal structural relationship (i.e., an acquisition) and outline the rationale for such a transaction.

3. Maintain contact after the meeting, even if the owner insists the company is not for sale. Call periodically and maintain a level of positive communication. Sometimes it takes years for owners to reach a decision to sell—and while you are not going to sit idly by, some companies may always be good acquisition targets. By

maintaining contact, you can develop a relationship with the seller and create an environment of mutual trust and respect.

When, and if, your candidate expresses interest, you will want to act quickly and establish momentum. Set up a meeting to learn the seller's personal objectives, review the company's operating and financial performance, and identify any concerns or reservations the seller may have. Your goal is to get the information you need to determine a preliminary price and to structure a letter of intent that outlines the key points of the proposed acquisition.

Dealing with the Seller's Management Team

If you are going to want the seller's key managers to stay on and help manage the integrated company, from the outset, you will need to allay their concerns about job security and career potential. Most managers will not believe that you intend to keep them all. It's likely that the best managers will leave if they feel their jobs are in jeopardy. Be prepared to answer the following questions:

- "What change can I expect as a result of this transaction?"
- "What is the direction of the combined entity?"
- "Will I still have a job?"
- "Will I continue in my present role?"
- "How will my performance be evaluated?"
- "Will I be better or worse off as a result of this transaction?"
- "What will I be paid?"

Communicating your vision and performance expectations is critical to obtaining management's commitment early on. A good way to do this is to have the seller's current management team play a role in developing the post-closing integration and communication plans. Here are other, more tangible ways of demonstrating your long-term commitment to the seller's managers, and thereby relieving any personal career anxieties:

1. Propose salary and wage adjustments, if appropriate, to bring compensation up to your company's or industry levels.

2. Establish an incentive bonus plan tied to realistic, attainable goals.
3. Provide employee contracts to key members of the management team.
4. Review the seller's benefit plans and assure employees that the transfer will be orderly and fair.
5. Explain any potential structural changes with care and clarity, ensuring that a history of good communication, equity, and trust is established.

In conclusion, the acquisition team's primary focus is to acquire companies that will enhance shareholder value and contribute to the growth and profitability of the combined entity. We find that a well-defined acquisition plan and the rigorous analysis of whether a potential target meets the criteria will help accomplish that goal. Following the steps set forth in this chapter is a great roadmap to use, as will the letter of intent and due diligence processes discussed in Chapters 4 and 5.

CHAPTER 4

The Letter of Intent and Other Preliminary Matters

At this stage of the transaction, both the seller and buyer (and their respective advisors) have developed a strategic plan and tentative timetable for completion of the deal, have completed their analysis as to why the transaction makes good sense for each party, and hopefully have taken the time to understand each other's perspective and competing objectives. The field of available candidates has been narrowed, the preliminary "get to know each other" meetings have been completed, and a tentative selection has been made. After the completion of the pre-sale review, the next step involves the preparation and negotiation of an interim agreement, which will guide and govern the conduct of the parties up until closing.

Although there are certain valid legal arguments against the execution of any type of interim document, especially since some courts have interpreted them to be binding legal documents (even if one or more of the parties did not initially intend to be bound), it has been my experience that a Letter of Intent, which includes a set of binding terms and nonbinding terms as a *roadmap* for the transaction, *is* a necessary step in virtually all mergers and acquisition transactions. I have found that most parties prefer the organizational framework and psychological comfort of knowing that there is some type of written document in place before proceeding further and before significant expenses are incurred. It is also critical to deal with as many of the potential due diligence problems or surprises at this early stage as possible. The ability to resolve problems that may derail a transaction is much stronger at the outset of the deal *before* each party has incurred significant expenses and becomes more entrenched in their position.

In addition to creating a framework for any potential deal with the prospective buyer, an LOI (letter of intent) is a catalyzing event in most deals. Receiving an LOI, even one that has unacceptable terms, provides the investment banker the opportunity to reach out to each of the target buyers and accelerate the "go or no-go" decision. In a normal process, the investment banker strives to keep the potential buyers on a common timeframe. However, the first LOI drives the timing of the process, and furthermore, provides a solid framework for more specific price negotiations. Finally, if the LOI received is at an acceptable price, the investment banker can now be more aggressive in price negotiations with the other interested parties. There is no event that allows the banker to create an auction more than an LOI, and as such, it is a tool that is welcomed, carefully managed, and ultimately used to obtain more value for the seller.

There are many different styles of drafting Letters of Intent, which vary from law firm to law firm and business lawyer to business lawyer. These styles usually fall into one of three categories: (a) binding; (b) nonbinding; and (c) hybrids, like the model in Exhibit 4-1. In general, the type to be selected will depend upon (a) the timing and the scope of the information to be released publicly concerning the transaction (if any); (b) the degree to which negotiations have been definitive and necessary information has been gathered; (c) the cost to the buyer and the seller of proceeding with the transaction prior to the making of binding commitments; (d) the rapidity with which the parties estimated a final agreement could be signed; (e) the valuation ranges which have been discussed to date for the seller's company; (f) the degree to which the buyer needs/wants a period of exclusivity (and the degree to which the seller is *willing* to grant an exclusivity period; and (g) the degree of confidence in the good faith of each party and the absence (or presence) of other parties competing for the transaction. In most cases the hybrid format, which contains both binding and non-binding terms is the most effective format to protect the interests of both parties and to level the playing field from a negotiations perspective.

Advantages and Disadvantages of Executing a Letter of Intent

Advantages

- Tests parties' seriousness.
- Mentally commits parties to sale.
- Sets out in writing certain key areas of agreement. Important since may be long delay before sales agreement is executed.
- Highlights remaining open issues, challenges to closing, valuation gaps and other related matters needing further negotiation.
- Discourages seller from shopping around for better deal.

Disadvantages

- May be considered a binding agreement. Important to state whether or not letter of intent is meant to constitute enforceable agreement.
- Public announcement of prospective sale may have to be made due to federal securities law if either company is publicly-held.

Although formally executed by the buyer and the seller, a Letter of Intent is often considered an agreement *in principle*. As a result, the parties should be very clear as to whether the Letter of Intent is a binding preliminary contract or merely a memorandum from which a more definitive legal document may be drafted upon completion of due diligence. Regardless of the legal implications involved, however, by executing a Letter of Intent, the parties make a psychological commitment to the transaction and provide a roadmap for expediting more formal negotiations. In addition, a well-drafted Letter of Intent will provide an overview of matters which require further discussion and consideration, such as the exact purchase price. Although an exact and final purchase price cannot realistically be established until due diligence has been completed, the seller may hesitate to proceed without a price commitment. Instead of creating a fixed price, however, the Letter of Intent will typically incorporate a price range that is qualified by a clause or provision which sets forth all of the factors that will influence and affect the calculation of a final fixed price, such as balance sheet adjustments, due diligence surprises or problems, a change in the health of the company or overall market conditions during the transaction period and even sometimes an "upside surprise" in favor of the seller when a significant *positive* development occurs during the transaction period (e.g., the settlement of litigation, the award of important intellectual property rights, a big new contract or customer commitment, etc.) which had not been integrated in establishing valuation ranges.

Proposed Terms

As you can see from the sample Letter of Intent in Exhibit 4-1, the first section addresses certain key deal terms such as price and method of payment, but these terms are usually nonbinding so that the parties have an opportunity to complete the due diligence and analysis and have room for further negotiation, depending on the specific problems uncovered during the investigative process.

Binding Terms

The sample Letter of Intent in Exhibit 4-1 also includes certain binding terms which will *not* be subject to further negotiation. These are certain issues that at least one side, and usually both sides, will want to ensure are binding, regardless of whether the deal is actually consummated. These include:

- *Legal Ability of Seller to Consummate the Transaction.* Before wasting too much time or money, the buyer will want to know that the seller has the power and authority to close the deal.
- *Protection of Confidential Information.* The seller in particular, and in general both parties, will want to ensure that all information

Exhibit 4-1. Sample letter of intent.

Ms. Prospective Seller
SellCo, Inc.
{address}

Re: *Letter of Intent Between BuyCo, Inc. and SellCo, Inc.*

Dear Ms. Prospective Seller:

This letter ("Letter Agreement") sets forth the terms by which BuyCo, Inc. ("BCI") agrees to purchase all of the issued and outstanding common stock of SellCo, Inc. (the "Company") in accordance with the terms set forth below. BCI and the Company are hereinafter collectively referred to as the "Parties."

Section I of this Letter Agreement summarizes the principal terms proposed in our earlier discussions and is not an agreement binding upon either of the Parties. These principal terms are subject to the execution and delivery by the Parties of a definitive Stock Purchase Agreement and other documents related to these transactions.

Section II of this Letter Agreement contains a number of covenants by the Parties, which shall be legally binding upon the execution of this Letter Agreement by the Parties. The binding terms in Section II below are enforceable against the Parties, regardless of whether or not the aforementioned agreements are executed or the reasons for nonexecution.

SECTION I—PROPOSED TERMS

1. Stock Purchase. The Parties will execute a Stock Purchase Agreement, pursuant to which, BCI will purchase ________ shares of a the Company's Common Stock (the "Shares"), from the schedule of Shareholders attached hereto for a total purchase price of not less than $________ the Company's Common Stock.

2. Employment Agreements. Prior to closing, the Company will enter into an individual employment agreement with ________ and ________ who are employed by the Seller for year-terms at the compensation levels of $________ and bonus plan eligibility of between $________ and $________ The Employment Agreement will contain such other terms and conditions as are reasonable and customary in the type of transaction contemplated hereby.

3. Closing and Documentation. The Parties intend that a closing of the agreements shall occur on or before ____________, 2006, at a time and place that is mutually acceptable to the Parties. BCI or its representatives will prepare and revise the initial and subsequent drafts of the necessary agreements.

SECTION II—BINDING TERMS

In consideration of the costs to be incurred by the Parties in undertaking actions toward the negotiation and consummation of the Stock Purchase Agreement and the related agreements, the Parties hereby agree to the following binding terms ("Binding Terms"):

4. Refundable Deposit. BCI will provide a refundable deposit in the amount of $________ to the Company at the time of the execution of this Letter Agreement. All sums paid hereunder shall be deductible from the purchase price to be

(continues)

Exhibit 4-1. Continued.

paid for the Shares as described in Paragraph 1. In the event that BCI does not complete the purchase of the Shares, the sums payable hereunder shall be referred to BCI (less ________) to be retained by the Seller for its expenses, with interest at the rate of 1.5% above the highest U.S. prime rate published in *The Wall Street Journal* from the date of execution of this Letter Agreement to the date of repayment. In the event that the closing is delayed beyond __________, 2006, BCI will make an additional deposit of $________ on ________, 2006 and $________ on ________, 2007.

5. Due Diligence. The directors, officers, shareholders, employees, agents and other representatives (collectively, the "Representatives") of the Company shall (a) grant to BCI and its Representatives full access to the Company's properties, personnel, facilities, books and records, financial and operating data, contracts and other documents; and (b) furnish all such books and records, financial and operating data, contracts and other documents or information as BCI or its Representatives may reasonably request.

6. No Material Changes. The Company agrees that, from and after the execution of this Letter Agreement until the earlier of the termination of the Binding Terms in accordance with Paragraph 12 below or the execution and delivery of the agreements described herein, the Company's business and operations will be conducted in the ordinary course and in substantially the same manner as such business and operations have been conducted in the past and the Company will notify BCI of any extraordinary transactions, financing or business involving the Company or its affiliates.

7. No-Shop Provision. The Company agrees that, from and after the execution of this Letter Agreement until the termination of the Binding Terms in accordance with Paragraph 12 below, the Company will not initiate or conclude, through its Representatives or otherwise, any negotiations with any corporation, person or other entity regarding the sale of all or substantially all of the assets or the Shares of the Company. The Company will immediately notify the other Parties regarding any such contact described above.

8. Lock-Up Provision. The Company agrees that, from and after the execution of this Letter Agreement until (a) the consummation of the transactions contemplated in Section I and the execution of definitive agreements thereby, or (b) in the event that definitive agreements are not executed, until the repayment of all amounts advanced hereunder, plus accrued interest, that without the prior written approval of BCI and subject to any anti-dilution provisions imposed hereunder, (x) no shares of any currently issued Common Stock of the Company shall be issued, sold, transferred or assigned to any party; (y) no such shares of Common Stock shall be pledged as security, hypothecated, or in any other way encumbered; and (z) the Company shall issue no additional shares of capital stock of any class, whether now or hereafter authorized.

9. Confidentiality. Prior to Closing, neither Party nor any of their Representatives shall make any public statement or issue any press releases regarding the agreements, the proposed transactions described herein or this Letter Agreement without the prior written consent of the other Party, except as such disclosure may be required by law. If the law requires such disclosure, the disclosing party shall notify the other Party in advance and furnish to the other Party a copy of the proposed disclosure. Notwithstanding the foregoing, the Parties acknowledge that certain disclosures regarding the agreements, the proposed transac-

tions or this Letter Agreement may be required to be made to each Party's representatives or certain of them, and to any other party whose consent or approval may be required to complete the agreements and the transactions provided for thereunder, and that such disclosures shall not require prior written consent. BCI and its employees, affiliates and associates will (a) treat all information received from the Company confidentially, (b) not disclose such information to third parties without the prior written consent of the Company, except as such disclosure may be required by law, (d) not use such information for any purpose other than the consideration of the matters contemplated by this Letter of Intent, including related due diligence, and (d) return to the Company any such information if this Letter Agreement terminates pursuant to Paragraph 12 below.

10. Expenses; Finder's Fee. The Parties are responsible for and will bear all of their own costs and expenses incurred at any time in connection with the transaction proposed hereunder up to $________. Any additional or extraordinary expenses above this amount shall be borne by BCI; provided, however, the Company shall be responsible for any finder's fees payable in connection with the transactions contemplated hereby.

11. Break-Up Fee. The Company agrees to pay BCI a break-up fee of $________ in the event that the sale and purchase of the shares contemplated in Section I is not accomplished by ___________, 2006 as a result of the Company's failure or refusal to close pursuant to the terms set forth above and not due to any refusal or delay on the part of BCI to close by that date.

12. Effective Date. The foregoing obligations of the Parties under Section II of this Letter Agreement shall be effective as of the date of execution by the Company, and shall terminate upon the completion of the transactions contemplated in Section I above or, if such transactions are not completed, then at such time as all of the obligations under this Section II have been satisfied, unless otherwise extended by all of the Parties or specifically extended by the terms of the foregoing provisions; provided, however, that such termination shall not relieve the Parties of liability for the breach of any obligation occurring prior to such termination.

Please indicate your agreement to the Binding Terms set forth in Section II above by executing and returning a copy of this letter to the undersigned no later than close of business on ___________, 20___. Following receipt, we will instruct legal counsel to prepare the agreements contemplated herein. The Binding Terms shall become binding on the Company upon the advance of deposit pursuant to Paragraph 4 and the execution of Promissory Note in consideration therefore.

Very truly yours,
/s/ Prospective Buyer
Prospective Buyer, President
BuyCo, Inc.

ACKNOWLEDGED AND ACCEPTED:
SellCo, Inc.

____

By: Prospective Seller, President

Dated:

____

provided in the initial presentation as well as during due diligence remains confidential.

- *Access to Books and Records.* The buyer will want to ensure that the seller and its advisors will fully cooperate in the due diligence process.

- *Break-Up or Walk-Away Fees.* The seller may want to include a clause in the Letter of Intent to attempt to recoup some of its expenses if the buyer tries to walk away from the deal, either due to a change in circumstances or the desire on the seller's part to accept a more attractive offer from a different potential buyer. The seller may want a reciprocal clause to protect against its own expenses if the buyer walks away or defaults on a preliminary obligation or condition to closing, such as an inability to raise acquisition capital.

- *No-Shop/Standstill Provisions.* The buyer may want a period of exclusivity where it has the confidence of knowing that the seller is not entertaining any other offers. The seller will want to place a limit or "outside date" to this provision in order to allow it to begin entertaining other offers if the buyer is unduly dragging its feet.

- *Good Faith Deposit: Refundable vs. Nonrefundable.* In some cases the seller will request a deposit or option fee and the parties must determine to what extent, if at all, this deposit will be refundable and under what conditions. There are often timing problems with this provision which can be difficult to resolve. For example, the buyer will want the deposit to remain 100 percent refundable if the seller is being uncooperative, or at least until the buyer and its team complete the initial round of due diligence to ensure that there are no major problems discovered which might cause them to walk away from the deal. The seller will want to set a limit on the due diligence and review period at which point the buyer forfeits all or a part of its deposit. The end result is often a progressive downward scale of refundability as the due diligence and the deal overall reach various checkpoints towards closing. To the extent that the buyer forfeits some or all of the deposit, and the deal never closes, the buyer may want to negotiate an eventual full or partial refundability if the seller finds an alternative buyer within a certain period of time, such as 180 days.

- *Impact on Employees.* Perhaps among the most challenging issue faced by sellers is the decision as to *who* is told *what, when* and *why* within the company. Sellers will typically want to "play their cards close to the vest" while buyers may want access to key executives and employees who are not yet in the loop as part of their due diligence perspective. From a human capital management perspective, if team members are told too soon then it may be hard to keep them from running out the door (due to uncertainty), and if they are told too late it may lead to resentment and frustration. If the communication of the possible sale is mishandled, then the employees may get the message that their jobs are unimportant or in jeopardy, or both. Supervisory personnel should be briefed first, and all of their questions should be answered so that they can inform their subordinates. After the closing, it is imperative that the top management of the acquiring company meet with the employees of the target company to discuss their post-closing roles, compensation and benefits. If there will be job cuts, discuss the methods as to how this will be determined and whether any training, resume writing skills or outplacement services will be offered.

• *Key Terms for the Definitive Documents*. It is often the case that the Letter of Intent will provide that it is subject to the definitive documents, such as the Purchase Agreement, and that those definitive documents will address certain key matters or include certain key sections, such as covenants, indemnification, representations and warranties, and key conditions for closing.

• *Conditions to Closing*. Both parties will want to articulate a set of conditions or circumstances stating that they will not be bound to proceed with the transaction if certain contingencies are not met, or if events subsequently happen after the execution of the Letter of Intent such as third party approvals, regulatory permission or related potential barriers to closing. Be sure to articulate these conditions clearly so that there are no surprises down the road.

• *Conduct of the Business Prior to Closing*. The buyer usually wants some protection that the general state of the company that he or she sees today will be there tomorrow. Thus, the seller will be obligated to operate its business in the ordinary course and that assets, customers and employees will not start disappearing from the premises, equipment left in disrepair, new customers not pursued, bonuses magically declared, personal expenses paid the night before and other steps which will deplete the value of the company prior to closing. If these things do occur, then the parties should anticipate a mechanism for adjusting the price based on the relating valuation of the lost contracts, relationships or human resources. These "negative covenants" help protect the buyer against unpleasant surprises at, or after, closing.

- *Limitations on Publicity and Press Releases*. The parties may want to place certain restrictions on the content and timing of any press releases or public announcements of the transaction and in some cases may need to follow SEC guidelines. If either are or both of the parties to the transaction are publicly traded, then the general rule is that once the essential terms of the transaction are agreed to in principle, such as through the execution a Letter of Intent, there must be a public announcement. The timing and content of this announcement must be weighed carefully by the parties, including an analysis as to how the announcement will affect the price of the stock. The announcement should not be too early or it may be viewed by the Securities and Exchange Commission ("SEC") as an attempt to influence the price of the stock.
- *Expenses/Brokers*. The parties should provide, where applicable, who shall bear responsibility for investment bankers fees, finder's fees, legal expenses, and other costs pertaining to the transaction.

Common Reasons Deals Die at an Early Stage

- Seller has not prepared adequate financial statements (*e.g.* going back at least two years and reflective of the company's current condition).
- Seller and its team are uncooperative during the due diligence process.
- Buyer and its team discover a "deal breaker" in the due diligence (*e.g.* large unknown or hidden actual or contingent liabilities, like an EPA clean-up matter).
- Seller has "seller's remorse," "cold feet," or has not properly thought through its after-tax consideration or compensation.
- Seller suffers from "don't call my baby ugly" syndrome and becomes defensive when the buyer and its team find flaws (and then focus on them in the negotiation) in the opera-

tions of the business, the valuation, the loyalty of the customers, the quality of the accounts receivable, the skills of the personnel, etc.

- There is a strategic shift (or extenuating set of circumstances) affecting the acquisition strategy or criteria of the buyer (*e.g., a* change in buyer's management team during the due diligence process).
- Seller is inflexible on price and valuation when buyer and its team discover problems during due diligence.

[For more on this topic, see Chapter 11, Keeping M&A Transaction Deals on Track.]

Preparation of the Work Schedule

Following the execution of the Letter of Intent, one of the first responsibilities of purchaser's legal counsel is to prepare a comprehensive Schedule of Activities ("Work Schedule"), which serves as a task checklist and assignment of responsibilities. This task should be accomplished well before the due diligence discussed in Chapter 5 begins. The primary purpose of the schedule is to outline all of the events that must occur and documents that must be prepared prior to the closing date and beyond. In this regard, purchaser's legal counsel acts as an orchestra leader assigning primary areas of responsibility to the various members of the acquisition team as well as to the seller and its counsel. Purchaser's counsel must also act as a "task master," to ensure that the timetable foreclosing is met. Once all tasks have been identified and assigned, along with a realistic timetable established for completion, then a firm closing time and date can be preliminarily determined.

Naturally, the exact list of legal documents which must be prepared and the specific tasks to be outlined in the Work Schedule will vary from transaction to transaction, usually depending on the specific facts and circumstances of each deal, such as: (a) whether the transaction is a stock or asset purchase; (b) the form and terms of the purchase price; (c) the nature of the business being acquired; (d) the nature and extent of the assets being purchased and/or liabilities being assumed; and (e) the sophistication of the parties and their respective legal counsel.

A sample Work Schedule for an asset purchase transaction, which is not intended to be overly complex or comprehensive, is shown in Exhibit 4-2.

Exhibit 4-2. Sample work schedule.

Timetable	Task	Responsible Parties
Six Weeks Before Closing	(a) Letter of Intent is Signed; Board Resolutions to Authorize Negotiations Obtained	Seller and Buyer and their counsel
	(b) Due Diligence Request Delivered to Seller	Buyer's Counsel
Five Weeks Before Closing	(a) Due Diligence Materials Organized and Delivered	Seller's Counsel
	(b) Review of Due Diligence Materials	Buyer's Counsel
	(c) Prepare Draft of Asset Purchase Agreement, Informational Schedules, and Exhibits to Purchase Agreement, Employment and Consulting Agreements, etc.	Buyer's Counsel
	(d) Order Lien Searches on Seller's Assets to Review Encumbrances	Buyer's Counsel
	(e) Comprehensive Review of Seller's Financial Statements	Buyer's Accounting Firm
Three to Four Weeks Before Closing	(a) Review, Negotiation and Redraft of Asset Purchase Agreement (may continue until the night before closing)	Buyer and Seller's Counsel
	(b) Preparation and Negotiation of Opinion(s) of Counsel	Buyer and Seller's Counsel
	(c) Complete Review of All Initial Due Diligence Materials and Make Follow-On Requests, Where Necessary	Buyer's Counsel
	(d) Ensure that All Board and Shareholder Approvals Have Been Obtained (as required by state law)	Buyer and Seller's Counsel
	(e) Prepare Checklist and Commence Process for All Third-Party Regulatory and Contractual Approvals (Banks,	Buyer and Seller's Counsel

		Landlords, Insurance Companies, Key Customers, etc.)	
Two Weeks Before Closing	(a)	Mutual Review of Press Releases or Other Third-Party Communications Regarding the Deal (or sooner as required by the SEC)	Buyer and Seller's Counsel
	(b)	Prepare Schedule of Closing Documents (including opinions, results of lien searches, compliance certificates, etc.)	Buyer's Counsel
One Week Before and Up to Closing	(a)	Finalize Any Last-Minute Negotiations to the Asset Purchase Agreement	Buyer and Seller's Counsel
	(b)	Obtain Closing Certificates from State Authorities (e.g., good standing certificates, taxes paid and current, charter and amendments)	Seller's Counsel
	(c)	Checklist to Ensure that All Conditions to Closing to Closing Have Been Met or Waived	Buyer and Seller's Counsel
	(d)	Dry-Run Closing to Identify Open Issues (Highly Recommended 2–3 days before closing)	Buyer and Sellers
	(e)	Closing	All Parties
	(f)	Resolution of Post-Closing Matters and Conditions	All Parties

Another Pre-Deal Task: The Growing Debate About the Role and Usefulness of Fairness Opinions

The collapse of Enron and the passage of Sarbanes-Oxley have forced boards of directors, particularly at publicly-traded companies, to reassess how they do M&A deals and on what basis they can represent to the shareholders that the deal is *fair* to all parties. Naturally, the board of the seller wants to be able to represent that it is being paid a fair price, and the board of the buyer wants to represent to its shareholders that it is not using company resources to *overpay* for a transaction. If the buyer intends to pay a price that is well above current market conditions, then it better be prepared to justify and defend the reasons for the higher valuation. Directors for decades have sought out "fairness opinions" written by consultants, investment bankers, or accountants, which justify the transaction and its price parameters in order to satisfy their duties and obligations to the shareholders. But fairness opinion practices have come under scrutiny as poor analysis, conflicts of interest, and a lack of due diligence to support the opinions began to surface.

Some boards have tried to correct previously flawed practices by making sure that: (a) the "author" of the fairness opinion is *truly independent* (e.g. not affiliated with any party to the deal, either directly or indirectly); (b) the "author" of the fairness opinion is *not* just "telling the directors what they want to hear" in hopes of obtaining business from the company down the road (the "beholden to management" dilemma); (c) success fees are removed as a component of the compensation paid to the author of the opinion; and (d) second and third opinions to the core fairness opinion are obtained. The process for selecting the firm to draft the fairness opinion should be competitive and well-documented and all potential conflicts avoided. The process should be especially rigorous if the transaction is high profile, controversial, or in any way contested, especially if key shareholders of the seller have expressed concern that their shares have been undervalued and/or if the shareholders of the buyer do not understand or agree with the underlying value proposition of the deal as proposed.

Due Diligence

Following the preparations of both teams, the narrowing of the field, and the execution of the letter of intent, both sides must begin preparing for the due diligence process. This process involves a legal, financial, and strategic review of all of the seller's documents, contractual relationships, operating history, and organizational structure. Due diligence is not just a process, it is also a reality test—a test of whether the factors driving the deal and making it look attractive to the parties are real or illusory. Due diligence is not a quest to find the deal breakers but a test of the value proposition underlying the transaction to make sure that the inside of the house is as attractive as the outside. Once the foundation has been dissected, it can either be rebuilt around a deal that makes sense or allow the buyer to walk away and prevent the consummation of a deal that doesn't make sense. It is also important to understand that in a post-Sarbanes-Oxley world, due diligence is typically wider and deeper in its scope than ever before, especially if the prospective buyer is a public company or a company with plans to go public within the next 18 months.

The seller's team must organize the documents, and the buyer's team must be prepared to ask all of the right questions, thereby conducting a detailed analysis of the documents provided. To the extent that the deal is structured as a merger, or where the seller will be taking the buyer's stock as all or part of its compensation, the process of due diligence is likely to be two-way, as the parties gather background information on each other.

The due diligence work is usually divided between two working teams: (1) financial and strategic, which is typically managed by the buyer's accountants and management team; and (2) legal, to be conducted by the buyer's counsel. Throughout the process, both teams compare notes on open issues and potential risks and problems. The legal due diligence focuses on the potential legal issues and problems that may serve as impediments to the transaction, as well as sheds light on how the transaction documents should be structured. The business due diligence focuses on the strategic and financial issues in the transaction, such as confirmation of the past financial performance of the seller; integration of the human and financial resources of the two companies; confirmation of the operating, production, and distribution synergies and economies of scale to be achieved by the acquisition; and the gathering of information necessary for financing the transaction.

Overall, the due diligence process, when done properly, can be tedious, frustrating, time consuming, and expensive. Yet it is a necessary prerequisite to a well-planned acquisition, and it can be quite informative and revealing in its analysis of the target company and its measures of the costs and risks associated with the transaction. Buyers should expect sellers to become defensive, evasive, and impatient during the due diligence phase of the transaction. Most business managers really don't enjoy having their business policies and decisions under the microscope, especially for an extended period of time and by a party searching for skeletons in the closet. Eventually, the seller is likely to give an ultimatum to the prospective buyer: "Finish the due diligence soon or the deal is off." When negotiations have reached this point, it is best to end the examination process some time soon thereafter. Buyers should resist the temptation to conduct a hasty "once over," either to save costs or to appease the seller. Yet at the same time, they should avoid "due diligence overkill," keeping in mind that due diligence is *not* a perfect process and should not be a tedious fishing expedition. Like any audit, a diligence process is designed to answer the important questions, and ensure with reasonable assurance that the seller's claims about the business are fair and legitimate.

Information will slip through the cracks, which is precisely why broad representations, warranties, liability holdbacks, and indemnification provisions should be structured into the final purchase agreement. These provisions protect the buyer, while the seller negotiates for carve-outs (e.g., a minimum "basket" of liabilities before the buyer may seek reimbursement for undisclosed or unexpected liabilities), exceptions, and limitations to liability that provide post-closing protections. The nature and scope of these provisions are likely to be hotly contested in the negotiations. Remember that the key objective of due diligence is not only to "confirm that the deal makes sense" (e.g., confirm the factual assumptions and preliminary valuations underlying the terms by which the buyer negotiates the transaction), but also to determine whether the transaction should proceed at all. The buyer must recognize at all times that there may be a need to "jump ship" if the risks or potential liabilities in the transaction greatly exceed what is anticipated.

Common Due Diligence Problems and Exposure Areas

There is virtually an infinite number of potential problems and exposure areas for the buyer which may be uncovered in the review and analysis of the seller's documents and operations. The specific issues and problems will vary based on the size of the seller, the nature of its business and the number of years that the seller (or its predecessors) have been in business.

- "Clouds" in the title to critical tangible (real estate, equipment, inventory) and intangible (patents, trademarks, etc.) assets: Be sure the seller has clear title to these assets and that they are conveyed without claims, liens and encumbrances.
- Employee matters: There is a wide variety of employment or labor law issues or liabilities that may be lurking just below the surface which will not be uncovered unless the right questions are asked. Questions designed to uncover

wage and hour law violations, discrimination claims, OSHA compliance, or even liability for unfunded persons under the Multi-Employer Pension Plan Act should be developed. If the seller has recently made a substantial workforce reduction (or if you as the buyer are planning post-closing layoffs), then the requirements of the Worker Adjustment and Retraining Notification Act (WARN) must have been met. The requirements of WARN include minimum notice requirements of 60 days prior to wide scale terminations.

- The possibility of environmental liability under CERCLA or related environmental regulations.
- Unresolved existing or potential litigation—these cases should be reviewed carefully by counsel.
- A seller's attempt to "dress-up" the financial statements prior to sale, often in an attempt to hide inventory problems, research and development expenditures, excessive overhead and administrative costs, uncollected or uncollectible accounts receivable, unnecessary or inappropriate personal expenses, unrecorded liabilities, tax contingencies, etc.

Effective due diligence is both an art and a science. The *art* is the style and experience to know which questions to ask and how and when to ask them. It's the ability to create an atmosphere of both trust and fear in the seller, which encourages full and complete disclosure. In this sense, the due diligence team is on a risk discovery and assessment mission, looking for potential problems and liabilities (the search), and finding ways to resolve these problems prior to closing and/or to ensure that risks are allocated fairly and openly after the closing.

The *science* of due diligence is in the preparation of comprehensive and customized checklists of the specific questions to be presented to the seller, in maintaining a methodical system for organizing and analyzing the documents and data provided by the seller, and in quantitatively assessing the risks raised by those problems discovered in the process. One of the key areas is detection of the seller's obligations, particularly those that the buyer will be expected or required to assume after closing (especially in a stock purchase transaction; in an asset purchase, purchased liabilities are specifically defined). The due diligence process is designed first to detect the *existence* of the obligation and second to identify any *defaults or problems* in connection with these obligations that will affect the buyer after closing.

The best way for the buyer to ensure that virtually no stone remains unturned is with effective due diligence preparation and planning. The legal due diligence checklist in the following section is intended to guide the company's management team while it works closely with counsel to gather and review all legal documents that may be relevant to the structure and pricing of the transaction; to assess the potential legal risks and liabilities to the buyer following the closing; and to identify all of the consents and approvals, such as an existing contract that can't be assigned without consent, which must be obtained from third parties and government agencies.

Common Mistakes Made by the Buyer During the Due Diligence Investigation

1. *Mismatch between the documents provided by the seller and the skills of the buyer's review team.* It may be the case that the seller has particularly complex financial statements or highly technical reports which must be truly understood by the buyer's due diligence team. Make sure there is a capability fit.
2. *Poor communication and misunderstandings.* The communications should be open and clear between the teams of the buyer and the seller. The process must be well-orchestrated.
3. *Lack of planning and focus in the preparation of the due diligence questionnaires and in the interviews with the seller's team.* The focus must be on asking the *right* questions, not just a lot of questions. Sellers will resent wasteful "fishing expeditions" when the buyer's team is unfocused.

4. *Inadequate time devoted to tax and financial matters*. The buyer's (and seller's) CFO and CPA must play an integral part in the due diligence process in order to gather data on past financial performance and tax reporting, unusual financial events or disturbing trends or inefficiencies.
5. *Lack of reasonable accommodations and support for the buyer's due diligence team.* The buyer must insist that its team will be treated like welcome guests, not enemies from the IRS! Many times buyer's counsel is sent to a dark room in the corner of the building to inspect documents without coffee, windows or phones. It will enhance and expedite the transaction if the seller provides reasonable accommodations and support for the buyer's due diligence team.
6. *Ignoring the real story behind the numbers*. The buyer and its team must dig deep into the financial data and test (and retest) the value proposition as to whether the deal truly makes sense. They must ask themselves, "Does the real value truly justify the price?" The economics of the deal may not hold water once a realistic look at cost allocation, inventory turnover, and capacity utilization is taken into account.

The checklist should be a guideline, not a crutch. The buyer's management team must take the lead in developing questions that pertain to the nature of the seller's business. These questions will set the pace for the level of detail and adequacy of the review. For example, I recently worked on a deal that involved the purchase of a hockey league in the Midwest. It was easy to prepare the standard due diligence list and draw up questions regarding corporate structure and history, the status of the stadium leases, team tax returns and to question the steps that had been taken to protect the team trademarks. The more difficult task was developing a customized list. In my role as legal counsel, I asked my client the question, "If you were buying a sports league, what would you need to review?"

The key point here is that every type of business has its own issues and problems, and a standard set of questions will rarely be sufficient. The list for this client included player and coaching contracts; stadium signage and promotional leases; league-wide and local-team sponsorship contracts; the immigration status of each player; team and player performance statistics; the status of contracts with each team's star players; scouting reports and drafting procedures; ticket sales (including walk-up, advance, season, group tickets, and coupons) for each team and game; promotional agreements with equipment suppliers and game-day merchandise, food and beverage concession contracts; the status of each team's franchise agreement; commitments made to cities for future teams; and unique per-team advertising rates for dasher boards (the signs for advertising that surround the rink).

When done properly, due diligence is performed in multiple stages. First, all the basic data are gathered and specific topics are identified. Follow-up questions and additional data gathering can be performed in subsequent rounds of due diligence; they must be custom-tailored to the target's core business industry trends and unique challenges.

Legal Due Diligence

In analyzing the company for sale, the buyer's team carefully reviews and analyzes the following legal documents and records, where applicable.

I. *Corporate Matters*
   A. Corporate records of the seller.
      1. Certificate of incorporation and all amendments.
      2. By-laws as amended.
      3. Minute books, including resolutions and minutes of all director and shareholder meetings.
      4. Current shareholders list (certified by the corporate secretary), annual reports to shareholders, and stock transfer books.
      5. List of all states, countries and other jurisdictions in which the seller transacts business or is qualified to do business.
      6. Applications or other filings in each state listed in (5), above, for qualification as foreign corporation and evidence of qualification.

    7. Locations of business offices (including overseas).

B. Agreements among the seller's shareholders.

C. All contracts restricting the sale or transfer of shares of the company, such as buy/sell agreements, subscription agreements, offeree questionnaires, or contractual rights of first refusal as well as all agreements for the right to purchase shares, such as stock options or warrants as well as any pledge agreements by an individual shareholder involving the seller's shares.

II. *Financial Matters*

A. List of and copies of management and similar reports or memoranda relating to the material aspects of the business operations or products.

B. Letters of counsel in response to auditors' requests for the preceding five (5) years.

C. Reports of independent accountants to the board of directors for the preceding five (5) years.

D. Revolving credit and term loan agreements, indentures and other debt instruments, including, without limitation, all documents relating to shareholder loans.

E. Correspondence with principal lenders to the seller.

F. Personal guarantees of seller's indebtedness by its shareholders or other parties.

G. Agreements by the seller where it has served as a guarantor for the obligations of third parties.

H. Federal, state and local tax returns and correspondence with federal, state and local tax officials.

I. Federal filings regarding the Subchapter S status (where applicable) of the seller.

J. Any private placement memorandum (assuming, of course, that the seller is not a Securities Act of 1934 "Reporting Company") prepared and used by the seller (as well as any document used in lieu of a PPM, such as an investment profile or a business plan).

K. Financial statements, which should be prepared in accordance with Generally Accepted Accounting Principles (GAAP), for the past five (5) years of the seller, including:

    1. Annual (audited) balance sheets.

2. Monthly (or other available) balance sheet.
3. Annual (audited) and monthly (or other available) earnings statements.
4. Annual (audited) and monthly (or other available) statements of shareholders' equity and changes in financial position.
5. Any recently prepared projections for the seller.
6. Notes and material assumptions for all statements described in K (1)-(5), above.

L. Any information or documentation relating to tax assessments, deficiency notices, investigations, audits or settlement proposals.

M. Informal schedule of key management compensation (listing information for at least the ten most highly compensated management employees or consultants).

N. Financial aspects of overseas operations (where applicable), including status of foreign legislations, regulatory restrictions, intellectual property protection, exchange controls, method for repatriating profits, foreign manufacturing, government controls, import/export licensing and tariffs, etc.

O. Projected budgets, accounts receivable reports (including detailed aging report, turnover, bad debt experience, and reserves) and related information.

III. *Management and Employment Matters*

A. All employment agreements.

B. Agreements relating to consulting, management, financial advisory services and other professional engagements.

C. Copies of all union contracts and collective bargaining agreements.

D. Equal Employment Opportunity Commission (EEOC) and any state equivalent) compliance files.

E. Occupational Safety and Health Administration (OSHA) files including safety records and worker's compensation claims.

F. Employee benefit plans (and copies of literature issued to employees describing such plans), including the following:

1. Pension and retirement plans, including union pension or retirement plans.
2. Annual reports for pension plans, if any.
3. Profit sharing plans.
4. Stock option plans, including information concerning all options, stock appreciation rights and other stock-related benefits granted by the company.
5. Medical and dental plans.
6. Insurance plans and policies, including the following:
   a. Errors and omissions policies.
   b. Directors' and officers' liability insurance policies.
7. Any Employee Stock Ownership Plan ("ESOP") and trust agreement.
8. Severance pay plans or programs.
9. All other benefit or incentive plans or arrangements not covered by the foregoing, including welfare benefit plans.

G. All current contracts agreements with or pertaining to the seller and to which directors, officers or shareholders of the seller are parties, and any documents relating to any other transactions between the seller and any director, officer or shareholders, including receivables from or payables to directors, officers or shareholders.

H. All policy and procedures manuals of the seller concerning personnel; hiring and promotional practices; compliance with the Family Leave Act, etc.; drug and alcohol abuse policies; AIDS policies; sexual harassment policies; vacation and holiday policies; expense reimbursement policies; etc.

I. The name, address, phone number and personnel file of any officer or key employee who has left the seller within the past three years.

IV. *Tangible and Intangible Assets of the Seller*

A. List of all commitments for rented or leased real and personal property, including location and address, description, terms, options, termination and renewal rights, policies regarding ownership of improvements, and annual costs.

B. List of all real property owned, including location and address, description of general character, easements, rights of way, encumbrances, zoning restrictions, surveys, mineral rights, title insurance, pending and threatened condemnation, hazardous waste pollution, etc.

C. List of all tangible assets.

D. List of all liens on all real properties and material tangible assets.

E. Mortgages, deeds, title insurance policies, leases, and other agreements relating to the properties of the seller.

F. Real estate tax bills for the real estate of the seller.

G. List of patents, patents pending, trademarks, trade names, copyrights, registered and proprietary Internet addresses, franchises, licenses and all other intangible assets, including registration numbers, expiration dates, employee invention agreements and policies, actual or threatened infringement actions, licensing agreements, and copies of all correspondence relating to this intellectual property.

H. Copies of any survey, appraisal, engineering or other reports as to the properties of the seller.

I. List of assets which may be on a consignment basis (or which may be the property of a given customer, such as machine dies, molds, etc.).

V. *Material Contracts and Obligations of the Seller*

A. Material purchase, supply and sale agreements currently outstanding or projected to come to fruition within 12 months, including the following:

1. List of all contracts relating to the purchase of products, equipment, fixtures, tools, dies, supplies, industrial supplies, or other materials having a price under any such contract in excess of $5,000.

2. List of all unperformed sales contracts.

B. Documents incidental to any planned expansion of the seller's facilities.

C. Consignment agreements.

D. Research agreements.
E. Franchise, licensing, distribution and agency agreements.
F. Joint venture agreements.
G. Agreements for the payment of receipt of license fees or royalties and royalty-free licenses.
H. Documentation relating to all property, liability and casualty insurance policies owned by the seller, including for each policy a summary description of:
   1. Coverage
   2. Policy type and number
   3. Insurer/carrier and broker
   4. Premium
   5. Expiration date
   6. Deductible
   7. Any material changes in any of the foregoing since the inception of the seller
   8. Claims made under such policies
I. Agreements restricting the seller's right to compete in any business.
J. Agreements for the seller's current purchase of services, including, without limitation, consulting and management.
K. Contracts for the purchase, sale, or removal of electricity, gas, water, telephone, sewage, power, or any other utility service.
L. List of waste dumps, disposal, treatment, and storage sites.
M. Agreements with any railroad, trucking, or any other transportation company or courier service.
N. Letters of credit.
O. Copies of any special benefits under contracts or government programs which might be in jeopardy as a result of the proposed transaction (*e.g.,* small business or minority set-asides, intrafamily transactions or favored pricing, internal leases or allocations, etc.).
P. Copies of licenses, permits and governmental approvals applied for or issued to the seller which are required in order to operate the businesses of the seller, such

as zoning, energy requirements (natural gas, fuel, oil, electricity, etc.) operating permits or health and safety certificates.

Note: This section is critical and will be one key area of the negotiations as discussed in Chapter 10. Therefore, it is suggested that the buyer and its advisory team request copies of *all* material contracts and obligations of the seller and then organize them as follows:

Schedule of All Contracts and Obligations of Seller Which Are to Be Assumed by Buyer After Closing*	Status of Each Contract or Obligation	To What Extent Will Third-Party Consents Be Required for the Assignment or Assumption of These Contracts or Obligations?
	Sample Responses:	*Sample Responses:*
A. ______________	Current	Not Required
B. ______________	Received Notice of Default on ________, 20__; cured on ____, 20__	Consent to Assignment Requested _____, 20__ and obtained _____, 20__
C. ______________	Notice of Default Received; Default Not Yet Cured!	Consent to Assumption Required But Not Yet Requested

*e.g., contracts which have a remaining term in excess of six months.

VI. *Litigation and Claims—Actual and Contingent*

A. Opinion letter from each lawyer or law firm prosecuting or defending significant litigation to which the seller is a party describing such litigation.

B. List of material litigation or claims for more than $5,000 against the seller asserted or *threatened* with respect to the quality of the products or services sold to customers, warranty claims, disgruntled employees, product liability, government actions, tort claims, breaches of contract, etc. including pending or threatened claims.

C. List of settlement agreements, releases, decrees, orders or arbitration awards affecting the seller.

D. Description of labor relations history.

E. Documentation regarding correspondence or proceedings with federal, state or local regulatory agencies.

Note: Be sure to obtain specific representations and warranties from the seller and its advisors regarding any knowledge pertaining to potential or contingent claims or litigation!

VII. *Miscellaneous*

A. Press releases (past two years)

B. Resumes of all key management team members

C. Press clippings (past two years)

D. Financial analyst reports, industry, surveys, etc.

E. Texts of speeches by the seller's management team, especially if reprinted and distributed to the industry or the media.

F. Schedule of all outside advisors, consultants, etc., used by the seller over the past five years (domestic and international).

G. Schedule of long-term investments made by the seller.

H. Standard forms (purchase orders, sales orders, service agreements, etc.).

Key Legal Questions

The buyer's acquisition team and its legal counsel gather data to answer the following ten legal questions during the legal phase of due diligence:

1. What legal steps will need to be taken to effectuate the transaction (e.g., director and stockholder approval, share transfer restrictions, restrictive covenants in loan documentation)? Has the appropriate corporate authority been obtained to proceed with the agreement? What key (e.g., FCC, DOJ) third-party consents (e.g., lenders, venture capitalists, landlords, key customers) are required?

2. What antitrust problems, if any, are raised by the transaction? Will filing with the FTC be necessary under the pre-merger notification provisions of the Hart-Scott-Rodino Act?

3. Will the transaction be exempt from registration under applicable federal and state securities loans under the "sale of business" doctrine?

4. What are the significant legal problems or issues now affecting the seller or that are likely to affect the seller in the foreseeable future? What potential adverse tax consequences to the buyer, seller, and their respective shareholders may be triggered by the transaction?

5. What are the potential post-closing risks and obligations of the buyer? To what extent should the seller be held liable for such potential liability? What steps, if any, can be taken to reduce these potential risks or liabilities? What will it cost to implement these steps?

6. What are the impediments to the assignability of key tangible and intangible assets of the seller company that are desired by the buyer, such as real estate, intellectual property, favorable contracts or leases, human resources, or plant and equipment?

7. What are the obligations and responsibilities of the buyer and seller under applicable environmental and hazardous waste laws, such as the Comprehensive Environmental Response Compensation and Liability Act (CERCLA)?

8. What are the obligations and responsibilities of the buyer and seller to the creditors of the seller (e.g., bulk transfer laws under Article 6 of the applicable state's commercial code)?

9. What are the obligations and responsibilities of the buyer and seller under applicable federal and state labor and employment laws (e.g., will the buyer be subject to successor liability under federal labor laws and as a result be obligated to recognize the presence of organized labor and therefore be obligated to negotiate existing collective bargaining agreements)?

10. To what extent will employment, consulting, confidentiality, or non-competition agreements need to be created or modified in connection with the proposed transaction?

Business and Strategic Due Diligence

At the same time as legal counsel is performing its legal investigation of the seller's company, the buyer assembles a management team to conduct business and strategic due diligence. The level and extent of this general business and strategic due diligence will vary, depending on the experience of the buyer in the seller's industry and its familiarity with the seller company. For example, a financial buyer entering into a new industry, and with no prior experience with the seller, should conduct an exhaustive due diligence—not only on the seller's company but also on any relevant trends within the industry that might directly or indirectly affect the deal. In contrast, a management buyout by a group of industry veterans who have been with the seller over an extended period of time will probably need to conduct only a minimum amount of business or strategic due diligence; in this case, the focus will be on legal due diligence and assessment and assumption of risk.

In conducting the due diligence from a business perspective, the buyer's team is likely to encounter a wide variety of financial problems and risk areas when analyzing the seller. These typically include an undervaluation of inventory; overdue tax liabilities; inadequate management information systems; related-party transactions (especially in small, closely held companies); an unhealthy reliance on a few key customers or suppliers; aging accounts receivable; unrecorded liabilities (e.g., warranty claims, vacation pay, claims, sales returns, and allowances); or an immediate need for significant expenditures as a result of obsolete equipment, inventory, or computer systems. Each of these problems poses different risks and costs for the acquiring company, and these risks must be weighed against the benefits to be gained from the transaction.

For the buyer just getting to know the seller's industry, the following two basic questions should be asked:

1. How would you define the market or markets in which the seller operates? What steps will you take to expedite your learning curve of trends within these markets? What third-party advisors are qualified to advise you on key trends affecting this industry?

2. What are the factors that determine success or failure within this industry? How does the seller stack up? What are the image

and reputation of the seller within the industry? Does it have a niche? Is the seller's market share increasing or decreasing? Why? What steps can be taken to enhance or reverse these trends?

The Emergence of Virtual Data Rooms

It appears that the age of bad hotel rooms, expensive travel costs and bad donuts in classic diligence data rooms may be slowly but surely being replaced with a "Virtual Data Room" or VDR's. Virtual Data Rooms use existing computer software and Internet technology to provide a secure and on-line format for reviewing and organizing due diligence information. The documents are easier to search and index when they are already online and prevent "water-cooler rumor mills" about what the guys in suits are doing in the corner conference room. It does require the company's IT department to be involved early and often in the overall selling process. The VDR also better facilitates the review of certain types of data which are easier to review online and in electronic form, such as CAD drawings, video files, patent filings, architectural drawings, etc. Are VDR's growing in acceptance? It appears so. Intra Links (www.intralink.com), a leading provider of VDR software and systems handled fifty (50) transactions in 2001, 450 in 2004 and predicts being a technology provider to 1500 transactions in 2005.

The following checklists are designed to provide the acquisition team with a starting point for analysis of the seller. They help to level the playing field in the negotiations, since the seller usually starts with greater expertise regarding its industry and its business. Here are some examples (these checklists are not intended to be exhaustive) of the topic areas and specific questions that should be addressed in due diligence on a given seller:

The Seller's Management Team: Checklist

- ❑ Has the seller's organization chart been carefully reviewed? How are management functions and responsibilities dele-

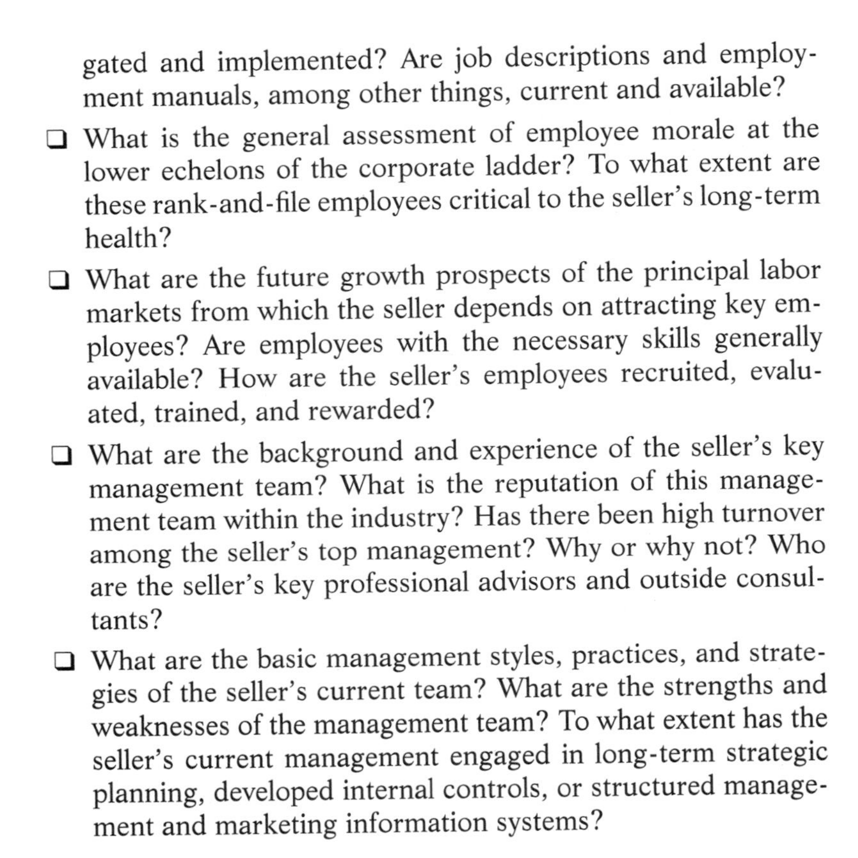

gated and implemented? Are job descriptions and employment manuals, among other things, current and available?

- ❑ What is the general assessment of employee morale at the lower echelons of the corporate ladder? To what extent are these rank-and-file employees critical to the seller's long-term health?
- ❑ What are the future growth prospects of the principal labor markets from which the seller depends on attracting key employees? Are employees with the necessary skills generally available? How are the seller's employees recruited, evaluated, trained, and rewarded?
- ❑ What are the background and experience of the seller's key management team? What is the reputation of this management team within the industry? Has there been high turnover among the seller's top management? Why or why not? Who are the seller's key professional advisors and outside consultants?
- ❑ What are the basic management styles, practices, and strategies of the seller's current team? What are the strengths and weaknesses of the management team? To what extent has the seller's current management engaged in long-term strategic planning, developed internal controls, or structured management and marketing information systems?

Operations of the Seller: Checklist

- ❑ What are the seller's production and distribution methods? To what extent are these methods protected either by contract or proprietary rights? Have copies of the seller's brochures and reports describing the seller and its products and services been obtained?
- ❑ To what extent is the seller operating at its maximum capacity? Why? What are the significant risk factors (e.g., dependence on raw materials or key suppliers or customers) affecting the seller's production capacity and ability to expand? What are the significant costs of producing the seller's goods and services? To what extent are the production and output of the seller dependent on economic cycles or seasonal

factors? *Note:* Obtain a breakdown of major sales by specific product and specific customer categories in order to fully assess the seller's financial performance, dependence on key customers, or product line susceptibility to risk.

- ❑ Are the seller's plant, equipment, supplies, and machinery in good working order? When will these assets need to be replaced? What are the annual maintenance and service costs for these key assets? At what levels are the seller's inventories? What are the break-even production efficiency and inventory turnover rates for the seller company and how do these compare with industry norms?
- ❑ Does the seller maintain production plans, schedules, and reports? Have copies been obtained and analyzed by the buyer? What are the seller's manufacturing and production obligations pursuant to long-term contracts or other arrangements? What long-term (post-closing) obligations or commitments have been made on the purchase of raw materials or other supplies or resources?
- ❑ What is the status of the seller's inventories (e.g., amount and balance in raw materials and finished goods in relation to production cycles and sales requirements)? What is the condition of the inventory? To what extent is it obsolete? *Note:* Be sure to get a breakdown and an analysis of all expenses (e.g., amounts, trends, categories) in order to assess the profitability of the seller's business, as well as to determine where post-closing expense savings can be obtained or economies of scale achieved.

Sales and Marketing Strategies of the Seller: Checklist

- ❑ What are the seller's primary and secondary markets? What is the size of these markets and what is the seller's market share within each market? What strategies are in place to expand this market share? What are the current trends affecting either the growth or the shrinkage of these particular markets? How are these markets segmented and reached by the seller?
- ❑ Who are the seller's direct and indirect competitors? What are the respective strengths and weaknesses of each competi-

tor? In what principal ways do companies within the seller's industry compete (e.g., price, quality, or service)? For each material competitor, the buyer should seek to obtain data on the competitor's products and services, geographic location, channel of distribution, market share, financial health, pricing, policies, and reputation within the industry.

- ❑ Who are the seller's typical customers? What demographic data have been assembled and analyzed? What are the customers' purchasing capabilities and patterns? Where are these customers principally located? What political, economic, social, or technological trends or changes are likely to affect the demographic makeup of the seller's customer base over the next three to five years? What are the key factors that influence the demand for the seller's goods and services?
- ❑ What are the seller's primary and secondary distribution channels? What contracts are in place in relation to these channels? How could these channels or contracts be modified or improved? How will these channels overlap or conflict with the existing distribution channels of the buyer?
- ❑ What sales, advertising, public relations, and promotional campaigns and programs are currently in place at the seller's company? To what extent have these programs been effectively monitored and evaluated?

Financial Management of the Seller: Checklist

- ❑ Based on the financial statements and reports collected in connection with the legal due diligence, what key sales, income, and earnings trends have been identified? What effect will the proposed transaction have on these aspects of the seller's financial performance? What are the various costs incurred in connection with bringing the seller's products and services to the marketplace? In what ways can these costs be reduced or eliminated?
- ❑ What are the seller's billing and collection procedures? How current are the seller's accounts receivables? What steps have been (or can be) taken to expedite the collection procedures and systems? How credible is the seller's existing accounting and financial control system?

- ☐ What is the seller's capital structure? What are the key financial liabilities and debt obligations of the seller? How do the seller's leverage ratios compare to industry norms? What are the seller's monthly debt-service payments? How strong is the seller's relationship with creditors, lenders, and investors?

A way for the buyer to ensure that the seller has been forthright in disclosing all material obligations and liabilities (whether actual or contingent) is to prepare an affidavit. An affidavit like the one shown in Exhibit 5-1 provides additional protection against misrepresentation or material omissions by the seller, its lawyers, and its auditors. The affidavit can be customized to a particular transaction and include the specific concerns that may arise during the transaction and afterwards.

Exhibit 5-1. Sample affidavit regarding liabilities.

State of ____________________ }
}ss.
County of ___________________ }

Prospective Seller, being of lawful age and being first duly sworn upon her oath states:

1. I am the sole shareholder of the S Corporation which trades under the name "SellerCo," and I have full right to sell its assets as described in the Bill of Sale dated ________. Those assets are free and clear of all security interests, liabilities, obligations, and encumbrances of any sort.

2. There are no creditors of SellerCo, or me, or persons known to me who are asserting claims against me or the assets being sold, which in any way affect the transfer to Prospective Buyer of the trade name SellerCo, its goodwill, and its assets, including the equipment as set forth in the Bill of Sale dated ________. I agree to pay all gross receipt and sales taxes and all employment taxes of any sort due through closing. I am current in regard to these taxes and all other taxes, and there are no pending disputes as to any of my taxes or the taxes of SellerCo.

3. There are no judgments against SellerCo or me in any federal or state court in the United States of America. There are also no replevins, attachments, executions, or other writs or processes issued against SellerCo or me. I have never sought protection under any bankruptcy law nor has any petition in bankruptcy been filed against me. There are no pending administrative or regulatory proceedings, arbitrations, or mediations involving SellerCo or me, and I do not know and have no reasonable ground to know of any proposed ones or any basis for any such actions.

(continues)

Exhibit 5-1. Continued.

4. There are no known outstanding claims by any employees of SellerCo or me, and I expressly recognize that no claims of, by, or on behalf of any employees arising prior to closing are being transferred to Prospective Buyer.

5. There are no and have been no unions that have been or are involved in any business that I own, and particularly, SellerCo. Furthermore, there currently is no union organizational activity underway in any business that I own, and particularly, SellerCo.

6. There are and have been no multi-employer pension plans or other pension or profit-sharing plans involved in any business that I own, and particularly, SellerCo.

7. I have always conducted SellerCo according to applicable laws and regulations.

8. From the time when the purchase agreement was executed through closing, I have conducted the business called SellerCo only in the usual and customary manner. I have entered into no new contracts and have assumed no new obligations during that time period.

9. I shall remain fully liable for payment of all bills, accounts payable, or other claims against SellerCo or me created prior to closing. None of them are being transferred to Prospective Buyer.

10. I hereby warrant and represent to Prospective Buyer that all statements in paragraphs one through nine of this Affidavit are true and correct.

11. a. I agree to indemnify and hold harmless Prospective Buyer in respect to any and all claims, losses, damages, liabilities, and expenses, including, without limitation, settlement costs and any legal, accounting, and other expenses for investigating or defending any actions or threatened actions, reasonably incurred by Prospective Buyer in connection with:
    i. Any claims or liabilities made against Prospective Buyer because of any act or failure to act of myself arising prior to closing in regard to SellerCo; or
    ii. Any breach of warranty or misrepresentation involved in my sale of SellerCo to Prospective Buyer.

    b. As to claims or liabilities against Prospective Buyer arising prior to closing in connection with SellerCo, or any claim arising at anytime in regard to any profit-sharing or pension plan started prior to closing involving SellerCo, or any breach of warranty or other material misrepresentation made by me, I agree that Prospective Buyer has the option to pay the claim or liability and deduct the amount of it from any money owed to me, after giving me reasonable notice of the claim and reasonable opportunity to resolve it. This right of setoff expressly applies to any damages Prospective Buyer suffers as a result of any breach of any warranty I have given to Prospective Buyer. Prospective Buyer's right of setoff against any money owed me shall not be deemed his exclusive remedy for any breach by me of any representations, warranties, or agreements involved in the sale of SellerCo to him, all of which shall survive the closing and any setoff made by Prospective Buyer.

12. I agree to execute any further documents to complete this sale.

____
Prospective Seller

Subscribed and Sworn to before me this _______ day of _______, 20_____.

____
Notary Public

My Commission Expires:

____

Note: Proper use of this affidavit depends on the purchase agreement used.

Conclusion

Due diligence must be a cooperative and patient process between the buyer's and seller's teams. Any attempts to hide or manipulate key data will only lead to problems down the road. Material misrepresentations or omissions can (and often do) lead to post-closing litigation, which is expensive and time consuming for both parties. Another mistake in due diligence often made by the seller is to forget the human element. I have worked on deals where the lawyers were sent into a dark room in the corner of the building, without any support or even coffee; on other deals, we were treated like royalty, with full access to support staff, computers, telephones, food, and beverages. It is only human, as buyer's counsel, to be a bit more cooperative in the negotiations when the seller's team is supportive and allows counsel to do his job.

An Overview of Regulatory Considerations

There is a wide variety of regulatory considerations in a merger or acquisition, usually falling into one of two categories: (a) *general* regulatory issues affecting all types of transactions and (b) *industry-specific* regulatory issues which affect only certain types of transactions in certain industries. The general regulatory considerations include issues such as antitrust, environmental, securities, and employee benefits matters, which are discussed below. There are also industry-specific regulatory issues where federal and state regulators may exercise rights of approval over those transactions which involve a change in ownership or control, or which may have an anti-competitive effect on a given industry.

Any transaction in the broadcasting, health care, insurance, public utilities, transportation, telecommunications, financial services or even the defense contracting industries should be analyzed carefully by legal counsel to determine what level of governmental approval may be necessary to close the transaction. These regulatory agencies such as the Federal Communications Commission (FCC) and the Pension Benefit Guaranty Corporation (PBGC) have broad powers to determine whether the proposed transaction will be in the best interests of the consuming general public, or, in the case of the PBGC, the employees and retirees of a given seller.

In certain regulated industries, these government approvals are needed to effectuate the transfer of government-granted licenses, permits or franchises. These may range from the local liquor board approving the transfer of a liquor license in a small restaurant acquisition or the need to obtain FCC approval for the transfer of multibillion dollar communication licenses, such as the transaction between MCI and Verizon.

The Impact of Sarbanes-Oxley

Since the collapse of Enron, Arthur Andersen, WorldCom, and investigations at AOL Time Warner, Tyco, Qwest, Global Crossing, ImClone, and many more, *the public's trust in our corporate leaders and financial markets*—either as employees, shareholders, or bondholders—has been virtually destroyed. And we all can agree that the market did not need this corporate governance crisis at this time—there were already plenty of factors at work in rattling the investor psyche, from the threat of war with Iraq, to the fighting in the Middle East, to threats of additional terrorist attacks on U.S. soil, to the disputes between Pakistan and India, coupled with the market corrections that we have all suffered through since March of 2000.

In response, Congress acted relatively swiftly (and some say hastily) in passing the Sarbanes-Oxley Act, which President George W. Bush signed into law on July 30, 2002. The SEC, NYSE, DOJ, NASDAQ, state attorney generals, and others have also responded quickly to create more accountability by and among corporate executives, board members, their advisors, shareholders, and employees. Central themes include more objectivity in the composition of board members; more independence and autonomy for auditors; more control over financial reporting; stiffer penalties for abuse of the laws and regulations pertaining to corporate governance, accounting practices and financial reporting; and new rules to ensure fair and prompt access to the information and current events that affect the company's current status and future performance.

Although some of the provisions and procedures under Sarbanes-Oxley have yet to be decided, the passage of this Act *has already had an impact on M&A transactions*. The standards for due diligence have changed—buyers and their counsel are digging deeper on a broader range of issues, and sellers need to be better prepared for the due diligence process than ever before. The financial statements of the seller will be scrutinized a lot more closely than ever before—particularly in transactions where there is a public buyer and a private seller. If there are any reporting or accounting irregularities in your financial systems (as a potential seller), then *now* is the time to fix them. It is also critical to understand that a private company's decision making and governance processes (e.g., how decisions are made, how well they are documented, how conflicts of interest have been avoided) will also be under a much larger microscope. Finally, potential sellers must also understand that all aspects of executive compensation, including the nature and structure of employee stock option plans will also be more closely scrutinized by public (or those intending to go public in the near future) buyers.

The passage and implementation of Sarbanes-Oxley also means all types of M&A advisors—from buyers to accountants to intermediaries—must understand how their roles and the nature of their advice must endure to meet these standards. M&A advisors must do a better job helping the seller clients get ready for the process and advising their buyer clients to ask all the right questions. Lawyers should expect to see tougher representations and warranties, holdbacks, and indemnification provisions to protect the buyers against the "inheritance" of problems that would raise issues for the buyer under Sarbanes-Oxley.

Environmental Laws

Prior to the 1970s, sellers normally had little or no legal obligation to disclose information concerning the presence or use of potentially hazardous substances on their premises, nor to report the release of such substances into the environment to the potential buyers of their business. What obligations did exist were imposed by state or local governments regulating public nuisances or engaging in emergency planning.

In the 1970s and early 1980s, as the federal government passed new laws concerning health and the environment, it created new obligations to report on the presence, use, and release of hazardous substances under certain circumstances. The Clean Water Act, the Toxic Substances Control Act (TSCA), the Resource Conservation and Recovery Act (RCRA), and the Comprehensive Environmental Response, Compensation, and Liability Act (CERCLA or Superfund), all contained provisions requiring notification of government authorities in the event of chemical releases and other emergencies. In addition, TSCA and regulations promulgated pursuant to the Occupational Safety and Health Act (OSHA) required chemical manufacturers and others to compile and report information on the presence and use of certain chemicals on their premises. Each of these laws had a unique, limited scope, for example, covering some substances but not others, and the result was a patchwork of different but sometimes overlapping reporting requirements.

In 1986, Congress enacted the Emergency Planning and Community Right-to-Know Act (EPCRA), found in Title III of the Superfund Amendments and Reauthorization Act of 1986 (SARA). Subchapter I of EPCRA creates a framework for state and local emergency response planning, and in that setting imposes on companies two types of reporting obligations: (1) the obligation to provide information about the presence of extremely hazardous substances so as to facilitate emergency planning; and (2) the obligation immediately to notify authorities in the event of a release. Subchapter II of EPCRA requires companies to file additional reports on the presence of hazardous substances at their facilities, and also to report on the periodic release of toxic chemicals. Unlike the other federal laws, much of the information that is reported under EPCRA is available to the public.

Not only did EPCRA not completely supersede other federal reporting provisions, it also did not preempt state law. Several states have passed "right-to-know" or other reporting laws and disclosure, the most aggressive being California's Proposition 65. However, because EPCRA's reporting requirements are fairly extensive and because they are implemented largely by the states themselves, in general the importance of state reporting laws has been diminished.

Any company that makes, uses, or otherwise is involved with potentially hazardous substances may be required under federal law to notify authorities of a release of such a substance into the environment. In many cases, a company's obligations will be satisfied by reporting under the Emergency Planning and Community Right-to-Know Act (EPCRA) and the Comprehensive Environmental Response, Compensation, and Liability Act (CERCLA), but in some cases the Clean Water Act, the Toxic Substances Control Act (TSCA), or the Resource Conservation and Recovery Act (RCRA) might be applicable.

This complex web of federal and state environmental laws creates legal issues for both buyer and seller in a proposed merger or acquisition, usually surrounding the problem of allocating liability for environmental problems under federal laws, such as RCRA and CERCLA, and state laws that address hazardous waste discharge and disposal. The seller should have its legal counsel obtain an environmental audit from a qualified consulting firm prior to the active recruitment of potential buyers in order to assess its own liability under the federal and state laws. Nonetheless, it is very likely that the buyer and its counsel will want to do their own independent review and assessment of the seller's sites, insurance policies, and possible areas of exposure.

The issue of potential liability under federal and state environmental laws is typically one of the broadest areas of coverage requested by buyers under the representations and warranties, such as those set forth below:

1. *Hazardous Material*. Other than as set forth on ____, (i) no amount of substance that has been designated under any law, rule, regulation, treaty or statute promulgated by any governmental entity to be radioactive, toxic, hazardous or otherwise a danger to health or the environment, including, without limitation, PCBs, asbestos, petroleum, urea-formaldehyde and all substances listed as hazardous substances pursuant to the Comprehensive Environmental Response, Compensation, and Liability Act of 1980, as amended, or defined as a hazardous waste pursuant to the United States Resource Conservation and Recovery Act of 1976, as amended, and the regulations promulgated pursuant to said laws (a "Hazardous Material"), and (ii) no underground or aboveground storage tanks containing Hazardous Material, are new or at any time have been present in, on or under any property, including the land and the improvements, ground water and surface water thereof, that either Seller has at any time owned, operated, occupied

or leased. Schedule ____ identifies all underground and above-ground storage tanks, and the registration/closure capacity, age, and the contents of such tanks, located on property owned, operated, occupied or leased by SellerCo.

2. *Hazardous Materials Activities*. SellerCo has not arranged for the transport of stored, used, manufactured, disposed of, released or sold, or exposed its employees or others to, Hazardous Materials or any product containing a Hazardous Material (collectively, "Seller's Hazardous Materials Activities") in violation of any rule, regulation, treaty or statute promulgated by any governmental entity.

3. *Environmental Permits and Compliance*. SellerCo currently holds all environmental approvals, permits, licenses, clearances, and consents (the "Environmental Permits") necessary for the conduct of Seller's Hazardous Material Activities and the business of SellerCo as such activities and business are currently being conducted. All Environmental Permits are in full force and effect. SellerCo (i) is in compliance in all material respects with all terms and conditions of the Environmental Permits and (ii) is in compliance in all material respects with all other limitations, restrictions, conditions, standards, prohibitions, requirements, obligations, schedules and timetables contained in the laws, rules, regulations, treaties or statutes of all governmental entities relating to pollution or protection of the environment or contained in any regulation, code, plan, order, decree, judgment, notice or demand letter issued, entered, promulgated or approved thereunder. To the best of SellerCo's knowledge after due inquiry, there are no circumstances that may prevent or interfere with such compliance in the future. Schedule ____ includes a listing and description of all Environmental Permits currently held by SellerCo. For purposes of this Agreement, knowledge of SellerCo includes the knowledge of the persons who, as of the Closing Date, were its officers, directors, and stockholders (including the trustees, officers, partners, and directors of stockholders that are not natural persons).

4. *Environmental Liabilities*. No action, proceeding, revocation proceeding, amendment procedure, writ, injunction, or claim is pending, or to the best knowledge of SellerCo, threatened against SellerCo or the business of SellerCo concerning any Environmental

Permit, Hazardous Material or the Seller's Hazardous Materials Activity or pursuant to the laws, rules, regulations, treaties or statutes of any governmental entity relating to pollution or protection of the environment. There are no past or present actions, activities, circumstances, conditions, events, or incidents that could involve either SellerCo (or any person or entity whose liability SellerCo has retained or assumed, either by contract or operation of law) in any environmental litigation, or impose upon SellerCo (or any person or entity whose liability either Seller has retained or assumed, either by contract or operation of law) any material environmental liability including, without limitation, common law tort liability.

Federal Securities Laws

Mergers and acquisitions among small and growing privately-held companies do not generally raise many issues or filing requirements under the federal securities laws. Where one or both of the companies are publicly traded and therefore have registered their securities under the Securities Act of 1933, however, a host of reporting obligations are triggered.

- *10-Q and 10-K Reports.* A discussion of the proposed transaction may need to be included in either or both of the acquiring company's and the target's quarterly and annual filing with the SEC. The acquiring company will usually be obligated to include the information in its scheduled SEC reports if the acquisition is deemed to be "significant." A significant acquisition is typically defined as one where the target's assets or pre-tax income exceeds ten percent (10%) of the acquiring company's assets or pre-tax income.
- *Registration Statements.* If the acquiring company plans to issue new securities as part of the consideration to be given to shareholders of the target, then a registration statement should be filed with the SEC.
- *Proxy Information.* If the proposed transaction must be approved by the shareholders of either the acquiring company or the target, then the SEC's special proxy rules and regulations must be carefully followed.

• *Tender Offers*. When a buyer of a publicly-held company elects to make a tender offer directly to the shareholders of the target, rather than negotiating through management, then the filing requirements in the Williams Act must be met. This includes the filing of the SEC's Schedule 13D whenever the purchaser becomes the beneficial owner of more than five percent (5%) of the target's equity securities, which gives notice to the SEC as well as the target company's officers and directors of the buyer's intentions.

Federal Antitrust Laws

The central concern of federal government policy is with those acquisitions that increase the dangers that companies in a particular market will have *market power*—the power to raise prices or limit production free from the constraints of competition. This danger increases when a market is dominated by a few large firms with substantial market shares. Federal antitrust laws prohibit any acquisition of stock or assets that tends to substantially lessen competition. Acquisitions of the stock or assets of a competitor or potential competitor ("horizontal acquisitions") are most likely to raise antitrust concerns, especially if they occur in markets that are already dominated by a few firms. Acquisitions involving companies in a supplier-purchaser relationship ("vertical acquisitions") also could raise antitrust concerns, but in general, vertical transactions are less of a concern from an antitrust perspective.

The Department of Justice (DOJ) and the Federal Trade Commission (FTC) may seek to stop acquisitions that they consider likely to significantly lessen competition. Furthermore, the Hart-Scott-Rodino Act generally requires that the FTC and DOJ be given advance notification of mergers and acquisitions involving companies and transactions above a specified minimum size, the details of which are discussed below.

Horizontal Acquisitions

The principal responsibility for enforcing antitrust laws with respect to business combinations continues to be exercised by the DOJ and the FTC. The agencies have jointly issued their own set of merger guidelines to help businesses assess the likelihood that their specific business transactions may be challenged under the federal antitrust laws. These federal agencies will consider a number of factors in assessing the legality of acquisitions involving companies competing in the same geographic market and offering competing products or services to generally the same targeted customers. However, the respective *market shares* of the combining companies, as well as the degree of "market concentration" continue to be the starting point for the government's analysis. Transactions that result in the combined companies' having a large share of the relevant market may raise antitrust concerns.

Because of the importance of market concentration, the definition of the relevant geographic and product "market" is critical. Among other things, the guidelines take into account reasonable product substitutes, production facilities which may be easily converted to making a particular product, and entry barriers. Once the market is defined, the guidelines seek to measure the extent to which the proposed transaction increases market concentration. While various tests are available, the guidelines measure concentration using the Herfindahl-Hirschmann Index (HHI). The HHI is calculated by adding the squares of the individual market shares of all competitors in the market. For example, a market consisting of four competitors that each has a 25 percent share of the market has an HHI of 2500 ($25^2 + 25^2 + 25^2 + 25^2 = 2500$). Under the guidelines, markets with HHIs over 1800 are presumed to be highly concentrated. The competitive significance of particular acquisitions is then examined both in terms of the level of the market's HHI following the acquisition and the extent to which the acquisition increases the HHI.

In addition to market shares and market concentration, federal enforcement agencies consider the degree of ease of entry into the market. The presence of barriers that would prevent a new competitor from entering a market—such as patents, proprietary technology, know-how, and high "sunk" capital investments—increase the likelihood that the agencies will seek to block the transaction. However, if the agencies conclude that it is relatively easy for new competitors to enter a market within a relatively short time (if prices rose to noncompetitive levels), it is unlikely that that they consider a merger in that market to be anti-competitive even though it produces a high post-acquisition HHI.

Other factors that will be given varying degrees of weight under the guidelines are changing market conditions that might undermine the significance of market shares, such as rapidly changing technology; the financial condition of a company which might affect its future competitive significance; characteristics of a product which make price collusion difficult or unlikely; and efficiencies resulting from the combination.

Vertical Acquisitions

Acquisitions involving suppliers and their customers could raise questions under the antitrust laws. Courts, as well as earlier federal enforcement policies, have expressed concerns that such acquisitions could foreclose access by competitors to necessary suppliers or distribution outlets. The foreclosure effect was measured by reference to the share of the market held by the supplier company and share of purchases of the product made by the customer company. Current federal enforcement policy is somewhat skeptical about claims that vertical acquisitions produce anti-competitive effects. It limits the inquiry primarily to the question of whether such an acquisition is likely to create unacceptable barriers to entry by making it necessary for any new entrant to enter at both the supplier and purchaser levels in circumstances where it is difficult to do so, and thus insulates concentrated markets at either level from new competition.

Hart-Scott-Rodino Act

The pre-merger notification requirements of the Hart-Scott-Rodino Act (H-S-R) can have an important impact on an acquisition timetable. Under H-S-R and the regulations issued under it by the FTC, acquisitions involving companies and transactions of a certain size cannot be consummated until certain information is supplied to the federal enforcement agencies and until specified waiting periods elapse.

The pre-merger notification program was established to avoid some of the difficulties that antitrust enforcement agencies encounter when they challenge anti-competitive acquisitions after they occur. The enforcement agencies have found that it is often impossible to restore competition fully because circumstances change once a merger takes place; furthermore, any attempt to reestablish competition is usually costly for the parties and the public. Prior review under the pre-merger notification program has created an opportunity to avoid these problems by enabling the enforcement agencies to challenge many anti-competitive acquisitions before they are consummated.

The Hart-Scott-Rodino Antitrust Improvements Act requires that persons contemplating proposed business transactions that satisfy certain size criteria report their intentions to the antitrust enforcement agencies before consummating the transaction. If the proposed transaction is reportable, then both the acquiring business and the business that is being acquired must submit information about their respective business operations to the Federal Trade Commission and to the Department of Justice and wait a specified period of time before consummating the proposed transaction. During that waiting period, the enforcement agencies review the antitrust implications of the proposed transaction. Whether a particular transaction is reportable is determined by application of the act and the pre-merger notification rules.

Hart-Scott-Rodino Act Reporting Rules

On January 25, 2005, the Federal Trade Commission announced that it had authorized the publication of a Federal Register Notice, required by the 2000 amendments to the Act, revising the notification thresholds and limitations in the Act and Rules. The new rules and regulations regarding increased notification thresholds took effect on March 2, 2005 and the new rules and regulations amending the reporting rules for unincorporated entities took effect on April 6, 2005.

Size of Transaction

There are two basic tests to determine if a transaction will be reportable. The first test is known as the "size of transaction" test. The minimum required value for any reportable transaction is currently $53.1 million (as adjusted), which was adjusted in March 2005 from $50 million, and will now be adjusted on an annual basis based upon changes in the GNP during the previous year. The size of transaction test is satisfied if, after consummation of the transaction, the acquiring person will hold voting securities or assets of the acquired person valued at $53.1 million (as adjusted) or more. Rather than amend the rules annually, each dollar threshold will be listed "as adjusted", which term is defined in the HSR Rules. Certain of the exceptions and exemptions to the reporting requirements are discussed below in paragraphs (a) and (d) under "Miscellaneous."

Size of Persons

The second test is known as the "size of person" test. This test only applies to transactions that are valued between $53.1-212.3 million (as adjusted). Deals that exceed $212.3 million (as adjusted) are reportable without regard to the size of the parties. If a transaction falls within the $53.1-212.3 million (as adjusted) range, in order for the transaction to be reportable, one party must have at least $106.2 million (as adjusted) in annual net sales and/or assets, and the other party must have at least $10.7 million (as adjusted) in annual net sales and/or assets. Total assets and total annual net sales of a person are determined by reference to the last regularly prepared balance sheet and annual income statement. When calculating the total assets and net sales, all entities that are controlled by such person must be included.

Filing Fee

The fees for filing a Pre-Merger Notification with the FTC and DOJ are staggered as follows:

- Deal value less than $106.2 million = $45,000
- Deal value at least $106.2 million, less than $530.7 million = $125,000
- Deal value $530.7 million or more = $280,000

The regulations provide for such fees to be paid by the acquiring person, however parties often agree to share such fees.

Waiting Periods
The parties to a reportable transaction may not consummate the transaction until the statutory waiting period detailed in the HSR Act has expired. The waiting period begins on the date that the FTC and DOJ receive the completed notification forms. The waiting period will end on the thirtieth (30th) day following such receipt (for cash tender offers and bankruptcy transactions the waiting period is 15 days). If any waiting period would expire on a Saturday, Sunday or legal holiday, the waiting period shall extend to the next regular business day. Parties can request "early termination" of the waiting period at the time of filing at no additional cost, but it is not guaranteed (although early termination is granted in most cases). When early termination is granted, it is usually within two weeks of the initial filing. It is important to note, however, that early terminations are reported in the Federal Register, listed on the FTC website and listed in the FTC's public reference room, therefore, *parties seeking to maintain the non-public nature of a transaction should not request early termination*.

During the waiting period, a transaction raising competitive concerns will be reviewed by only one of the agencies, being assigned to either the DOJ or the FTC through a clearance procedure. Prior to the expiration of the waiting period, either the FTC or the DOJ can issue a "second request" for additional documents and information, but second requests are not common. In fact, over the last ten years, the number of second requests has never exceeded 4.3% of the total number of transactions in which a second request could have been issued.

The issuance of a second request extends the waiting period until thirty days after the date the parties certify that they have substantially complied with the second request (the extension for cash tender offers and bankruptcy transactions is 10 days). Responding to a second request will often take between sixty and ninety days, depending on the size of the companies, the number of product markets and the amount of material to be reviewed. During this time, the responsible agency will be evaluating the relevant markets and interviewing suppliers, customers and competitors to learn more about the anti-competitive effects of the transaction.

The first step in determining reportability is to determine who the "acquiring person" is and who the "acquired person" is. These technical terms are defined in the rules and must be applied carefully. In an assets acquisitions, the acquiring person is the buyer, and the acquired person is the seller. In a voting securities acquisition, the acquiring person is the voting securities to be acquired. Thus, in many voting securities acquisitions, the FTC imposes a reporting obligation on the acquired person despite the fact that, in such voting securities transactions, the acquired person may have no direct dealings with the acquiring person. The rules require that a person proposing to acquire voting securities directly from shareholders rather than from the issuer itself serve notice on the issuer of those shares to make sure the acquired person knows about its reporting obligation.

Once you have determined who the acquiring and acquired persons are, you must determine whether the size of each person meets the act's minimum size criteria. This "size of person" test generally measures a company based on the company's last regularly-prepared balance sheet (see box). The size of a person includes not only the business entity that is making the acquisition or the business entity whose assets are being acquired or which issued the voting securities being acquired, but also the parent of that business entity and any other entities that the parent controls.

The next step is to determine what voting securities, assets, or combination of voting securities and assets are being transferred in the proposed transaction. Then you must determine the value of the voting securities and/or assets or the percentage of voting securities that will be "held as a result of the transaction." Calculating what will be held as a transaction is complicated, and it requires application of several complex rules. The securities "held as a result of the transaction" include those that will be transferred in the proposed transaction as well as certain assets of the acquired person that the acquiring person has purchased within certain time limits. In some instances, a transaction may not be reportable even if the size of person and the size of transaction tests have been satisfied. The act and rules set forth a number of exemptions, describing particular transactions or classes of transactions that need not be reported despite fact that the threshold criteria have been satisfied. The acquisition of voting securities of a foreign issuer may be exempt if the foreign company did no business in the United States and holds no assets in the United States.

Once it has been determined that a particular transaction is reportable, each party must submit its notification to the Pre-Merger Notification Office of the Federal Trade Commission and to the Director of Operations of the Antitrust Division of the Department of Justice for a calculation of the new filing fees (see box).

Labor and Employment Law

There are a wide variety of federal and state labor and employment law issues which must be addressed by the buyer and its counsel as part of its overall due diligence on the seller's business. This includes a comprehensive review of the seller's employment practices and manuals to ensure historical compliance with the laws governing employment discrimination, sexual harassment, drug testing, wage and hour laws, etc., as well as its compliance with the Family and Medical Leave Act (FMLA), the Americans with Disabilities Act (ADA), and the Worker Adjustment and Retraining Notification Act (WARN), which governs plant closings and retraining requirements.

Where applicable, it will also be necessary to review collective bargaining agreements, with a particular focus on the buyer's duty to bargain with the union as a "successor" employer.

The buyer must also be aware of the wide range of potential ERISA liability issues which it may confront if the employee benefit plans established by the seller are not properly structured or funded. The buyer must also develop a strategy for the integration of the seller's plan(s) into its own, which may involve transferring plan assets in whole or in part or the utilization of surplus plan assets.

There are many different types of employee benefit plans, including a "qualified" plan (that provides certain favorable tax consequences currently such as deductions for plan contributions and deferral of income for plan participants) or unqualified plans (such as deferred compensation arrangements, which do not provide favorable tax consequences currently).

Retirement plans are generally known as "defined contribution plans" or "defined benefit plans." *Defined contribution plans* include profit sharing plans with or without a 401(k) feature, thrift or savings plans, money purchase pension plans, target benefit plans, stock bonus plans, employee stock ownership plans, simplified employee pensions (SEP), savings incentive match plans for employees (Simple Plans), and certain funded executive compensation plans. A *defined benefit plan* is a retirement plan other than a defined contribution plan. The traditional defined benefit pension plan is one in which the employer takes financial responsibility for funding an annuity payable over an employee's life or as a joint and survivor annuity to the employee and his or her spouse.

Employee benefit plans can represent one of the largest potential liabilities of a business enterprise. The types of employee benefit plans involving the greatest potential liabilities are defined benefit pension plans, post-retirement medical and life insurance benefits, and deferred compensation programs for executives. In many cases, the liability for an employee benefit plan shown on the financial statements may not be an adequate portrayal of the true liability. A buyer is well advised to have an actuary compute the value of the employee benefits, both retirement plans and retiree medical plans, in order to be sure that the balance sheet provision is adequate. The treatment of employee benefit plans in corporate acquisition, merger and disposition situations has taken on greater and greater importance since the passage of the Employee Retirement Income Security Act of 1974 (ERISA).

The importance of employee benefits plans grows with each new development in the benefits arena including the following:

Multiemployer Pension Plan Amendments Act of 1980 (MEPPAA)
Deficit Reduction Act of 1984 (DRA)
Retirement Equity Act of 1984 (REA)

Omnibus Budget Reconciliation Act of 1986 (OBRA)
Consolidated Omnibus Budget Reconciliation Act of 1986 (COBRA)
Single Employer Pension Plan Amendments Act of 1986 (SEPPAA)
Tax Reform Act of 1986 (TRA 86)
Omnibus Budget Reconciliation Acts of 1987 (OBRA 87)
Technical and Miscellaneous Revenue Act of 1988 (TAMRA)
Omnibus Budget Reconciliation Act of 1989 (OBRA 89)
Omnibus Budget Reconciliation Act of 1990 (OBRA 90)
Tax Extension Act of 1991 (TEA 91)
Unemployment Compensation Act of 1992 (UCA)
Unemployment Compensation Amendments of 1992
Omnibus Budget Reconciliation Act of 1993 (OBRA 93)
Retirement Protection Act of 1994 (RPA)
Small Business Job Protection Act of 1996 (SBJPA)
Health Insurance Portability and Accountability Act of 1996 (HIPAA)
Taxpayer Relief Act of 1997 (TRA 97)
Internal Revenue Service Restructuring and Reform Act of 1998 (IRSRRA)
Tax Relief Extension Act of 1999 (TRE 99)
Community Renewal Tax Relief Act of 2000 (CRTRA)
Economic Growth and Tax Relief Reconciliation Act of 2001 (EGTRRA)
Consolidated Appropriations Act of 2001 (CAA)
Sarbanes-Oxley Act of 2002 (Sarbanes-Oxley)
Job Creation and Worker Assistance Act of 2002 (JCWAA)
Medicare Prescription Drug, Improvement, and Modernization Act of 2003
Pension Funding Equity Act of 2004 (PFEA)
Statements 87, 88 and 106 132R of the Financial Accounting Board (F.A.S. 87, 88 and 106 132R)

Employee benefit plans can be the source of major off-balance sheet liabilities, which have to be dealt with by the parties to the transactions. In some cases, employee benefit plans will dictate whether the transaction will be structured as a sale of stock or a sale of assets. In a few cases, employee benefit plans may result in the deal falling through. In still other situations, employee benefit plans can be utilized to accomplish the transaction.

Generally, employee benefit plan considerations do not dictate the structure of a corporate acquisition. There are, however, a few exceptions. A seller which faces a potentially large withdrawal liability with respect to a multiemployer pension plan may insist on a sale of stock rather than a sale of assets. On the other hand, a buyer which does not want to inherit a burdensome plan from the seller may insist on a sale of assets. In the case of a sale of assets, the buyer is not generally obligated to assume the plans of the seller. This decision will depend on the nature of the plans, their funding status, their past history of compliance with the laws, and the nature of the adjustment in the purchase price with respect to the plans.

The biggest difficulty related to employee benefit liabilities in a merger or acquisition is to determine the appropriate adjustment of the purchase price. Since the liabilities involve actuarial calculations, they are totally dependent upon the assumptions as to interest rates, life expectancies, the selection of mortality tables and other factors that will impact on the ultimate liability under the plan. The parties have to agree to these assumptions or to a method of arriving at these assumptions in order to calculate whether the plan is overfunded or underfunded.

One such method for a pension plan would be to value the plan's liabilities using the PBGC's assumptions for terminated pension plans. While the PBGC rates are not the most favorable rates in the market place, they do represent the rates which will be utilized to determine whether the plan is underfunded in the even the plan should terminate. Another approach is to value the liability on an ongoing basis rather than on a termination basis.

The most important aspect of the acquisition process for the buyer is to start its investigation of the employee benefit plans early and to do as thorough a job as possible. The buyer should be especially concerned with identifying items which are hidden liabilities. Obviously, a buyer should review the plans and their summary plan descriptions. Annual Form 5500's for the last three years should be examined by professionals. To the extent there are actuarial reports for the plans, the buyer should examine copies of them, and make sure they reflect any recent plan amendments increasing benefits.

Collective bargaining agreements should also be examined to determine if they provide for benefit increases which were not contemplated in the most recent actuarial report. With respect to welfare plans, buyers should determine if they are obligated to provide for increases pursuant to "maintenance of benefit provisions" in collective bargaining agreements. If a union negotiated plan bases benefits on the compensation of the employees, the buyer should check to see if large wage increases have been negotiated. Finally, the buyer should review any post-retirement medical or life insurance benefits provided by the seller.

The purchase agreement should contain detailed and explicit provisions with respect to the handling of employee benefits. If responsibility for a benefit program has to be divided between the buyer and the seller, it is easier to have a fair division of the responsibility if it is negotiated in advance. Buyers rarely get significant concessions from sellers after the deal has closed. A set of sample representations and warranties to cover these issues is set forth below.

1. *Definitions.*
   (a) "Benefit Arrangement" means, whether qualified or unqualified any benefit arrangement, obligation, custom, or practice, whether or not legally enforceable, to provide benefits, other than salary, as compensation for services rendered, to present or former directors, employees, agents, or independent contractors, other than any obligation, arrangement, custom or practice that is an Employee Benefit Plan, including, without limitation, employment agreements, severance agreements, executive compensation arrangements, incentive programs or arrangements, rabbi or secular trusts, sick leave, vacation pay, severance pay policies, plant closing benefits, salary continuation for disability, consulting, or other compensation arrangements, workers' compensation, retirement, deferred compensation, bonus, stock option, ESOP or purchase, hospitalization, medical insurance, life insurance, tuition reimbursement or scholarship programs, employee discount arrangements, employee advances or loans, any plans subject to Section 125 of the Code, and any plans or trusts providing benefits or pay-

ments in the event of a change of control, change in ownership, or sale of a substantial portion (including all or substantially all) of the assets of any business or portion thereof, in each case with respect to any present or former employees, directors, or agents.

(b) "Seller Benefit Arrangement" means any Benefit Arrangement sponsored or maintained by SellerCo or with respect to which SellerCo has or may have any liability (whether actual, contingent, with respect to any of its assets or otherwise), in each case with respect to any present or former directors, employees, or agents of SellerCo as of the Closing Date.

(c) "Seller Plan" means any Employee Benefit Plan for which SellerCo is the "plan sponsor" (as defined in Section 3(16)(B) of ERISA) or any Employee Benefit Plan maintained by SellerCo or to which SellerCo is obligated to make payments, in each case with respect to any present or former employees of SellerCo as of the Closing Date.

(d) "Employee Benefit Plan" has the meaning given in Section 3(3) of ERISA.

(e) "ERISA" means the Employee Retirement Income Security Act of 1974, as amended, and all regulations and rules issued thereunder, or any successor law.

(f) "ERISA Affiliate" means any person that, together with SellerCo, would be or was at any time treated as a single employer under Section 414 of the Code or Section 4001 of ERISA and any general partnership of which either Seller is or has been a general partner.

(g) "Pension Plan" means any Employee Benefit Plan described in Section 3(2) of ERISA.

(h) "Multiemployer Plan" means any Employee Benefit Plan described in Section 3(37) of ERISA.

(i) "Welfare Plan" means any Employee Benefit Plan described in Section 3(1) of ERISA.

2. *Schedule.* The schedule contains a complete and accurate list of all Seller Plans and Seller Benefit Arrangements. With respect, as applicable to Seller Plans and Seller Benefit Arrangements, true,

correct, and complete copies of all the following documents have been delivered to GCC and its counsel: (A) all documents constituting the Seller Plans and Seller Benefit Arrangements, including but not limited to, insurance policies, service agreements, and formal and informal amendments thereto, employment agreements, consulting arrangements, and commission arrangements; (B) the most recent Forms 5500 or 5500 C/R and any financial statements attached thereto and those for the prior three years; and (C) the most recent summary plan description for the Seller Plans.

3. Neither SellerCo nor any ERISA Affiliate maintains, contributes to, or is obligated to contribute to, nor has either SellerCo or any ERISA Affiliate ever maintained, contributed to or been obligated to contribute to, any Pension Plan or Multiemployer Plan. Neither SellerCo nor any ERISA Affiliate has any liability (whether actual or conditional, with respect to its assets or otherwise) to or resulting from any Employee Benefit Plan sponsored or maintained by a person that is not a Seller or any ERISA Affiliate. Neither Seller nor any ERISA Affiliate has or has ever had any obligations under any collective bargaining agreement. The Seller Plans and Seller Benefit Arrangements are not presently under audit or examination (nor has notice been received of a potential audit or examination) by the IRS, the Department of Labor, or any other governmental agency or entity. All group health plans of each Seller and their ERISA Affiliates have been operated in compliance with the requirements of Sections 4980B (and its predecessors) and 5000 of the Code, and each Seller has provided, or will have provided before the Closing Date, to individuals entitled thereto all required notices and coverage under Section 4980B with respect to any "qualifying event" (as defined therein) occurring before or on the Closing Date.

4. *Schedule 3.19(d)* hereto contains the most recent quarterly listing of workers' compensation claims of the Sellers for the last three fiscal years.

Structuring the Deal

There is virtually an infinite number of ways in which a corporate merger or acquisition may be structured. There are probably as many potential deal structures as there are qualified and creative transactional lawyers and investment bankers. The goal is not to create the most complex, but rather to create a structure which fairly reflects the goals and objectives of the buyer and seller. Naturally, not all of the objectives of each party will be met each time—there will almost always be a degree of negotiation and compromise. Virtually all structures, even the most complex, are at their roots basically either mergers or acquisitions, including the purchase or consolidation of either stock or assets. The creativity often comes in structuring the deal to achieve a particular tax or strategic result or to accommodate a multistep or multiparty transaction. This chapter will look at some of the typical structures as well as a few alternative types of transactions such as spin-offs, shell mergers, and ESOP's.

At the heart of each transaction are the following key issues which will affect the structure of the deal:

- How will tangible and intangible assets be transferred to the purchaser from the seller?

- At what price and according to what terms?
- What issues discovered during due diligence may affect the price, terms or structure of the deal?
- What liabilities will be assumed by the purchaser? How will risks be allocated among the parties?
- What are the tax implications to the buyer and seller?
- What are the long-term objectives of the buyer?
- What role will the seller have in the management and growth of the underlying business after closing?
- To what extent will third-party consents or governmental filings/approvals be necessary?
- What arrangements will be made for the key management team of the seller (who may not necessarily be among the selling owners of the company)?
- Does the buyer currently have access to all of the consideration to be paid to the seller or will some of these funds need to be raised from debt or equity markets?

There is a wide variety of corporate, tax and securities law issues that affect the final decision as to the structure of any given transaction. Each issue must be carefully considered from a legal and accounting perspective. However, at the heart of each structural alternative are the following basic questions:

- Will the buyer be acquiring *stock* or *assets* of the target?
- In what form will the consideration from the buyer to the seller be made (e.g., cash, notes, securities, etc.)?
- Will the purchase price be fixed, contingent or payable over time on an installment basis?
- What are the tax consequences of the proposed structure for the acquisition (see Chapter 6)?

Stock vs. Asset Purchases

Perhaps the most fundamental issue in structuring the acquisition of a target company is whether the transaction will take the form of an asset or stock purchase. Each form has its respective advantages and disadvantages, depending on the facts and circumstances sur-

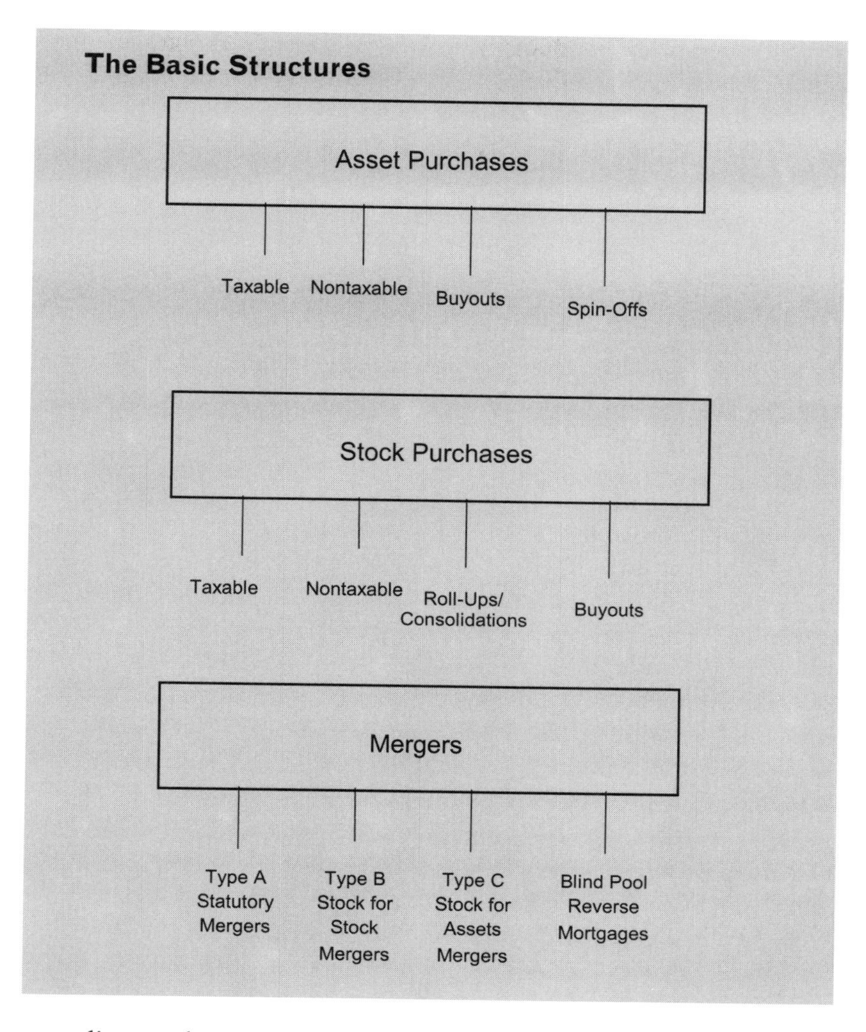

rounding each transaction. The buyer and seller should consider the following factors in determining the ultimate form of the transaction:

Stock Purchases

The Buyer's Perspective: Advantages

1. Tax attributes carryover to buyer (e.g., net operating loss and credit carryforwards).

2. Avoids many of the restrictions imposed on sales of assets in loan agreements and potential sales tax.
3. Preserves the right of the buyer to use seller's name, licenses and permits.
4. No changes in corporation's liability, unemployment or workers' compensation insurance ratings.
5. Nontransferable rights or assets (e.g., license, franchise, patent, etc.) can usually be retained by the buyer.
6. Continuity of the corporate identity, contracts and structure.

The Seller's Perspectives: Advantages

1. Taxed only on the sale of stock.
2. All obligations (i.e., disclosed, not disclosed, unknown and contingent) and nontransferable rights can be transferred to the buyer.
3. Gain/loss is usually capital in nature.
4. If stock held by individuals is IRC Section 1244 stock and is sold at a loss, the loss is generally treated as ordinary.
5. May permit sellers to report gains from sale of stock on the installment basis.
6. Does not leave the seller with the problem of disposing of assets which are not bought by the purchaser.

The Buyer's Perspective: Disadvantages

1. Less flexibility to cherry pick key assets of seller.
2. The buyer may be liable for unknown, undisclosed or contingent liabilities (unless adequately protected in the purchase agreement).
3. No step-up in basis (i.e., seller's basis is carried over to the buyer at historical tax basis).
4. Normally does not terminate existing labor union collective bargaining agreement(s) and generally results in the continuation of employee benefit plans.
5. Dissenting shareholders' have a right of appraisal for the value of their shares with the right to be paid appraised value or remain a minority shareholder.

The Seller's Perspective: Disadvantages

1. Offer and sale of the company's securities may need to be registered under certain circumstances.
2. Seller cannot pick and choose assets to be retained.
3. May not use the corporation's net operating loss and credit carryforwards to offset gain on sale.
4. Loss on sale of stock may not be recognized by corporate shareholder who included the company in its consolidated income tax return.

Asset Purchases

The Buyer's Perspective: Advantages

1. The buyer can be selective as to which assets of target will be purchased.
2. The buyer is generally not liable for seller's liabilities unless specifically assumed under contract.
3. Step-up in basis of assets acquired equal to purchase price allowing higher depreciation/amortization deductions.
4. Buyers are generally free of any undisclosed or contingent liabilities.
5. Normally results in termination of labor union collective bargaining agreement(s) and employee benefit plans may be maintained or terminated.
6. Buyers may elect new accounting methods.

The Seller's Perspective: Advantages

1. Sellers maintain corporate existence.
2. Ownership of nontransferable assets or rights (e.g. licenses, franchises, patents, etc.) are usually retained.
3. Corporate name and goodwill can generally be maintained.
4. Corporation's tax attributes (e.g., net operating loss and credit carryforwards) are retained.

The Buyer's Perspective: Disadvantages

1. No carryover of seller corporation's tax attributes (e.g., net operating loss and credit carryforwards).

2. If a bargain purchase, step-down in basis of assets.
3. Nontransferable rights or assets (e.g., license, franchise, patent, etc.) cannot be transferred to buyers.
4. Transaction more complex and costly in terms of transferring specific assets/liabilities (i.e., title to each asset transferred and new title recorded; state sales tax may apply).
5. Lender's consent may be required to assume liabilities.
6. Loss of corporation's liability, unemployment or workers' compensation insurance ratings.

The Seller's Perspective: Disadvantages

1. Double taxation if the corporation also liquidates.
2. Generates various kinds of gain or loss to sellers based on the classification of each asset as capital or ordinary.
3. Transaction more complex and costly in terms of transferring specific assets/liabilities (i.e., title to each asset transferred and new title recorded; state sales tax may apply).
4. Bill of Sale must be comprehensive with exhibits attached in order to ensure that no key assets are overlooked and as a result not transferred to the buyer.
5. A variety of third-party consents will typically be required to transfer key tangible and intangible assets to the buyer.
6. Seller will be responsible for liquidation of the remaining corporate "shell" and distributing the proceeds of the assets sale to its shareholders, which may result in a double taxation unless a Section 338 election is made.
7. Asset acquisition requires compliance with applicable state bulk sales statutes, as well as state and local sales and transfer taxes.

Tax and Accounting Issues Affecting the Structure of the Transaction

In a given merger or acquisition, there is a wide variety of tax and accounting which must be considered and understood as part of the negotiation and structuring of the transaction. These issues will affect the valuation and pricing as well as the structure of the deal and may be a condition precedent to closing. This section will provide an *overview* of the basic tax and accounting issues to be addressed in a merger or acquisition, but will be limited to a summary because the tax laws are very complex and constantly changing. You should discuss the accounting issues with the Certified Public Accountant (CPA) who will serve as a part of the acquisition team.

Mergers and acquisitions may be completely tax-free, partially tax-free or entirely taxable to the seller. Each party and their advisors will have their own, often differing, views on how the transaction should be structured from a tax perspective, depending on the non-tax strategic objectives of both buyer and seller in the transaction and the respective tax and financial position of each party. In some cases the tax consequences will be the primary driving force in the transaction and in other cases the tax issues are secondary or even a non-issue. In addition to the taxable aspects of the structure of the transaction, there will be a wide variety of other tax issues to be considered, such as the tax basis of the assets acquired, the impact of the imputed interest rules on the transaction, and the tax aspects of any deferred consideration and/or incentive compensation to the seller.

It is relevant to highlight an example that conveys the degree to which tax can be an impediment to a transaction. In one situation the CEO of the seller had negotiated a "carve-out" with his board, and received some of the new combined company's stock as personal income. That income, however, created over a million dollars in cash tax liability. This tax liability presented a significant challenge to getting the deal done. The CEO, who deserved credit for the deal, now had a strong incentive to prevent the deal from happening. Navigating tax liability issues, like the one in this example, are critical steps to successful deal closure.

The general tax-related goals of the seller usually include:

- *Deferring the taxation* of the gain realized on the sale of the business to a future date (such as if the seller acquires the buyer's securities, which may appreciate in value, but the seller need not generally pay taxes on these gains until these securities are sold).

- Classifying the income which is recognized as *capital gain and not as ordinary income.*

• Ensuring that *cash is available to pay for taxes* as they become due, and to avoid the "double tax" at both the corporate and the shareholder level.

Again, the strategic objectives must be balanced against the tax consequences. If the seller has an immediate need for liquidity or has no desire to receive the buyer's securities (the seller may not accept the buyer's post-closing vision and plans for the combined entities), then it will be difficult to achieve nontaxable status.

Over the years, the changes to the federal tax laws have chipped away at the buyer's motivations for having the transaction characterized as tax-free. The buyer's ability to "carry over" favorable tax attributes of the seller has been diminished such that the buyer's use of its own securities as consideration to pay the seller often have to do more with preservation of cash than with applicable tax laws.

If the transaction is taxable, then the "stepped-up" basis will be increased to equal to the fair market value of the consideration paid to the seller. If the transaction is non-taxable, the buyer is able to "carry over" the seller's tax basis to its own financial statements. If the buyer would prefer to carry these assets on the balance sheet at the stepped-up tax basis (such as if the buyer is paying much more than the seller's tax basis) or if the buyer would prefer not to issue securities to the seller to prevent dilution of ownership, then the buyer should opt for a taxable transaction. Based upon our experience, resolving the tax issues effectively between the parties is critically important. This issue directly impacts the price of the transaction and each party's perception of the fair value.

Taxable vs. Non-Taxable Deals

Taxable

Purchase of *stock* for cash, promissory notes or other non-equity consideration

Purchase of *assets* for cash, promissory notes or other non-equity consideration

Taxable transactions generally anticipate that the seller will have little or no continuing equity participation in the acquired company.

Nontaxable

An exchange of the *buyer's stock* for the seller's stock	An exchange of the *buyer's stock* for all or substantially all of the seller's assets

Nontaxable transactions generally anticipate a continuing, direct or indirect equity participation in the acquired company by the seller or its shareholders.

Most corporate acquisitions will be deemed to be taxable transactions if structured as either a purchase of stock or assets in exchange for cash, promissory notes or other forms of consideration. Nontaxable transactions usually fall more into the category of a merger in that they involve an exchange of the target company's stock or assets for the purchaser's equity securities or of a subsidiary created by the purchaser, coupled with some direct or indirect continuing relationship between the buyer and the seller and their respective shareholders. These nontaxable transactions must fall within one of several reorganization categories contained in IRS Code Section 368.

Tax-Free Reorganizations

If the parties choose to structure the transaction as a tax-free reorganization, then the requirements set forth below must be followed:

The three principal forms of "Tax-Free Reorganizations Under the Internal Revenue Code" are: (a) Type A Statutory Merger, (b) Type B "Stock-for-Stock" Merger, and (c) Type C "Stock-for-Assets" Merger.

"A" Reorganizations

A Type A reorganization is a statutory merger or consolidation under state law. No express limitations are imposed on the type of consideration that can be used in the transaction or on the disposition of assets prior to the merger. This is a very flexible acquisition device that permits shareholders to receive property including cash in addition to stock of the acquiring corporation.

"B" Reorganizations

Type B reorganizations are an acquisition by one corporation, in exchange solely for all or part of its voting stock or that of its controlling company. If, immediately after the acquisition, the acquiring corporation has control (at least 80 percent of the total combined with power of all classes of stock and at least 80 percent of the total number of shares of all other classes of stock) of such other corporation (whether or not the acquiring corporation had control immediately before the acquisition). Counsel to the buyer, however, must be particularly sensitive to any cash payment, such as a finder's fee or the payment of appraisal rights to dissenting shareholders.

"C" Reorganizations

Type C reorganizations are an acquisition by one corporation, in exchange solely for all or part of its voting stock (or that of its parent) and of "substantially all" of the properties of another corporation. The transferor corporation must distribute the stock, securities, and other properties it receives from the acquiring corporation, as well as any retained assets, as part of the plan of reorganization.

The tax aspects of the proposed transaction are among the most important issues to be addressed by the acquisition team. These laws are complex and are constantly changing. Therefore, knowledgeable advisors should be carefully consulted.

Accounting Issues

The pooling-of-interests method of merger accounting ended on June 30, 2001, almost without fanfare. Companies, especially financial firms and those in the high technology and pharmaceutical industries, often chose pooling as their way of avoiding the long-term earnings dilution from the amortization of goodwill against earnings. Goodwill was defined as the excess of cost of an acquired entity over the net of the amounts calculated for assets acquired and liabilities assumed.

The elimination of pooling has been muted to a large degree because of the new rules for treating acquired goodwill and intangibles in a purchase acquisition. Instead of the old approach of amortization of goodwill for up to forty years, companies now must subject the acquired goodwill to a complex annual "impairment test" aimed at determining whether there has been a decline in the value of that goodwill. Write-offs would be required only if the value has been impaired. The impact will be initially positive because of the goodwill aspect no longer requiring automatic amortization.

The new approach of the Financial Accounting Standards Board (FASB) is more complicated than amortization. Under the new FASB goodwill and intangible-asset measurement standards, companies generally must perform an impairment test yearly for each reporting unit. It is a two-step test that first determines whether the book value of acquired assets of the reporting unit exceeds the unit's so-called fair value—typically measured through discounted cash-flow estimates. If fair value is lower than book value, the company then must determine whether the fair value of the unit's goodwill is less than the goodwill's book value, which would necessitate an impairment loss being recognized. Companies have six months after adopting the new rules to perform the first step.

Since companies do not know in what year goodwill may become impaired, financial personnel may be challenged to predict earnings internally to a greater degree. Further, tension of FASB's new criteria for determining whether some acquired intangible assets, like patents, should be recognized separately from goodwill, and perhaps amortized over the asset's perceived life span, is created as a result of the new rules.

One Step vs. Staged Transactions

Another key issue regarding the structure of the deal is whether the entire transaction will be completed in one step or whether it will occur over a series of steps. The parties may want to get to know each other better before considering a full-blown merger or there may be some contingencies affecting the value of the company which are driving the buyer, or even the seller, to want to slow things down and consider a preliminary transaction as the first step. It is also plausible that the seller believes that the long-term value of the company may be much higher and as a result would prefer to keep "some of his chips still on the table."

The Five Structural Alternatives

1. Asset

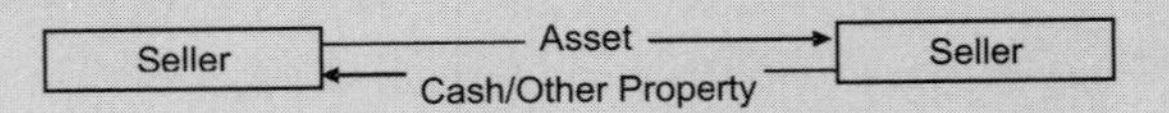

This is often the simplest of structures with the buyer purchasing a set of selected assets from the seller in exchange for cash or other assets.

2. Stock Purchase

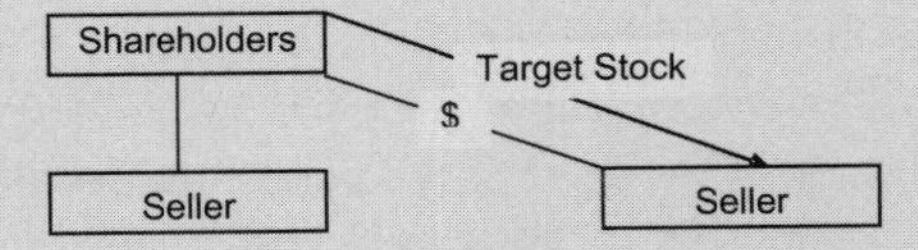

The shareholders of the seller sell their shares to the buyer in exchange for cash or other assets.

3. Statutory Merger

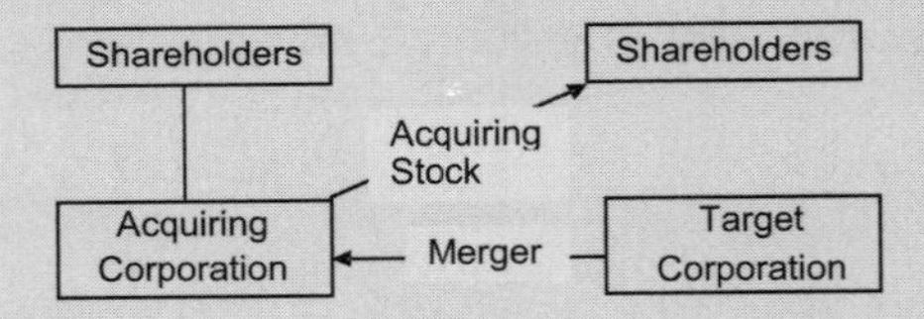

A statutory merger is a nontaxable acquisition in which one corporation completely absorbs another by virtue of a merger under state corporate law.

4. Stock-for-Stock Acquisition

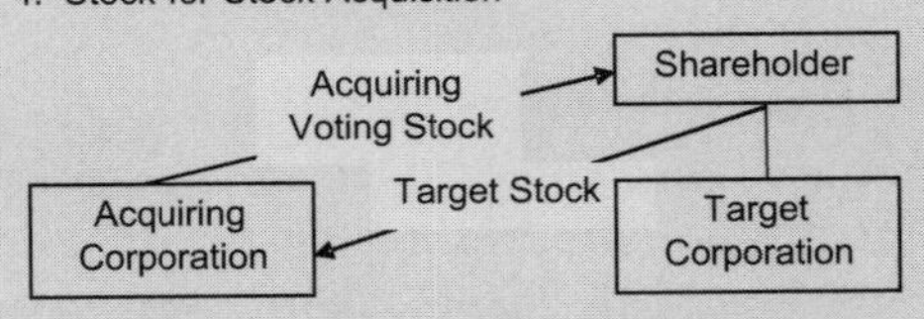

The acquiring company exchanges its voting stock for the stock of the acquiring company.

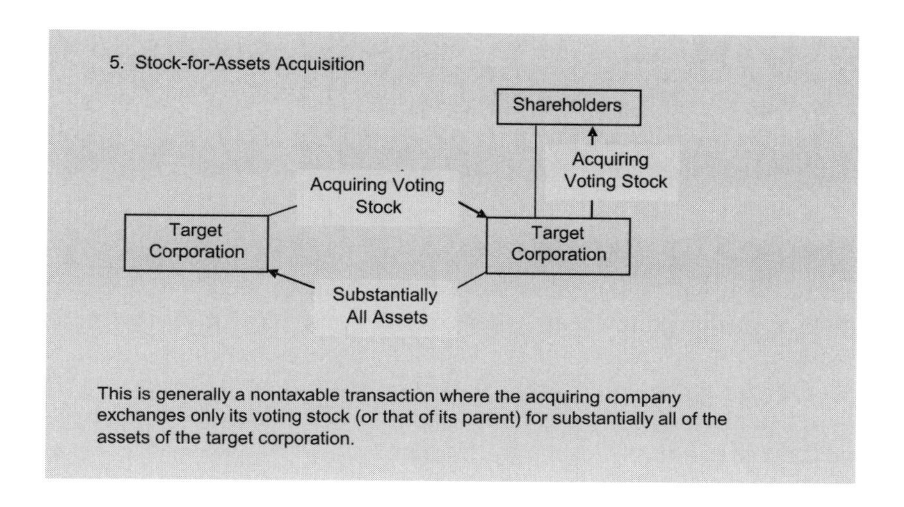

This is generally a nontaxable transaction where the acquiring company exchanges only its voting stock (or that of its parent) for substantially all of the assets of the target corporation.

For example, from the buyer's perspective, there may be certain governmental approvals needed which affect the seller's valuation, such as the approval of the Food and Drug Administration (FDA) for a new line of pharmaceutical or medical devices. These approvals may be two years away and if not obtained would significantly affect the value of the seller's business. In such a case, the buyer may want to consider an alternative and more preliminary initial structure, such as a strategic alliance (as a first step towards a merger) or a technology licensing agreement (as a first step towards an acquisition). There may even be certain shares exchanged to allow cross-ownership or the buyer may want to purchase a minority interest in the seller with an option to purchase the balance within six months after obtaining FDA approval.

Even the seller may have certain reservations about the buyer or want to see certain contingencies met before it commits to selling 100 percent of its business. The buyer may be waiting for some key third-party approval or event to take place, before which the seller is reluctant to commit, such as the buyer being in the process of filing for approval of an initial public offering (IPO) of its securities. If these securities are to serve as part of the seller's compensation, then it may be wise to wait to ensure that there will be a secondary market (and hence liquidity) for the shares before moving forward. In such cases, the parties would enter into a letter of intent but there would typically be a clause that allows the seller to walk away from the deal if the offering is unsuccessful.

Some transactions are multi-staged for strategic reasons and some may be structured to be one stage with the possibility of being multi-staged if certain post-closing contingencies are not met.

Method of Payment

The way in which the seller will be paid is quite clearly one of the most important aspects of structuring the deal. The method of payment for the acquisition of stock or assets ordinarily involves a balancing of business and tax considerations. Often a particular fact or set of circumstances will outweigh the others and determine the method of payment. Although the personal, strategic and tax needs of all parties must be considered, there are a wide variety of forms of payment which should be considered before a final decision is determined. These include cash, marketable securities, parcels of real estate, the rights to intangible assets (licenses, franchises, etc.), secured and unsecured promissory notes, the common and preferred securities of the purchaser (or their affiliates) (and often with the promise that these securities will one day be publicly-traded), earn-outs, consulting and employment agreements, royalty and license agreements or even the exchange of another business. All of these tools should be considered in structuring the elements of the purchase price.

For example, a seller concerned about the financial and/or business viability or the creditworthiness of a buyer will demand payment in cash for assets or stock being sold. Alternatively, a seller reluctant to completely dispose of an interest in a business or who wishes to defer tax to a later taxable year may be willing to take the buyer's stock and/or take back a promissory note as part of the consideration. Tax considerations may dictate the form of payment. From a buyer's perspective, debt is often preferable to stock since interest may be tax deductible. For example, in a leveraged acquisition the business assets acquired are expected to generate sufficient cash flow to pay off the debt incurred to acquire the assets.

Cash

It is often said that "cash is king." Although at first blush, most sellers envision that an all-cash deal is the preferred route, sellers must consider a wide variety of payment methods which in the long run may result in a much greater total price. There are certain circumstances, however, when an all-cash transaction makes sense, such as when the seller suspects that the buyer will be unable to honor the types of consideration mentioned above, which may rely on the buyer's long-term viability and credibility. From a buyer's perspective, an all-cash transaction can be internally financed, financed through an equity raise or in conjunction with a private equity fund, or financed through the cash flow of the combined companies and/or the acquired company, or even financed through asset-based lending, to be collateralized by the business assets or stock acquired.

Debt

If the creditworthiness of the buyer is high, then sellers may be willing to accept promissory notes from the buyer as part of the consideration. These promissory notes may be secured by the assets of the buyer, or by the seller's assets, or not at all. It is also possible that the notes will be subordinated to a senior commercial lender if the buyer borrows money from a bank as part of its capital to acquire the seller's business.

Stock

The securities of the buyer may constitute all or part of the payment to the seller for the business assets or stock. In some situations, common stock of the buyer or the newly-formed subsidiary (or even a new class of preferred stock) will be issued to encourage a seller to maintain an economic interest in the ongoing viability of the business assets or stock being sold. Under this type of payment structure, a seller can participate as a shareholder in any future growth in value or profits derived from the combined entities and is motivated to ensure the success of the business.

Convertible Securities

Convertible debt securities often enable buyers and sellers to obtain the benefits of both the stock and debt form of payment. From a seller's perspective, convertible debt securities provide "downside" protection and a fixed return while allowing the opportunity to reap the benefits of growth in value or profits derived from the combined entities. From a buyer's perspective, they provide the tax advantages of interest deductions while enabling buyers to avoid payments of principal at maturity should such instrument be converted into equity.

Contingent Payments

Often buyers and sellers will be unable to agree on the determination of the value of the assets or stock being sold or may want to reserve the right to adjust the terms of transactions in light of changes in circumstances or expectations. *Contingent consideration* provides for additional payments based on factors such as revenue targets, cash flow goals, or synergies achieved.

Similarly, the parties to an acquisition may provide for the repayment of cash or other considerations, through the use of escrows or other security arrangements, upon the occurrence of specified contingencies.

Nontraditional Structures and Strategies

There is a wide variety of nontraditional deal structures and acquisition strategies that are not as straightforward as a stock or asset purchase, such as spin-offs, roll-ups, leveraged buy-outs, and employee stock ownership plans. These deal structures are often a smaller slice of an overall corporate restructuring but nevertheless have grown as an increasingly larger part of the annual merger and acquisition activity.

An Introduction to Spin-Offs

Spin-offs are transactions designed to divest non-core operating divisions or assets (or divisions which have matured to the point of deserving or requiring standalone status) into their own independent operating company.

Although some respectable companies have been created as a result of spin-offs, it has also been said that "you don't spin off your crown jewels for no reason." Many spin-offs have been criticized by the IRS as trying to dump liabilities to spin-off entities which then have balance sheets laden with debt and a core focus with limited potential.

To qualify for favorable tax treatment, the transaction must meet the rigorous Internal Revenue Service business-purpose test designed to ensure that a spin-off has a valid business reason. Among the purposes which are acceptable to the IRS are that a deal will help with access to capital markets, debt-financing prospects, competitive position, management direction, or retention of key employees.

Leveraged Buy-Outs

A leveraged buy-out (LBO) is a transaction in which capital borrowed from a commercial lender is used to fund a large portion of the purchase. Generally, the loans are arranged with the expectation that the earnings of the business will easily repay the principal and interest. The LBO potentially has great rewards for the buyers who, although they frequently make little or no investment, own the target company free and clear after the acquisition loans are repaid by the earnings of the business. LBOs are often arranged to enable the managers of subsidiaries or divisions of large corporations to purchase a subsidiary or division which the corporation wants to divest, known as an "MBO," or management buy-out.

The LBO transaction will generally take one of two basic forms: the sale of assets or the cash merger. Under the *cash merger format*, the acquired company disappears upon merger into the acquiring company and its shareholders receive cash for their shares. Under the *sale of assets format*, on the other hand, the operating assets become part of the buying company but the selling company will generally be given the option of either receiving cash or continuing to hold their shares in the selling company.

At the heart of the LBO transaction are the dynamics of financing the acquisition by employing the assets of the acquired company as a basis for raising capital. Large unused borrowing capacity is the characteristic which typically enables a purchaser to use the seller's assets to borrow the purchase price. Specific factors which may exist to enhance borrowing capacity are: (1) large amounts of excess cash and cash equivalents such as certificates of deposit and other short term paper; (2) a limited amount of current debt; (3) demonstrated ability over a number of years to achieve substantial earnings; (4) substantial undervalued assets, which, when taken individually have a market value in excess of the depreciated value at which they are carried on the seller's balance sheets, sometimes called "hidden equity;" (5) subsidiaries with operations in unrelated industries which possess large amounts of excess properties that can be readily liquidated for cash without detriment to ongoing operations; and (6) the potential for "hidden cash flow" for the purchaser arising from income sheltered by depreciable property, the basis of which is readjusted upward as a consequence of the sale. Because of the complexities and uncertainties associated with arranging financing of this nature, the purchase agreement should provide that the obtaining of the financing by the purchaser is a condition precedent to the purchaser's obligations under the agreement.

Consolidations/Roll-Ups

Another major structural trend or strategy that became popular during the 1990s has been the consolidation or "roll-up." Under such a strategy, the buyer is a holding company which has targeted an industry which may be ripe for consolidation within a given region or market niche. The roll-up strategy may be horizontal or vertical in nature, but typically involves the aggressive acquisition of competitors in a given market to achieve operating efficiencies, synergies and market dominance. Obviously, antitrust laws are an issue (see Chapter 6) and some acquisitions will be friendly and some hostile. The consideration paid to the seller is usually the securities of the buyer. It is best to devise a plan and compensation strategy that provides incentive for the current management to stay in place and build up the value of their equity in the consolidated entity. The roll-up buyer must look at each deal to see how the target fits into the overall strategy and to look at the impact of the given acquisition on the earnings, valuation and taxes of the consolidated entities. If the consolidator (the buyer in a roll-up strategy) is public or close to an initial public offering, they must also consider the reaction of Wall Street, the business media and the investment bankers to each transaction.

Some "roll-up" companies are the result of certain private equity or venture capital firms picking target industries, hiring management teams to manage the consolidation process, and then financing the deals with their own capital resources. The well-managed roll-up companies have a specific strategic focus and rigid criteria for evaluating deals and are not just haphazardly accumulating companies to build an asset base or a revenue stream through consolidation. These better-managed companies are constantly searching for cross-marketing opportunities and operating efficiencies by and among their operating divisions to their customers as well as ancillary yet related products and services which can be added to the menu. From the seller's perspective, if you are approached by a consolidator who is offering primarily its own securities in order to "join the team," be sure to realize that most of your upside in the deal is tied to the ability of the buyer to successfully execute its business and consolidation plan. Make sure that you understand and agree with the buyer's strategy and vision, and that you are clear as to your role on a post-closing basis.

Selling to Your Staff: ESOPs as an Acquisition/Exit Strategy for Sellers

An employee stock ownership plan (ESOP) is an alternative available to sellers for disposing of their business which offers certain tax advantages to both seller and lender. There is a wide range of small- and middle-market companies who can not find a suitable buyer (or who choose to "sell" the company to their employees) and who therefore create an ESOP to buy all or substantially all of the company using deferred compensation. Two general categories of ESOP's are:

1. *Leveraged ESOP.* Uses borrowed funds (either directly from the company or from a third-party lender based on the guaranty of the company, with the securities of the employer as collateral) to acquire the employer's securities. The loan will be repaid by the ESOP from employer and employee contributions, as well as any dividends which may be paid on the employer's securities.

2. *Non-Leveraged ESOP.* A stock bonus plan (or contribution stock bonus plan with a money purchase pension plan) which pur-

chases the employer's securities with funds from the employer which would have been paid as some other form of compensation (that *were not* provided by a third-party lender).

General Legal Considerations in Structuring an ESOP

ESOP's, as with all types of deferred compensation plans, *must* meet certain requirements set forth by the IRS. Failure to meet these requirements will result in the contributions by the sponsoring employer *not* being tax deductible. To ensure that you're in compliance with IRS regulations, when creating your ESOP you must:

- Establish a trust in order to make contributions. The trust must be for the exclusive benefit of the participants and their beneficiaries.
- Avoid discrimination in favor of officers, major shareholders or highly compensated employees, particularly regarding allocation of assets and income distribution. A good rule of thumb is that at least *70 percent of all non-highly compensated employees must be covered* by the plan.
- Benefit no fewer than the lesser of: (1) 50 employees or (2) 40 percent or more of the employees of the plan sponsor.
- Invest primarily in the securities of the sponsoring employer. Although there are no strict guidelines, it is assumed that the ESOP portfolio will include at least 50 to 60 percent of the employer's securities at any given time.
- Vest in compliance with one of the minimum vesting schedules set forth by the IRS. The plan must adopt one of the following: (1) five-year "cliff" vesting (employee is vested after five years of service) or; (2) (7) seven-year "scheduled" vesting (20 percent fully vested after three years, increasing 20 percent per year until 100 percent vesting is reached after seven years).
- Establish voting requirements which conform to those of the IRS. Under the Code, voting rights may be vested in the trust's fiduciary, except under certain circumstances where rights must be passed through to the plan's participants. Generally, passing through becomes an issue when the vote will involve mergers, consolidations, reorganizations, recapitalizations, liquidations, major

asset sales and the like. Voting rights *in toto* may be passed through to employees, however, at the discretion of the employer in structuring the plan. Failure to fully "pass through" these rights may raise personnel and productivity problems (if the employees do not feel like true owners and as a result are cynical about the ESOP) thereby defeating a major incentive for adopting the ESOP.

• Comply with IRS rules regarding the distribution of ESOP benefits/assets. The plan must provide for a prompt (within one year) distribution of benefits to the participant following *retirement, disability,* or *death*. The nature and specific timing of the distribution will depend in part on the *cause* for separation from service with the company as well as whether the sponsoring employer is closely-held as opposed or publicly-traded.

• The employer's contributions should be based on a specific percentage of payroll, such as a money-purchase pension plan, or based on some other formula, such as a percentage of profits, as is the case with some profit sharing plans. This form provides for maximum flexibility in that contributions are in the complete discretion of the employer. Each year the employer simply makes a determination of the appropriate amount of contribution. It should be noted that the plan provides for a minimum contribution sufficient to permit the plan to pay any principal and interest due with respect to a loan used to acquire employer securities. The employers' contribution may be made in cash or other property, including employer's securities. In the event that the employer contributes its own securities, it may obtain a so-called "cashless deduction." The employer is entitled to deduct the fair market value of the securities so contributed, and the contribution involves no cash outlay by the employer.

• Provide "adequate consideration" in connection with the purchase of employer stock in an ESOP. This requires some method for valuation of the shares be available. For publicly-traded companies, this is generally not a problem, since the prevailing market price is a sufficient indication of value. For privately-held companies, however, value must be determined by the fiduciaries of the plan acting in good faith. This will generally require an *independent appraisal* by a qualified third-party appraisal firm, initially upon the establishment of the ESOP, and at least annually thereafter (the *cost* and *impact* of such an appraisal on a closely-held company should be considered before adopting an ESOP plan).

Key Legal Documents in the Establishment of an ESOP

There is a wide variety of legal documents which must be prepared in connection with the organization and implementation of an ESOP by a seller. These documents must be prepared by counsel, however, only after input has been received by all key members of the company's ESOP Team (financial and human resources staff, accountants, investment bankers, commercial lenders, the designated trustee, the designated appraisal firm, etc.). The preliminary analysis which should be conducted *prior to* the preparation of the documents should include:

- Impact on dilution, ownership, control and earnings of the company
- Type of securities to be issued (common vs. preferred)
- Tax deductibility of contributions and related tax issues
- Registration of the securities, where required, under federal and state securities laws
- Employee motivation and productivity improvement analysis
- Current and future capital requirements and growth plans of the company
- Interplay of the ESOP with other current or planned employee benefit plans within the company
- Timetable for planning, organization and implementation of the ESOP

ESOP Documentation

Once these and other factors have been considered, and strategic decisions made, counsel may be instructed to prepare the necessary documentation. In a leveraged-ESOP, the documents may include: (a) ESOP Plan; (b) ESOP Trust Agreement (which may be combined with the Plan); (c) ESOP Loan Documentation, such as a loan agreement or note guaranty (the initial set of documents may be from the commercial lender to the sponsoring employer, with a "mirror-image" loan being made by the employer to the ESOP); (d) ESOP Stock Purchase Agreement (where stock is purchased from the employer or its principal shareholders); (e) Corporate Charter Amendments and Related Board Resolutions; and (f) Legal Opinion and Valuation Reports.

The primary issues to be addressed by each of these documents are as follows:

The ESOP Plan (Where Trust Agreement is Self-Contained)

1. Designation of a name for the ESOP
2. Definition of key terms (*e.g.*, "participant," "year of service," "trustee")
3. Eligibility to participate (standards and requirements)
4. Contributions by employer (designated amount or formula; discretionary)
5. Investment of trust assets (primarily in employer securities, plans for diversification of the portfolio; purchase price for the stock; rules for borrowing by the ESOP, etc.)
6. Procedures for release of the shares from encumbrances (formula as ESOP obligations are paid down)
7. Voting rights (rights vested in trustee; special matters triggering employee voting rights)
8. Duties of the trustee(s) (accounting, administrative, appraisal, asset management, recordkeeping, voting obligations, preparation of annual reports, allocation and distribution of dividends, etc.)
9. Removal of trustee(s)
10. Effect of retirement, disability, death and severance of employment
11. Terms of the put option (for closely held companies)
12. Rights of first refusal upon transfer
13. Vesting schedules

ESOP Stock Purchase Agreement

1. Appropriate recitals
2. Purchase terms for the securities
3. Conditions to closing
4. Representations and warranties of the seller
5. Representations and warranties of the buyer

6. Obligations prior to and following the closing
7. Termination
8. Opinion of counsel
9. Exhibits, attachments, and schedules

Structuring the Offer to Meet the Needs of Both Parties

Seller's Needs

1. Price
2. Form of Consideration (e.g., cash, stock, notes)
3. Continuing Employment or Involvement
4. Important Qualitative Concerns
5. "Hidden" Agenda

Buyer's Needs

1. Control
2. Return on Investment
3. Minimal Cash Equity
4. Retention of Key Managers
5. Structured to Meet Lenders' Needs

Tools to Bridge the Gap

1. Cash is "King" (try to limit net worth)
2. Unsecured, Subordinated Long-Term Notes with Low Fixed Interest Rates
3. Employment and Consulting Contracts
4. Non-Compete Agreement
5. Earn-Outs

CHAPTER 8

Valuation and Pricing of the Seller's Company

Price is the paramount issue in a merger and acquisition transaction. It, beyond anything else, determines the amount of value that is transferred to the seller in exchange for ownership of the business for sale. It is the number one concern for both buyers and sellers, and ultimately determines whether or not a transaction can be consummated. Fortunately, there are several established valuation methods used to estimate the price range in which a business will be sold. The actual price, however, is only determined by what companies are actually willing to pay, the market price.

Although a formal valuation of the seller's business is a vital component of the buyer's analysis of the proposed transaction, it is important to realize that valuation is not an exact science nor will valuation alone typically drive the terms and pricing of the transaction. There are numerous acceptable valuation methods and, in most situations, each will yield a different result. Unfortunately, no method will answer the question, "How much is the business actually worth?" That question can only be answered in the receipt and negotiation of term sheets. The reality is that the market determines the price, and valuation, while an important exercise, is only indicative of what the market has paid for similar companies in the past. That said, there is clearly utility in the exercise of valuation because both buyers and sellers use these tools to gain insight into whether their perception of value will likely intersect the other party's perception of value.

To determine the value of a company, several key questions must be addressed. To whom is the asset valuable? In what context is the asset worth paying for? Before we get into the specifics of how businesses are valued, it is important to understand how prices are set in the real world.

A Quick Introduction to Pricing

The key question in pricing is: how do I, the seller, extract as much value from the buyer as possible? The obvious answer is, "as much as it is worth to the buyer!" While this would certainly maximize the price paid, there are certain real world constraints that prevent this from happening. First, people generally do not advertise how much something is worth to them. A man dying from thirst will value a glass of water far more than someone who just drank a glass of water; however, unless the potential water customers are willing to identify themselves as such, the water vendor may be only able to charge a single price. Similarly, just as a computer is worthless to someone who does not have electricity, worth a small amount to a three-year-old child, and potentially, millions to a technology entrepreneur, it is impossible to charge a single price and capture all of the value provided to each of the three of the potential computer customers.

In the real world, this problem is addressed through versioning where customers are forced to identify in what segment they belong by providing them different options that appeal to each segment differently. For the child, a basic kid's computer is all that is necessary. The technology entrepreneur, on the other hand, will likely prefer a more high-end computer and will pay a substantially different price as a result. Similarly, a Tiffany's diamond, while often the same quality as diamonds sold at other retail locations, commands a 30 to 50 percent premium because the Tiffany's brand is attached.

There are several key lessons from the world of pricing:

- Each potential buyer will value a business differently.
- Getting buyers to identify themselves (or intentions) helps de-

termine what good should be offered, and how that good will be valued.

- Cost is often not relevant in determining market value (i.e., the price of bottled water is not at all related to the cost of the water, which is ostensibly free).
- A single set price will exclude certain buyers from bidding and will not ensure the maximum price is paid.

An auction pricing format is generally believed to be the best way for a seller to maximize the price paid by the buyer. There are several different auction formats, each with generally the same principles: (1) a competitive process ensures the price offered is near the maximum price that any individual buyer is willing to pay; (2) the "winner" pays more than all the other bidders are willing to pay; and (3) the "winner" generally pays just a little bit more than what the second highest bidder was willing to pay.

When applied to businesses, there are several key differences. First, no business buyer likes to participate in an auction as they understand the principle and expected outcome, and second, it is generally very difficult to ensure that each potential bidder adheres to the same process and schedule as the other bidders. Nevertheless, the concept of an auction is a valuable tool for a seller and should be simulated, as much as is reasonably possible, during a sales process.

Finally, an auction, while great for actually maximizing the price paid, still does not help inform the buyer or seller what the likely outcome of the auction process will be. For that, we turn to a more traditional valuation exercise.

Valuation Overview

The valuation of a business may be done by the seller prior to entertaining prospective buyers, by a buyer who identifies a specific target, by an investment banker or other intermediary involved in the transaction process, or by all parties during negotiations to resolve a dispute over price. The fair market value of a business is generally defined as the amount at which property would change hands between a willing seller and a willing buyer when neither is under compulsion and both have reasonable knowledge of the relevant facts. However, this is often an unrealistic scenario as buyers and sellers are forced to consider "investment" or "strategic" value beyond a street analysis of fair market value.

Determining Strategic Value

In the context of a proposed acquisition, a proper valuation model will evaluate what the seller's business would look like under the umbrella of the prospective buyer's company (i.e., create a forward-looking *pro forma* financial model). The first step is to normalize current operating results to establish "net free cash flow." Next, it is important to examine "what if" scenarios to determine how specific line items would change under various circumstances. This exercise identifies a range of *strategic values* based on the projected earnings stream of the seller's company under its proposed new ownership. The greater the synergy, the higher this earnings stream and the higher the purchase price.

To arrive at this "strategic value," large amounts of financial data and general information on many aspects of the seller's business are required, such as the quality of management or overlapping functions within both businesses. The valuation exercise will attempt to assess how the value of the target company will be affected by any changes to the operations or foundation of the company as a result of the proposed transaction, such as a loss of key customers or key managers.

A thorough valuation should also examine the seller's "intangible assets" when determining strategic value. The list of intangible assets should include items such as customer lists, brands, intellectual property, patents, license and distributorship agreements, regulatory approvals, leasehold interests, and employment contracts. To the extent that the seller can supply specifics on its intangibles, since certain intangibles may not be readily apparent, the more likely it is that they will enhance the valuation.

The Basic Methods of Valuation

There are three main approaches to valuation: comparables company and comparable transaction analysis, asset valuation, and discounted cash flow (DCF) valuation. The first approach looks at companies that are comparable to the one in question, and looks at their performance ratios (e.g., value as a ratio of revenue) as guidance in valuing the business in question. The second approach is a process relevant to businesses with high levels of fixed assets and involves valuing the measurable pieces of the business in order to determine the value of the whole. The final approach looks at the amount of cash the business is likely to produce each year going forward, and equates those future cash flows into present value (i.e., today) terms.

Of the three main methods of valuation, no single method will provide a price that cannot be questioned. The methods are useful in that they provide points from which to start and supply a range of reasonable values grounded in reasonable assumptions and actual facts. In the end, it is vital to remember that the value or price of a company is largely dependent on the true motivations and goals of the key players involved and on the transaction's timing.

Comparable Company and Comparable Transaction Analysis

The notion of comparable worth pertains to the use of performance and price data of publicly and privately held companies in order to estimate the value of a similar business. The premise of *comparable company analysis* is that by examining publicly held companies that operate in the same or similar industry, one can infer how shareholders would value the target company were it traded publicly. Since market theory purports that publicly traded companies are valued "fairly" given all available information, then any public business that is similar to the target would be valued using similar metrics. This is not to say that "since our company is a large retailer, we are worth the same as other large retailers" but rather, that the relative value of a large retailer as a percentage of sales may be a good way to value a private retailer. In May 2005, Wal-Mart, for example, traded at 0.77 times the last twelve months of revenue. A business like Wal-Mart might use a 0.77 multiple of its last twelve months of revenue to determine what it would be worth were it traded in public markets. Similarly, *comparable transaction analysis* is done by identifying transactions of privately held companies with similar operations to the target. By examining the consummated transaction value in relation to relevant company metrics, a value for the target can be inferred.

The justification for this method lies in the premise that potential buyers will not pay more for the target company than what they would spend for a similar company that trades publicly or has been sold in a recent transaction. The challenge of this approach is that the comparison is only good to the extent that the companies chosen for the analysis are truly comparable to the target. Obviously, the companies should be as similar to the target as possible, particularly in regard to product offering, size of revenue base, and growth rate.

Once a preliminary range of valuations based on this method is determined, it is often necessary to adjust the price for situations particular to the target company. If, for example, the target company has profits that are consistently above industry averages due to an unusually low cost structure, then the value of the target firm must be adjusted upward from the comparables in order to account for that competitive advantage. In the example just mentioned, the buyer must be able to see and understand the justification for the target company's being valued higher than the comparable analysis dictates, or he or she will not be willing to pay the premium.

In some cases, a comparable analysis may not be possible or may yield unrealistic results. If the target company is closely held, comparable company or transaction analysis may be difficult or impossible as the necessary metric may not be available to make crucial judgments. In addition, the goals of financial reporting for a publicly held company can be quite different from those of a private company. While a publicly held company's management strives to show high earnings on its financial reports in order to attract investors, a closely held private company's management may be a sole entrepreneur or small group that wishes to minimize the earnings shown on its financial reports in order to minimize the tax burden. While both goals are legitimate, the key financial ratios of a target company that is closely held may vary widely with similar public companies in the industry.

Asset Valuation Method

If the operation of a target company's business relies heavily on fixed assets, a prospective buyer may conduct an asset valuation when attempting to determine a price for the business. The justification for an asset valuation in this case is that the buyer should pay no more for the target company than he or she would pay to obtain or build a comparable set of assets on the open market. Within these guidelines, the buyer can choose how to value these substitute assets using (1) the "cost of reproduction" or (2) the "cost of replacement" methods. The *cost of reproduction* takes into account the cost to construct a substitute asset using the same materials as the original at current prices, while the *cost of replacement* utilizes the cost to replace the original asset at current prices adhering to current standards. In either case, it is also necessary to consider the time that would be required assemble the assets and initiate normal operations.

When using the asset valuation method, all assets of the target company, both tangible and intangible, must be considered. Tangible assets, as the name implies refers to actual physical things like machinery and equipment, real estate, vehicles, office furniture and fixtures, land, and inventory. Markets exist were these assets are actively traded and as such, their value is fairly easy to determine. Intangibles assets include patents, trade secrets, brands, customer lists, supplier relationships, and other similar items that do not trade actively in an established market. These intangibles often are referred to as the company's goodwill, and defined as the difference in value between the company's hard assets and the true value of the company. While intangibles do have legitimate value, it is often difficult to convince a buyer of the exact value that an intangible asset provides. Generally it is in the seller's best interest to supply an acquirer with as much information about the company's intangibles as possible. The greater value of goodwill that can be attributed to specific, well-defined intangibles, the higher the price at which the company is likely to be valued. For example, rather than lumping patents that a company holds under "Intangible Goodwill" or as a single line item, each patent should be listed separately and supporting documentation provided that details crucial facts like patent scope, dates of expiration, and individual effects on the company's operations.

Discounted Cash Flow Valuation Method

Perhaps the most commonly used method for determining the price of a company is the discounted cash flow (DCF) valuation method.

In a DCF valuation, projections of the target company's future free cash flow are discounted to the present and summed to determine the current value. The implication of a DCF valuation is that when ownership of the target company changes hands, the buyer will own the cash flows created by continued operations of the target. Key elements of the DCF model are financial projections, the concepts of free cash flow, and the cost of capital used to calculate an appropriate discount rate.

The first step in a DCF valuation is developing projections of the target company's financial statements. Intimate knowledge of the target company's operations, historical financial results, and numerous assumptions as to the implied future growth rate of the company and its industry are key elements of grounded financial projections. In addition, it is necessary to determine a reasonable forecast horizon, which depending on industry and company stage, can range between five and ten years.

The next step in a DCF valuation is determining the target company's future free cash flows. The most basic definition of *free cash flows* is cash that is left over after all expenses (including cost of goods sold, operating and overhead expenses, interest and tax expenses, and capital expenditures) have been accounted for; it is capital generated by the business that is not needed for continued operations and accordingly, it is the capital available to return to shareholders without impairing the future performance of the business. Determining the free cash flows of a business is a function of understanding and utilizing the basic financial data provided in the target's projected financial statements. That being said it is extremely important in determining a company's free cash flows to have both general knowledge of financial statements and a thorough understanding of the target company's accounting practices as projections are often heavily influenced by historical financial statement data.

After determining the free cash flows for the target over the designated forecast period (typically five years), a terminal value is assigned to all future cash flows (everything post five years), which should be consistent with both industry growth rates and inflation predications. (**Note**: During the Internet bubble, optimistic entrepreneurs often made the mistake of assuming their company's growth rate would forever exceed that of the U.S. economy, yielding sizeable yet unrealistic valuations). Two primary methods are used for assigning a terminal value: (1) perpetual growth, which assumes that the target's free cash flow will grow indefinitely at a given rate, and (2) exit multiples implied by comparable company or transaction multiples described in previous sections.

Perhaps the most crucial concept of the discounted cash flow valuation method is that of a discount rate. As future free cash flows occur in the future and the target business is being valued today, it is necessary to adjust future inflows of capital to today's dollars. This discount rate encapsulates the idea the money today is worth more than money in future. If given the choice between $100 today and $100 two years from now, most people would choose the former as they would have the opportunity to invest that money and reasonably expect to receive more than $100 two years from now. This same concept, the time value of money, is used to apply an appropriate discount rate to the future free cash flows and the terminal value of a target business.

Finally, after discounting all future cash flow to today's dollar, the target company's cash flows can be summed to yield a final implied valuation. Unfortunately, like the other valuation methods described, the DCF valuation method has its flaws—the most prominent being that it is grounded in assumptions and financial projections that are prone to human error.

The Challenges of Valuing a Smaller Company

As discussed in Chapter 1, the transactional focus of this book is for deals ranging in the $1 million to $100 million range, and as a result, smaller, nonpublic companies will be the target business. These smaller, closely-held businesses will be more difficult to value, due to the following informational challenges and risks, which in turn result in lower valuations.

Smaller firms, in general, present certain "information risks," which make valuation more difficult due to:

- Lack of externally generated information, including analyst coverage, resulting in a lack of forecasts

- Lack of adequate press coverage and other avenues to disseminate company generated information
- Lack of internal controls
- Possible lack of internal reporting

In addition, there are numerous firm-specific reasons why small firms are more difficult to analyze from a valuation perspective, such as:

- Inability to obtain any financing or reasonably priced financing
- Lack of product, industry, and geographic diversification
- Inability to expand into new markets
- Lack of management expertise
- Higher sensitivity to macro- and microeconomic movements
- Lack of dividend history
- More sensitivity of business risks, supply squeezes, and demand lulls
- Inability to control or influence regulatory activity and union activity
- Lack of economies of scale or cost disadvantages
- Lack of access to distribution channels
- Lack of relationships with suppliers and customers
- Lack of product differentiation or brand name recognition
- Lack of deep pockets necessary for staying power

Because investors in private companies assume a higher degree of risk, they expect higher rates of return than they would of investments in public market securities. As a result, private company valuations tend to be lower. This discount, know aptly as the "private company discount," can range from 20 percent to 50 percent and depends on the type of business and the numerous factors outlined above. While the selling company can estimate that the discount will be based on assumptions of the acquirer's perceived risk, the actual discount can not be determined until a transaction is consummated.

While the detailed methods of valuation described in this chapter can provide a decent starting point for estimating the price at which a transaction will occur, unfortunately, that is often all that they provide. The final negotiated price can vary widely and is dependent on diverse factors, including the market conditions, the timing of the negotiations and of the valuation date, the internal motivation and goals of both the buyer and seller, the operating synergies which will result from the transaction, the structure of the transaction, and other factors that may not even be defined explicitly. When all is said and done, only a consummated transaction will provide a 100 percent accurate valuation.

Financing the Acquisition

Let's assume that the buyer's team has followed all of the steps in the process thus far: It has identified its strategic objectives, prepared the acquisition plan, identified the qualified candidates, narrowed the field, negotiated and signed the letter of intent, conducted the valuation and negotiated the purchase price, completed due diligence, and instructed counsel to start working on the definitive documents. The team breathes a sigh of relief until it realizes: *How will we finance this transaction?*

There are a wide range of options to finance a transaction from a simple equity financing to a layered transaction with multiple levels of debt and equity. Since each transaction is unique, the structures will vary. Each deal presents its own challenges, its own set of seller's needs, its own financial market conditions, and so forth. Overall, the key factors that affect the structure are size and complexity of the transaction, the buyer's cash position, the market for the buyer's securities, the terms of the purchase price, and the macro financial market conditions.

A key to the type and availability of funding is determined by the company being acquired. A company with little debt, significant assets, and strong cash flow is a good candidate for acquisition with long-term debt financing. On the other hand, your options will be limited if the company has poor cash flow, existing debt, and encumbered assets.

Three primary issues to address as you plan your acquisition financing are finding the ideal amount of debt that should be raised, determining a capital structure with the future success of the company in mind, and the cost of the funds.

This chapter looks at some common sources of debt and equity financing used by buyers in connection with acquisition financing.

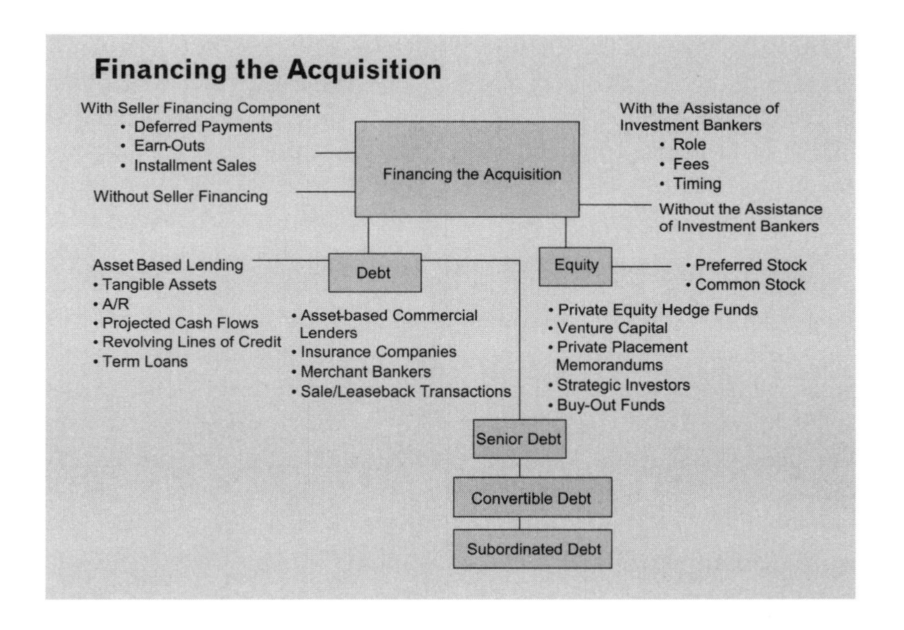

The Seller as a Source of Financing

For small- and middle-market transactions, seller financing or "take back" paper is a common practice. The basic mechanics of seller financing are detailed below. The simplest way to provide seller financing is to have the buyer make a down payment, with seller carrying a note for the rest of the purchase price. The business itself, and the significant business assets, provide the primary collateral for the note. A lien on the property is filed with the secretary of state's office to further document the transaction. If the buyer defaults on the note, the seller is the first in line to step back in and take over the business. In this situation, the buyer is agreeing to pay the seller according to the terms of the promissory note. The terms of the promissory note (interest rate, length, principal payments, etc.) can vary depending on the negotiated agreement.

For the seller, taking back a note for part or the entire purchase price may be the only way to sell the business, since banks have fairly strict lending criteria for acquisition loans. For the buyer, seller financing can be important due to less rigorous qualification standards and more lenient terms than a bank would have.

In these types of transaction, a buyer will typically use a bank for primary financing but may need a seller note in order to bridge a purchase price gap. The seller note, in this case, is subordinated and second in line to the commercial bank if the buyer defaults on the primary loan.

Additional security is sometimes requested for the seller note above and beyond the business itself. Types of security can include a personal residence as additional collateral, commercial real estate, investments, or even a personal guarantee.

The buyer may use seller financing to either keep the seller motivated to contribute to the company's future success or force the seller to prove that the business truly has the upside potential that has been represented. In other words, this form of financing requires the seller to absorb some of the risk. We have described above seller financing that is *fixed,* such as a simple installment sale or unsecured promissory note.

Other types of seller financing are *equity,* such as taking some of the buyer's common or preferred stock (or convertible debt) as payment; *contingent,* such as warrants (options to purchase the shares at a fixed price at a later point in time); or other types of conditional payments, such as *earn-outs*. With an earn-out, the seller receives additional payments only if the acquired business performs above a specified level in the future, or in the event that a specific post-closing condition is met, or if a certain event occurs (or does not occur), such as FDA approval or the issuance of a patent. Sellers that agree to accept a portion of their consideration in this manner must recognize the economic risks. If the buyer defaults on its obligations, the seller could ultimately end up owning the business again.

Debt Financing Alternatives

Asset-Based Lending

Although the many types and sources of debt financing should be considered, a traditional commercial bank loan is the most common source of acquisition capital for small and growing buyers. Asset-based lending is a key driver for financing acquisitions. The bank will loan money based on the amount of collateral (inventory, accounts receivable, and fixed assets). Banks will often lend up to 80 percent of the eligible collateral. The buyer/borrower is responsible for obtaining the balance of the purchase price. The buyer/borrower is also responsible for ensuring that there is sufficient working capital after making loan payments to continue operations and execute the business plan.

Cash Flow Financing

Another type of financing available for acquisitions is cash flow lending. This is an option for firms with predictable cash flows. The bank will want proof that the cash flows are sustainable in the future based on the historical financials. The financial institution will determine the loan structure based on the ability of the cash flows to meet the debt obligation.

Subordinated Mezzanine Debt

Subordinated debt financing can include both debt and equity. Compared to traditional debt and equity, there are dramatically fewer sources of subordinated debt. This type of debt is much riskier than senior debt and, thus, more expensive. To secure this type of financing, one should expect to pay a higher interest rate and give equity, typically in the form of warrants.

Equity

Equity financing has the greatest risk as it is lowest in the pecking order in case of a bankruptcy. To compensate for the risk, equity investors demand higher returns than the other financing sources. In many small- and middle-market transactions, the buyer provides the equity. If additional equity is needed, however, there are numerous sources, including private equity firms, venture capitalists, strategic investers, angel investors, and even hedge funds. There is a tremendous amount of equity funding available in today's market for M&A deals with an estimated $600 billion just in private equity firms ready for investment.

Understanding the Lender's Perspective

In recent years, commercial lending banks have changed the way in which they make loans for merger and acquisition deals. The local approval of loans is a steadily fading practice, while the loan-approval process has come to resemble the due diligence review of a securities offering. Lenders now behave like investors, conducting competitive analyses, determining market share trends, and so forth. These stricter loan standards mean that buyers must have more equity than before. In most instances, sellers' take-back notes must be entirely subordinated to the institutional financing. The classic leveraged buyout of the 1980s is a rarity for banks today, primarily because collateral alone is no longer sufficient; cash flow and balance sheet strength have become equally important.

These stricter loan standards mean fewer debt-driven deals are getting done, but the deals that are being done are at lower interest rates and have generally lower default rates. In addition, virtually all institutional lenders have taken a harder line on collateralized financing. Inventories, once a building block of many merger and acquisition loans, are becoming extremely difficult to finance. Rapidly changing technology can make high-tech goods obsolete almost overnight, while the steady increase in retail chain store failures threatens the worth of surviving stores' merchandise.

The real estate component may also be difficult to finance. Money is available, but underwriting requirements are increasingly onerous. Whereas once the loan-to-market-value ratio was 60 or 65 percent, now lenders will advance only 50 or 60 percent of the appraised value. For loans to manufacturers and distributors, lenders usually restrict their loans to high-ceiling, general-purpose buildings—a criterion that can sink many potential LBOs. All would-be borrowers are subject to often daunting scrutiny regarding soil contamination and other environmental hazards. Finally, real estate lenders, like institutional lenders in general, now place great emphasis on cash flow, both historical and projected.

Before attempting to understand the types of loans available from commercial banks, it is important to understand the perspective of the average commercial bank when it analyzes the buyer's loan proposal. Banks are in the business of selling money, and capital is the principal product in their inventory. Bankers, however, are both statutorily and personally averse to risk. The bank's shareholders and board of directors expect that loan officers will take all necessary steps to minimize the risk to the institution in each transaction and obtain the maximum protection in the event of default. Therefore, the types of loans available to the buyer/borrower, the terms and conditions of loan agreements, and the steps taken by the bank to protect its interest all have a direct relationship to the level of risk that is perceived by the lending officer and the loan committee. The management team that has been assigned to obtain the acquisition financing from a commercial bank must be in a position to show how the typical risks in an acquisition will be mitigated in preparation for the negotiation of the loan documentation.

Steps in the Loan Process

There are three key steps in obtaining acquisition financing from typical commercial lenders.

STEP 1: Preparing the Loan Proposal

The loan proposal should focus on the history of the buyer, the performance of the seller, and the reasons why the proposed deal makes sense. The loan proposal should also contain a copy of the signed letter of intent, as well as the financial statements of both parties. From the buyer/borrower's perspective, this will mean a loan proposal package that demonstrates the presence of a strong management team; an accounts receivable management program; the ability of the combined entity to service the debt, shown in financial statements and projections; the stability of the company through its longstanding and synergistic relationships with suppliers, distributors, and employees; and an understanding of the trends in the marketplace. The loan proposal should also explain the structure of the proposed transaction and give the underlying rationale for selecting this structure. All of these factors will be assessed by a loan officer in determining the merits of the proposed deal and the relative risk to the bank in making a loan in connection with the proposed acquisition.

Although the exact elements of a buyer/borrower's loan proposal will vary depending on the size of the company, its industry, and the terms of the proposed transaction, most lenders want the following fundamental questions answered:

- Who is the borrower?
- How much capital is needed and when?
- How will the capital be allocated and for what specific purposes?
- Why does the proposed transaction make sense from a financial, strategic, and operational perspective?
- What additional market share, cost savings, or other efficiencies will be achieved as a result of this transaction?
- How will the combined entity service its debt obligations (e.g., application and processing fees, interest, principal, or balloon payments)?
- What protection (e.g., tangible and intangible assets to serve as collateral) can the borrower provide the bank in the event that the company is unable to meet its obligations?

Although the answers to these questions are all designed to assist the banker in an assessment of the risk factors in the proposed transaction, they are also intended to provide the commercial loan officer with the information necessary to persuade the loan committee to approve the transaction. You must understand that the loan officer, once convinced of the merits of the deal, will then serve as an advocate on behalf of the buyer/borrower in presenting the loan proposal to the bank's loan committee. The loan documentation, terms, rates, and covenants that the loan committee will specify as a condition for making the loan will be directly related to the ways in which the buyer/borrower is able to demonstrate its ability to mitigate and manage the risk to the lender in connection with financing the proposed transaction.

The loan proposal should include the following categories of information, many of which can be borrowed or modified from the acquisition plan:

- *Summary of the Request.* An overview of the history of the buyer and the seller, the amount of capital needed, the proposed repayment terms, the intended use of the capital, and the collateral available to secure the loan.
- *History of the Borrower.* A brief background of the buyer and/or the seller; its capital structure; the key founders; the stage of development and plans for growth; a list of key customers, suppliers, and service providers; management structure and philosophy; plant and facility; the key products and services offered; and an overview of any intellectual property owned or developed.
- *Market Data.* An overview of trends in the industry; the size of the market; the buyer's and/or seller's market share; an assessment of the competition (direct and indirect); proprietary advantages; marketing, public relations, and advertising strategies; market research studies; and future industry prospects.
- *Financial Information.* Pro forma post-acquisition balance sheets and projected income statements; federal and state tax returns; appraisals of key assets or company valuations; current balance sheet; credit references; and a two-year income statement. The role of the capital requested (with respect to the buyer's and/or seller's plans for growth), an allocation of the loan proceeds, and the buyer's and/or seller's ability to repay must be carefully explained, and a discussion of its ability to service the debt must be supported by a three-year projected cash flow statement on a monthly basis.
- *Schedules and Exhibits.* A schedule of supporting documents (such as a letter of intent between buyer and seller) and background information on the seller's performance. Resumes of the buyer's principals, recent articles about the buyer or seller, a schedule of patents and trademarks, a picture of the seller's products or site, and an organization chart of the proposed management structure for the post-closing business should also be appended as exhibits to the loan proposal.

STEP 2: Understanding the Types of Commercial Bank Loans

During the process of planning the capital structure and in preparing the loan proposal, it is important for the buyer/borrower to understand the various types of loans that are available from a commercial bank (one or more of which could be tailored to meet specific requirements) in the context of a proposed acquisition. Loans are usually categorized by the term of the loan, the expected use of the proceeds, and the amount of money to be borrowed. The availability of these various loans depends on both the nature of the industry and the bank's assessment of the company's creditworthiness.

The following are typical loan categories:

• *Short-Term Loans.* Ordinarily used for a specified purpose, with the expectation by the lender that the loan will be repaid at the end of the project. For example, a seasonal business may borrow capital in order to build up its inventory in preparation for the peak season. When the season comes to a close, the lender expects to be repaid immediately. Similarly, a short-term loan could be used to cover a period when the company's customers or clients are in arrears; when the accounts receivable are collected, the loan is repaid. Short-term loans are usually made in the form of a promissory note (see discussion of loan documentation below) payable on demand, and may be secured by the inventory or accounts receivable that the loan is designed to cover; or it may be unsecured, in which case no collateral will be required.

Unless the company is a startup or operates in a highly volatile industry (thereby increasing the risk in the eyes of the lender), most short-term loans will be unsecured, thereby keeping the loan documentation and the bank's processing time and costs to a minimum. Lenders generally view short-term loans as self-liquidating in that they can be repaid by foreclosing on the current assets that the loan has financed. The fact that the bank's transactional costs are low, along with its perception of the lower risk during this short period of time, makes short-term borrowing somewhat easier for a growing business to obtain and serves as an excellent means for establishing a relationship with a bank and demonstrating creditworthiness.

• *Operating Lines of Credit.* Consist of a specific amount of capital that is made available to the company on an "as needed" basis over a specified period of time. A line of credit may be short term (60 to 120 days) or intermediate term (one to three years), renewable or nonrenewable, and at a fixed or fluctuating rate of interest. Borrowers should be especially careful to negotiate ceilings on interest rates; to avoid excessive commitment, processing, application, and related upfront fees; and to ensure that repayment schedules will not be an undue strain for the company. The company should also ensure that its obligations to make payments against the line of credit are consistent with its own anticipated cash-flow projections.

• *Intermediate-Term Loans.* Usually provided over a three- to five-year period for the purposes of acquiring equipment, fixtures, furniture, and supplies; expanding existing facilities; acquiring another business; or for working capital. The loan is almost always secured, not only by the assets being purchased with the loan proceeds but also by the other assets of the company, such as inventory, accounts receivable, equipment, and real estate. The loan usually calls for a loan agreement, which typically includes restrictive covenants that govern the operation and management of the company during the term of the loan. The restrictive covenants (discussed in greater detail below) are designed to protect the interests of the lender and ensure that all payments are made on a timely basis, before any dividends, employee bonuses, or noncritical expenses are paid.

Tips for Managing Tripartite Transactions

The buyer/borrower faces the challenge of trying to keep its transactions for raising debt or equity capital on track along with its deal with the seller. These tripartite transactions can be difficult to manage, but the following tips should keep everything in harmony for a synchronized closing.

• Timing is everything. Like an orchestra leader, the buyer must ensure that the lender is in the loop at all appropriate times on due diligence, deal negotiations, pre-closing conditions, and the coordination of closing. It is incumbent on the buyer to make sure that the financing transaction closes prior to the closing of the acquisition itself.

- The lender will be doing due diligence on the buyer as well as its own independent due diligence on the seller. The lender's due diligence will not only be on the two companies but also on the viability of the post-closing integration plan and the documentation of the transaction. The lender will want to see the executed confidentiality agreements, executed letters of intent, responses to due diligence requests, and all other documents that may directly or indirectly affect its rights as a lender.
- The lender will want to review the buyer's acquisition plan, with a particular focus on the value of the collateral securing the loans (where applicable), the historical earnings and cash flows of the seller, the track record and experience of the buyer, trends within the seller's industry, and the pro forma financial projections for a post-closing consolidated company.
- The buyer must pay careful attention to *cost-of-capital* issues and debt-to-equity ratios, which will vary from transaction to transaction. The sources of capital and their expected return on investment will also vary. For example, a senior lender, who will insist on a preferred position over other creditors, such as the subordinated lender, will often lend up to 70 percent of the purchase price, depending on the amount of assets available for collateral and the strength of the projected (as well as the historical) cash flows. If the senior lenders are properly secured, then they may not be as difficult in the negotiation of loan covenants and minimum interest rates. The subordinated lenders, on the other hand, are typically willing to provide 10 to 30 percent of the purchase price, but will generally demand a 15 to 30 percent annual return over a five-to-ten-year investment horizon. Both the senior lender and the subordinated lender will usually look to the buyer to provide between 15 and 30 percent of the total capital required for the transaction. The general rule is, the larger the lender's portion of the acquisition financing puzzle, the higher its expected

return on investment. If the buyer turns to the equity markets, it should be aware that most buyout funds, venture capitalists, and private investors will be looking for 20 to 30 percent returns on their investments.

Equity Financing

Equity financing involves the offer and sale of the buyer's securities for the purposes of raising the capital to pay the seller as well as to provide working capital for the new combined company. Securities are sold via private placements, negotiations with buyout or venture funds, and strategic investors. There are a wide variety of resources available to identify sources of equity capital including:

Regional Investment Bankers Association (RIBA)
171 Church Street, Suite 260
Charleston, SC 29401
(803) 557-2000
Jeff Adduci, president

Pratt's Guide to Venture Capital Firms
Published by Venture Economics (a subsidiary of Securities Data Publishing)
40 West 57th Street, 11th Floor
New York, NY 10019
(800) 455-5844

Directory of Buyout Financing Sources
Published by the Buyout Directories
40 West 57th Street, 11th Floor
New York, NY 10019
(212) 765-5311

National Venture Capital Association (NVCA)
1655 Fort Myer Drive
Suite 700
Arlington, VA 22209
(703) 351-5269

National Association of Small Business Investment Companies (NASBIC)
1199 N. Fairfax Drive
Suite 200
Alexandria, VA 22314
(703) 683-1601

In addition to these directories, buyers should consider contacting national underwriters and even insurance companies that have participated in the equity financing of larger acquisitions.

Before turning to a few of these strategies in more detail, let's take a look at the types of equity securities which may be offered and sold by the buyer/offeror to acquisition financing sources. The various forms of equity securities include common stock, preferred stock, and warrants and options. Each type of equity security will carry with it a different set of rights, preferences, and potential rates of return in exchange for the capital contributed to the company. For example, the typical growing company (whose value to an investor is usually greatly dependent on intangible assets such as patents, trade secrets or goodwill, and projected earnings) will tend to issue equity securities before incurring additional debt typically because its balance sheet lacks the assets necessary to secure the debt while additional debt is likely to increase the risk of company failure to unacceptably dangerous levels.

The three types of equity securities are:

1. *Common Stock*. An offering of common stock and the related dilution of interest are often a traumatic experience for owners of growing companies who currently operate closely-held corporations. The need for growth capital beyond what is available through personal savings or corporate retained earnings, results in a realignment of the capital structure and a redistribution of ownership and control. Although the offering of additional common stock is generally costly and will entail a surrender of some ownership and control, it does offer the company an increased equity base and a more secure foundation upon which to build a company, while the likelihood of obtaining future debt financing is greatly increased.

2. *Preferred Stock*. In exchange for their capital, purchasers of preferred stock receive dividends at a fixed or adjustable rate of

return (similar to a debt instrument), with priority over dividends distributed to the holders of the common stock, as well as a preference on the distribution of assets in the event of liquidation. The preferred stock may or may not have certain rights with respect to voting, convertibility to common stock, anti-dilution rights, or redemption privileges, which may be exercised either by the company or the holder.

Although the fixed dividends payments are not tax-deductible and ownership of the company is still diluted, the balance between risk and reward is still achieved because the principal invested need not be returned (unless there are provisions for redemption). In addition, the preferred stockholders' return on investment is limited to a fixed rate of return (unless there are provisions for conversion of the preferred stock into the common), and the claims of the preferred stockholders are subordinated to the claims of creditors and bondholders in the event of a failure to pay dividends upon the liquidation of the company. The use of convertible preferred stock is especially popular with venture capitalists.

3. *Convertible Securities*. Convertible securities provide the holder with an option to convert the underlying security, such as a note or preferred stock (based on specified terms and conditions), into common stock. The incentive for conversion is usually the same as for the exercise of a warrant, namely, that the price of the common stock is higher than the current rate of return provided by the convertible security. Convertible securities offer several distinct advantages to a company such as:

- An opportunity to obtain growth capital at lower interest rates and with less restrictive covenants in exchange for a chance to participate in the company's success if it meets its projections and objectives
- A means of generating proceeds 10 percent to 30 percent above the sale price of common stock at the time the convertible security is issued
- Greater earnings per share because the company can obtain the same capital by selling fewer shares of convertible securities than by selling common stock
- A general broadening of the market of prospective purchasers for the securities since certain buyers may wish to avoid a di-

rect purchase of common stock but would consider an investment in convertible securities.

Private Placement Offerings

The private placement offering is any type of offering of securities by a small or growing company, which does *not* need to be registered with the Securities and Exchange Commission ("SEC"). In order to determine whether a private placement is a sensible strategy for raising acquisition capital, it is imperative that the buyer/offeror has a fundamental understanding of federal and state securities laws affecting private placements (which are provided below as an overview), is familiar with the preparation requirements, and has a team of qualified legal and accounting professionals to assist with the preparation of the offering documents or Private Placement Memorandum (or "PPM").

The private placement generally offers reduced transactional and ongoing costs for the offeror because of its exemption from many of the extensive registration and reporting requirements imposed by federal and state securities laws. The private placement alternative usually also offers the ability to structure a more complex and confidential transaction, since the offerees will typically consist of a small number of sophisticated investors. In addition, a private placement permits a more rapid penetration into the capital markets than would a public offering.

Federal Securities Law

As a general rule, the Securities Act of 1933 requires the filing of a registration statement with the SEC prior to the offer to sell any security in interstate commerce unless an exemption is available, of which private placement is the most commonly recognized. The penalties for failing to register or for disclosing inaccurate or misleading information are quite stringent. Registration is also an expensive and time-consuming process and a network of underwriters and broker/dealers must be assembled to make a market for the security. In addition, a registrant is also subject to strict periodic reporting requirements.

To qualify for a private placement, the buyer/offeror must work

Range of Some of the Buyer's Options to Raise Acquisition Capital from Simplest to Most Complex

Simplest ⟶ Most Complex

1	2	3	4	5	6
Buyer uses its own cash or securities* to pay seller	Buyer uses cash/securities and seller provides some financing through notes and loan-outs	Buyer provides equity for 25 percent to 50 percent of purchase price and balance is provided by senior lender—a revolver for the deal and post-closing working capital	Buyer provides equity for 25 percent of purchase price, with 50 percent from senior lender and 25 percent from subordinated lender	Buyer provides equity for 30 percent of purchase price (which must be raised through a securities offering or negotiations with a buyout fund) and 50 percent from a senior lender and 20 percent from a subordinated lender	The total purchase price is a combination of: • cash from buyer (equity) • notes taken back by seller • securities of the buyer • cash from senior lender • cash from subordinated lender • cash from equity source, such as buyout fund, PPM, or venture capitalist

*Although paying the seller with your own stock appears to be the simplest option, be sure to work with counsel to ensure that these shares are properly issued and authorized and that the impact on valuation and dilution is considered carefully.

with legal counsel to structure the transaction within the various categories of exemptions available. They include: *Section 4(2)* (the broad "private offering" exemption designed for "transaction(s) not involving any public offering"); *Section 3(a)(11)* (an intrastate exemption); and (c) the most common, *Regulation D* (which encompasses three specific transactional exemptions from Sections 3(b) and 4(2)).

Section 4(2)

Section 4(2) allows an exemption from registration for transaction(s) by an issuer not involving a public offering. The vague language of the act has been a source of much controversy and confusion in the legal and financial communities. Over the years, court cases have established that to qualify for this exemption, targeted investors in a 4(2) offering must have access to the same kind of information that would be available if the issuer were required to register. However, terms like "access to" and "same kind" generally leave discretion to the company and its attorney of the exact method of presenting the necessary information. In relying on an exemption under Section 4(2), the offering should be structured in accordance with the following guidelines:

1. The offering should be made directly to prospective investors without the use of any general advertising or solicitation.
2. The number of offerees should be limited.
3. The offering should be limited to either insiders (such as officers of the company or family members) or sophisticated investors who have a pre-existing relationship with you or the company.
4. The prospective investor should be provided with (at a minimum) recent financial statements, a list of critical risk factors (which influence the investment) and an open invitation to inspect the company's facilities and records.
5. If in doubt as to whether Section 4(2) applies to a particular offering, d*o not rely on it*. Rather, attempt to structure the transaction within one of the Regulation D exemptions.

Section 3(a)(11)

Section 3(a)(11) allows for an exemption for "any security which is part of an issue offered and sold only to persons resident within a single state by an issuer which is a resident and doing business within such state." The key issue in relying on this exemption is ensuring that the offering is truly an intrastate offering. This test is deceptive; however, the SEC has adopted Rule 147 to assist in determining whether the requirements of Section 3(a)(11) have been met. Precautionary steps must be taken to ensure that all offerees are residents of the particular state because even one nonresidential offeree will jeopardize the availability of the exemption.

Rule 504

Rule 504 under Regulation D permits offers and sales of not more than $1,000,000 during any 12-month period by any issuer that is not subject to the reporting requirements of the Securities Exchange Act of 1934 and that is not an investment company. Rule 504 places virtually no limit on the number or the nature of the investors that participate in the offering. The SEC also requires that its Form D be filed for all offerings under Regulation D within 15 days of the first sale. *But even if accreditation is not required, it is strongly recommended that certain baseline criteria be developed and disclosed in order to avoid unqualified or unsophisticated investors.*

Even though no formal disclosure document or prospectus needs to be registered and delivered to offerees under Rule 504, there are many procedures that still must be understood and followed, and a disclosure document is nevertheless strongly recommended. An offering under Rule 504 is still subject to the general anti-fraud provisions of the Exchange Act; thus, every document or other information that is actually provided to the prospective investor must be accurate and not misleading by virtue of its content or its omissions. Finally, a buyer/offeror seeking to raise capital under Rule 504 should examine applicable state laws very carefully because although many states have adopted overall securities laws similar to Regulation D, many of these laws do not include an exemption similar to 504 and as a result, a formal memorandum (which is discussed later in this chapter) may need to be prepared.

Rule 505

Rule 505 under Regulation D is selected over Rule 504 (by many companies) as a result of its requirements being consistent with many state securities laws. Rule 505 allows for the sale of up to $5,000,000 of the issuer's securities in a 12-month period to an unlimited number of "accredited investors" and up to thirty-five non-accredited investors (regardless of their net worth, income, or sophistication). An "accredited investor" is any person in at least one of the eight categories set out in Rule 501(a) of Regulation D. Included in these categories are officers and directors of the company who have "policy-making" functions as well as outside investors who meet certain income or net worth criteria. Rule 505 has many of the same filing requirements and restrictions imposed by Rule 504 (such as the need to file a Form D), in addition to an absolute prohibition on advertising and general solicitation for offerings and restrictions on which companies may be an issuer. Any company that is subject to the "bad boy" provisions of Regulation A is disqualified from being a 505 offeror; this applies to persons who have been subject to certain disciplinary, administrative, civil or criminal proceedings, or sanctions that involve the company or its predecessors.

Rule 506

Rule 506 is similar to Rule 505; however, the issuer may sell its securities to an unlimited number of accredited investors and up to thirty-five non-accredited investors. For buyer/borrowers needing over $5,000,000 to complete the proposed acquisition, this exemption is the most attractive because it has no maximum dollar limitation. The key difference under Rule 506 is that any non-accredited investor must be "sophisticated." A "sophisticated investor" is one who does not fall within any of the eight categories specified by Rule 501(a), and is believed by the issuer to "have knowledge and experience in financial and business matters that render him capable of evaluating the merits and understanding the risks posed by the transaction (either acting alone or in conjunction with his "purchaser representative"). The best way to remove any uncertainty over the sophistication or accreditation of a prospective investor is to request that a comprehensive Confidential Offeree Questionnaire be completed before the securities are sold. Rule 506 does eliminate the need to prepare and deliver disclosure documents in any specified format, if exclusively accredited investors participate in the transaction. As with Rule 505, an absolute prohibition on advertising and general solicitation exists.

State Securities Laws

Regulation D was designed to provide a foundation for uniformity between federal and state securities laws. This objective has been met in some states but still has a long way to go on a national level. Full compliance with the federal securities laws is only one level of regulation that must be taken into account when developing plans and strategies to raise capital through an offering of securities. Whether or not the offering is exempt under federal laws, registration may still be required in the states where the securities are to be sold under blue sky laws.

The level of review varies widely among the states, ranging from very tough "merit" reviews designed to ensure that all offerings of securities are fair and equitable, to very lenient "notice only" filings designed to promote full disclosure. The securities laws and requirements of each state where an offer or sale will be made should be checked very carefully prior to the distribution of the offering documents. Every state in the nation does, in fact, have some type of statute governing securities transactions and securities dealers. When drafting the offering, these laws should be reviewed to determine:

- If the particular limited offering exemption selected under federal law will also apply in the state
- Which pre-sale or post-sale registration with the applicable states or mandatory state legends is required
- The remedies available to an investor who has purchased securities from a company that has failed to comply with applicable state laws
- Who may offer securities for sale on behalf of the company

Small Corporate Offering Registration

Most states have now adopted the Small Corporate Offering Registration ("SCOR"), which simplifies Regulation D as a source of acquisition financing for small businesses. SCOR allows for a question-and-answer format disclosure document, which you can fill in with the assistance of your accountant or attorney. This new format significantly reduces the cost of compliance without sacrificing the quality of information available to prospective investors to reach an informed decision. There are restrictions on the structure of offerings that can be made under the U-7, the details of which should be discussed carefully with your attorney.

Preparing the Private Placement Memorandum

The offeror should work with legal counsel to prepare the document and exhibits that will constitute the "Private Placement Memorandum" (known as the "PPM"). The PPM describes the background of the company, the details of the proposed transaction, the historical performance of the seller, the risks to the investor, and the terms of the securities being sold. In determining the exact degree of "disclosure" that should be included in the document, there are several factors which affect the type of information that must be provided and the format in which the data is to be presented, such as the:

- Minimum level of disclosure that must be made under federal securities laws (which depends, in part, on the exemption from registration being relied upon).
- Minimum level of disclosure that must be made under an applicable state's securities laws (which naturally depends on in which state or states an offer or sale of the securities is to be made).
- Expectations of the targeted investors. Some investors will expect a certain amount of information presented in a specified format regardless of what the law may require.
- Complexity or the nature of the company and the terms of the offering.

Many offerors should prepare detailed disclosure documents regardless of whether or not they are required to do so in order to avoid liability for misstatements, fraud or confusion, especially if the nature of the company and/or the terms of its offering are very complex.

Each transaction or proposed offering of securities must be carefully reviewed by legal counsel to first determine the minimum level of disclosure that must be provided to prospective investors under applicable federal and state laws. Once this is established, the costs of preparing a more detailed document than may be required should be weighed against the benefits of the additional protection provided to the company by a more comprehensive prospectus. The key question will always be, "What is the most cost-effective vehicle for providing the targeted investors with the information that they require and that both applicable law and prudence dictate they must have?" There are no easy answers.

The specific disclosure items to be included in the PPM will vary depending on the size of the offering and nature of the investors under federal securities laws and any applicable state laws. The text should be descriptive not persuasive and allow the reader to reach his or her own conclusions as to the merits of the securities being offered by the company. At the minimum every good PPM must include the following material.

- *Introductory Materials.* These introduce the prospective investor to the basic terms of the offering. A cover page should include a brief statement about the buyer and seller and the core business of each company; the terms of the offering (often in table form); and all required "legends" required by federal and state laws. The cover page should be followed by a summary of the offering, which serves as an integral part of the introductory materials and cross-reference point for the reader. The third and final parts of the introductory materials are usually a statement of the investor suitability standards, which includes a discussion of the federal and state securities laws applicable to the offering and the definitions of an accredited investor as applied to the offering.
- *Description of the Company.* This is obviously a statement of the buyer's and seller's history and should include a discussion of each company's history; its principal officers and directors; products and services; management and operating policies; performance history and goals; competition; trends in the industry; advertising

and marketing strategy; suppliers and distributors; intellectual property rights; key real and personal property; customer demographics; and any other material information that would be relevant to the investor.

• *Risk Factors.* This is usually the most difficult section to write, yet it's viewed by many as clearly one of the most important to the prospective investor. Its purpose is to outline all of the factors that make the offering or the projected acquisition plans risky or speculative. Naturally, the exact risks to the investors posed by the offering will depend on the nature of the company and the trends within that industry.

• *Capitalization of the Issuer.* This should be discussed providing the capital structure of the buyer/offeror both before and after the offering and before and after the proposed acquisition. For the purposes of this section in the PPM, all authorized and outstanding securities must be disclosed (including all long-term debt).

• *Management of the Company.* This should include: a list of the names, ages, special skills or characteristics, and biographical information on each officer, director, or key consultant; compensation and stock option arrangements; bonus plans; special contracts or arrangements; and any transactions between the company and individual officers and directors (including loans, self-dealing, and related types of transactions). The role and identity of the buyer/offeror's legal and accounting firms should also be disclosed, as well as any other "expert" retained in connection with the offering.

• *Terms of the Offering.* This should describe the terms and conditions, the number of shares and the price. If the securities are to be offered through underwriters, brokers or dealers, then the names of each distributor, the terms of the relationship, the commissions to be paid, the obligations of the distributor (e.g., guaranteed or best efforts offering), and any special rights, such as the right of a particular underwriter to serve on the board of directors, any indemnification provisions or other material terms of the offering.

• *Allocation of Proceeds.* This must state the principal purposes for which the net proceeds will be used and the approximate amount intended to be used for each purpose. You should give careful thought to this section because any deviation from the use of funds as described in the PPM could trigger liability.

• *Dilution.* This should include a discussion of the number of shares outstanding prior to the offering, the price paid, the net book value, the effect on existing shareholders of the proposed offering, as well as dilutive effects on new purchasers at the completion of the offering. Often the founding shareholders (and sometimes their key advisors or the people who will help promote the PPM) will have acquired their securities at prices substantially below those in the prospective offering.

• *Description of Securities.* This should explain the rights, restrictions and special features of the securities being offered. It should also explain provisions of the articles of incorporation or by-laws that affect capitalization (such as pre-emptive rights, total authorized stock, different classes of shares or restrictions on declaration, and distribution of dividends).

• *Financial Statements.* Financial statements to be provided by the issuer will vary depending on the amount of money to be raised, applicable federal and state regulations, and the company's nature and stage of growth. Provide a discussion and explanation of these financial statements and an analysis of its current and projected financial condition.

• *Exhibits.* Exhibits such as the articles of incorporation and by-laws; key contracts; or leases, brochures, news articles, marketing reports; and resumes of the principals may be appended as exhibits to the PPM.

Subscription Materials

Once the prospective investors and their advisors have made a decision to provide capital to the buyer/offeror in accordance with the terms of the PPM, there is a series of documents which must be signed to evidence the investors' desire to subscribe to purchase the securities offered by the PPM. The various subscription materials that should accompany the PPM serve several purposes, such as to protect the company against a claim of noncompliance and screen out potentially difficult investors. The two key documents are the:

• *Subscriber Questionnaire,* which is developed in order to obtain certain information from prospective offerees and then serve as evidence of the required sophistication level and the ability of offerees to fend for themselves as required in a PPM. You should obtain information regarding the prospective purchaser's background, citizenship, education, employment, investment and/or business experience.

- *Subscription Agreement*, which is the contract between the purchaser (investor) and the issuer of the securities. It should contain acknowledgment of:

1. The receipt and review by the subscriber of the PPM
2. The restricted nature of the securities to be acquired and knowledge of the fact that the securities were acquired under an exemption from registration
3. Any particularly significant suitability requirements (such as amount of investment or passive income, tax bracket, and so forth) that the issuer feels may be crucial to the purchaser's ability to obtain the benefits of the proposed investment
4. An awareness of specific risks disclosed in the information furnished
5. The existence of the purchaser representative (if one is used)

The Subscription Agreement should also require a signature to confirm the accuracy and completeness of the information contained in the offeree or purchaser questionnaire and the number and price of the securities to be purchased and the manner of payment.

The Subscription Agreement often contains an agreement on the part of the purchaser to indemnify the issuer against losses or liabilities resulting from any misrepresentations on the part of the prospective purchaser that would void or destroy the exemption from registration that the issuer is attempting to invoke. The Subscription Agreement should also contain representations on the part of the subscriber with respect to its authority to execute the agreement.

Venture Capital Funds

A buyer/offeror whose transaction does not qualify for debt financing from a commercial bank or where a private placement is not appropriate might consider an institutional venture capital or buy-out as a source of acquisition financing. The term "venture capital" has been defined in many ways, but refers generally to relatively high-risk, early-stage financing of young, emerging growth companies. The professional venture capitalist is usually a highly trained finance professional who manages a pool of venture funds for investment in growing companies on behalf of a group of passive investors.

Another major source of venture capital available to buyer/offerors who meet certain minimum size requirements is a Small Business Investment Company ("SBIC"). An SBIC is a privately organized investment firm which is specially licensed under the Small Business Investment Act of 1958 to borrow funds through the Small Business Administration for subsequent investment in the small business community. Finally, some private corporations and state governments also manage venture capital funds which may be available sources of equity capital for acquisition financing.

The Investment Decision

Regardless of the buyer/offeror's particular stage of development or the specific details of the proposed acquisition transaction, there are several key variables that all venture capital firms will consider in analyzing the Acquisition Plan presented. These variables generally fall into four categories: (1) the management team; (2) products and services offered; (3) the markets in which the target company and the buyer/offeror compete; and (4) the anticipated return on investment. In determining whether the growing company would qualify for venture capital, its management team must be prepared to answer the following questions:

Management Team

- What are the background, knowledge, skills and abilities of each member?
- How is this experience relevant to the specific industry in which the buyer/offeror competes?
- How are the risks and problems often inherent to the buyer/offeror's industry handled by the members of the management team?

Products and Services

- At what stage of development are the buyer/offeror's products and services?
- What is the specific market opportunity which has been identified by the proposed transaction?
- How long will this "window of opportunity" remain open?
- What steps are necessary for the company to exploit this opportunity?
- To what extent are the company's products and services unique, innovative and proprietary?

The Growing Company's Targeted Markets

- What is the stage in the life cycle of the industry in which the buyer/offeror plans to operate on a post-closing consolidated basis?
- What is the size and projected growth rate of the company's targeted market?
- What methods of marketing, sales and distribution will be utilized in attracting and keeping customers?
- What are the strengths and weaknesses of each competitor (be it direct, indirect, or anticipated) in the targeted market?

Return on Investment

- What are the buyer/offeror's current and projected valuation and performance in terms of sales, earnings and dividends?
- To what extent have these budgets and projections been substantiated?
- Has the company overestimated or underestimated the amount of capital that will be required for the growth and development of its acquisition plan?
- How much money and time has already been invested by the owners and managers?

Negotiating and Structuring the Investment

The negotiation and structuring of most venture capital transactions revolves around the need to strike a balance between the concerns of the buyer's management team (such as dilution of ownership and loss of control) and the concerns of the venture capitalist (such as return on investment and mitigating the risk of company failure). The typical end result of these negotiations is a *term sheet* which specifies the key financial and legal terms of the transaction and then serves as a basis for the negotiation and preparation of the definitive legal documentation. The buyer/offeror should work with its legal counsel in order to understand the many traps and restrictions, such as contingent proxies and super majority voting provisions that are typically found in venture capital financing documents. The term sheet may also contain rights and obligations including an obligation to maintain an agreed valuation of the company; responsibility for certain costs and expenses in the event the proposed transaction does not take place; or secure commitments for financing from additional sources prior to closing.

The initial negotiation of the term sheet and eventually the definitive documents will usually center on the types of securities to be issued and the principal terms, conditions, and benefits offered by the securities. The type of securities ultimately selected will usually fall within one of the following categories:

- *Preferred Stock* is the most typical form of security issued in connection with a venture capital financing because of the many advantages offered to an investor (such as convertibility into common stock, dividend and liquidation preferences over the common stock, anti-dilution protection (allowing the venture capitalist to maintain its ownership position), mandatory or optional redemption schedules (allowing the company to repurchase the shares or the investors to "put" them back to the buyer), and special voting rights and preferences).
- *Convertible Notes* are often preferred by a venture capitalist in connection with higher-risk transactions because he or she is able to enjoy the senior position of a creditor over a shareholder, until the risk of the company's failure has been mitigated.
- *Debt Securities with Warrants* are also preferred by venture capitalists because they protect the downside by earning debt payments and protect the upside by including warrants to purchase common stock at favorable prices and terms. The use of a warrant enables the investor to buy common stock without sacrificing the

position as a creditor, as would be the case if only convertible debt was used in the financing.

- *Common Stock* is rarely preferred by venture capitalists (especially at early stages of development) because it does not offer the investor any special rights or preferences, a fixed return on investment, special ability to exercise control over management, and liquidity to protect against downside risks. One of the few times that common stock might be selected is when there are tax advantages to preserving the buyer's Subchapter S status under the Internal Revenue Code which might be jeopardized if a class of preferred stock (with different economic terms) were to be authorized by an amendment of the buyer's corporate charter.

Once the type of security is designated by the venture capitalist, steps must be taken to ensure that the authorization and issuance of the security is properly made under applicable state corporate laws. For example, if the company's charter does not provide for a class of preferred stock, then the articles of amendment must be prepared, approved by the board of directors and shareholders, and filed with the appropriate state corporation authorities. The articles of amendment will include new provisions on voting rights, dividend rates and preferences, mandatory redemption provisions, anti-dilution protection (also called "ratchet clauses" because the price of the shares upon conversion is "ratcheted" down if the buyer's company issues shares below the conversion price), and related special rights and features. If debentures are selected, then negotiations will typically focus on term, interest rate and payment schedule, conversion rights and rates, extent of subordination, remedies for default, acceleration and pre-payment rights and underlying security for the instrument, as well as the terms and conditions of any warrants which are granted along with the debentures.

The legal documents involved in a venture capital financing must reflect the end-result of the negotiation process and must contain all of the legal rights and obligations. These documents generally include the following:

- Preferred stock or debenture purchase agreement ("Investment Agreement")

- Stockholders' agreement
- Employment and confidentiality agreements
- Warrant (where applicable)
- Debenture or notes (where applicable)
- Preferred stock resolution (to amend the corporate charter) (where applicable)
- Contingent proxy
- Legal opinion of company counsel
- Registration rights agreement

The following is a brief overview of the nature and purposes of some of these documents:

- *The Investment Agreement* describes all of the material terms and conditions of the financing. It also serves as a type of disclosure document because certain key historical and financial information is disclosed in the representations and warranties made to the investors. The representations and warranties (along with any exhibits) are designed to provide full disclosure to the investors, which will then provide a basis for evaluating the risk of the investment and structure of the transaction. The Investment Agreement will also provide for certain conditions precedent which must be met by the company prior to the closing. These provisions require the company to perform certain acts at (or prior to) closing as a condition to the investor providing the venture capital financing. The conditions to closing are often used in negotiations to mitigate or eliminate certain risks identified by the investor (such as a class action suit by a group of disgruntled employees) but usually are more of an administrative checklist of actions which must occur at closing, such as the execution of the stockholders', employment and confidentiality agreements.
- *The Stockholders' Agreement* will typically contain certain restrictions on the transfer of the company's securities, voting provisions, rights of first refusal, and co-sale rights in the event of a sale of the founder's securities, anti-dilution rights, and optional redemption rights for the venture capital investors. Venture capitalists will often require the principal stockholders to become parties to the stockholders' agreement as a condition to closing on the in-

vestment. Any existing stockholders or buy/sell agreements will also be carefully scrutinized and may need to be amended or terminated as a condition to the investment. For example, the investors may want to reserve a right to purchase additional shares of preferred stock (in order to preserve their respective equity ownership in the company in the event that another round of the preferred stock is subsequently issued). This is often accomplished with a contractual pre-emptive right (as opposed to such a right being contained in the corporate charter, which would make these rights available to all holders of the company's stock).

• *Employment and Confidentiality Agreements* will often be required of key members of the management team as a condition to the investment. These agreements define the obligations of each employee, the compensation package, the grounds for termination, the obligation to preserve and protect the company's intellectual property, and post-termination covenants (such as covenants not to compete or to disclose confidential information).

• *The Contingent Proxy* provides for a transfer of the voting rights attached to any securities held by a key principal to the venture capitalist upon the death or disability of such personnel. The proxy may also be used as a penalty for breach of a covenant or warranty included in the Investment Agreement.

• *The Registration Rights Agreement* would require the venture capital investors to convert their preferred stock or debentures prior to the time that a registration statement is approved by the SEC, and it is often required since these registration rights are limited to the company's common stock. Many venture capitalists view the eventual public offering of the company's securities (pursuant to a registration statement filed with the SEC under the Securities Act) as the optimal method of achieving investment liquidity and maximum return on investment. As a result, the venture capitalist will protect his or her right to participate in the eventual offering with a Registration Rights Agreement. The registration rights may be in the form of "demand rights" (which are the investors' right to require the company to prepare, file and maintain a registration statement) or "piggyback rights" (which allow the investors to have their investment securities included in a company-initiated registration). The number of each type of demand or piggyback rights, the percentage of investors necessary to exercise these rights, the allocation of expenses of registration, the minimum size of the offering, the scope of indemnification, and the selection of underwriters and broker/dealers will all be areas of negotiation in the Registration Rights Agreement.

A well-prepared Acquisition Plan, an understanding of the analysis conducted by the venture capitalist and an understanding of the legal documents typically prepared in a venture capital financing will significantly increase your company's ability to gain access to this growing source of acquisition financing.

The Acquisition Agreement and Related Legal Documents

Once the due diligence has been completed, valuations and appraisals conducted, terms and price initially negotiated, and financing arranged, the acquisition team must work carefully with legal counsel to structure and begin the preparation of the definitive legal documentation which will memorialize the transaction. The drafting and negotiation of these documents will usually focus on the key terms of the transactions, the past history of the seller, the present condition of the business, and a description of the rules of the game for the future. They also describe the nature and scope of the seller's representations and warranties, the terms of the seller's indemnification of the buyer, the conditions precedent to closing of the transaction, the responsibilities of the parties during the time period between execution of the purchase agreement and actual closing, the terms and structure of payment, the scope of post-closing covenants of competition and related obligations, the deferred or contingent compensation components, and what will happen if things go awry post-closing, such as any predetermined remedies for breach of the contract.

Buyers and sellers of companies look to their legal counsel for guidance on a wide variety of strategic, regulatory and financial tasks beyond the obvious roles typically played in the due diligence process and in preparing and negotiating the acquisition documents. In a larger "Wall Street-style" transaction, the advisory team is often very large and the role of counsel is often narrower and more clearly defined. However, in deals by and between smaller and midsize companies, the role of the business lawyer is often expanded to include a wide variety of responsibilities, from financial advisor to corporate strategist to creative problem solver to quasi-investment banker to emotional sounding board to family business counselor. To be an effective advisor in one or more of these roles, a business lawyer will need to really understand the key aspects of the client's business model and plans as well as trends in the industry. It may also require training and expertise in fields as wide-ranged as strategic planning, accounting and finance, tax, and even psychology.

It is critical to understand that for many sellers of a business that has been owned and grown over a long period of time, the sale of the company will not only be the most important financial event of their lives but also the most emotional. An effective business lawyer will help his client prepare for this transaction at an early stage in the process, with a focus on a legal audit to identify potential problems and prepare for the buyer's due diligence request, the review of the offering memorandum, the review of the projected valuation and pro forma or restated financials and estate planning and related issues which will be relevant following the closing of the transaction. Exhibit 10-1 provides an overview of each attorney's role, which is driven by the role of the client in a given transaction.

The goal is to compare the acquisition objectives described in the Acquisition Plan with the strengths and weaknesses of each seller to ensure that the acquisition team has a clear idea as to *how* the targeted companies will complement the buyer's strengths and/or mitigate the buyer's weaknesses. The specific qualitative and quantitative screening criteria help assist the buyer and its team to ensure that the right candidates are selected. They are intended to "filter out" the wrong deals and mitigate the chances of post-closing regrets and problems.

Keys to Preparing an Effective Acquisition Agreement

Following the negotiation and execution of the Letter of Intent and concurrent with the due diligence process, the buyer's lawyer will

Exhibit 10-1. Roles of counsel: mergers and acquisitions transactions.

	Seller's Counsel	Buyer's Counsel
Early Stage	• Legal Audit/preparing for the due diligence process • Review of Offering Memorandum and presentation materials	• Assist the development of the Acquisition Plan and screening process • Preliminary due diligence on wide range of targets
LOI/Due Diligence	• Prepare document/ data room for due diligence • Review and negotiate Letter of Intent	• Legal and strategic due diligence on target • Review and negotiate the Letter of Intent
Acquisition Documents	• Review and negotiate the definitive documents • *Narrow* the R&Ws and Covenants and shift Allocation of Risk	• Review and negotiate the definitive documents • *Widen* the scope of the R&Ws and covenants and shift Allocation of Risk
Post-Closing	• Enforce any post-closing compensation terms and covenants • Work with seller on asset/estate protections and post-closing projects	• Enforce post-closing obligations of the seller • Work on post-closing integration issues • Work with buyer on asset transaction

Regulatory Counsel	Third Party Counsel
• Works to obtain regulatory approvals to allow for the closing of the transactions • Advises on post-closing regulatory issues • Represents the debt and equity sources of capital that may be required to finance the transaction	• Represents lenders, venture investors, vendors, customers, landlords etc. that may be required to approve the proposed deal • Investment bankers and other advisors may also have their own counsel

typically begin preparing the definitive Acquisition Agreement and related documents. Preparing an effective Acquisition Agreement starts first with the buyer's business lawyer's understanding the key issues and challenges to the closing of the transaction, the key factors motivating the transaction, and the special issues and risks that will need to be dealt with in the documents based upon the results of the due diligence process. The motivation for the deal to happen and the underlying goals and objectives for the transaction on a post-closing basis will often affect the structure of the transaction (e.g. stock vs. asset acquisitions), pricing and valuation issues, and the ability to obtain necessary third-party or governmental approvals.

The heart and soul of the Acquisition Agreement is, in many ways, merely a tool for *allocating risk*. The buyer will want to hold the seller accountable for any post-closing claim or liability which arose relating to a set of facts which occurred while the seller owned the company, or which has occurred as a result of a misrepresentation or material omission by the seller. The seller, on the other hand, wants to bring as much finality to the transaction as possible to allow some degree of sleep at night. When both parties are represented by skilled negotiators, a middle ground is reached both in general as well as on specific issues of actual or potential liability. The buyer's counsel will want to draft changes, covenants, representations and warranties which are strong and absolute and the seller's counsel will seek to insert phrases like, ". . . except insignificant defaults or losses which have not, or are not likely to, at any time before or after the closing, result in a material loss or liability to or against the buyer . . .", leaving some wiggle room for insignificant or nonmaterial claims. The battleground will be the indemnification provisions and any exceptions, carve-outs, or baskets which are created to dilute these provisions.

Exhibit 10-2 is designed to be a diagnostic tool to ensure that all parties to the transaction understand the acquisition documents and to ensure that all key categories of issues have been addressed and that the definitive documents are reflective of the business points reached between the parties.

Case Study: GCC Acquires TCI

Assume for the balance of this chapter that Growth Co. Corp. ("GCC") has identified Target Co., Inc. ("TCI"), a closely-held manufacturer, as an acquisition candidate, but is concerned about unknown or contingent liabilities stemming from some prior product liability claims against TCI which may resurface. A Memorandum of Understanding is negotiated so GCC will acquire substantially all of the assets of TCI for $10 million. The financing

Exhibit 10-2. Understanding key components of the acquisition agreement: consideration, mechanics, and risk allocation.

Consideration	Mechanics	Allocation of Risk
• Structure • Scope of purchase • Price • How/when paid • Deferred consideration/security • Earn-outs and contingent payments • Other ongoing financial relationships between buyer and seller • Employment/ consultant agreements • Post-closing adjustments	• Conditions to closing • Timetable • Covenants (including covenants not to compete) • Third-party and regulatory approvals • Schedules (exceptions/ substantiation • Opinions • Dispute resolution	• Representations and warranties (R&Ws) two-way street (due diligence driven) • Indemnification • Holdbacks and baskets • If seller is taking buyer's stock or notes, then R&Ws are a two-way street • Collars • R&W insurance • Methods for dealing with surprises

arranged by GCC will come from the following sources. (Note that this financing structure may be more complex than the typical asset acquisition at this level; however, it is designed to provide the reader with some different approaches for structuring such an acquisition.)

1. $2,000,000 in cash from the internal capital reserves and retained earnings of GCC.

2. $3,000,000 in debt financing provided by Business Bank Corp. ("BBC"), which will be secured by the assets of TCI.

3. $4,500,000 in seller's take-back financing by TCI and in the securities of GCC, payable as follows:
   a. $2,000,000 Subordinated Five-Year Promissory Note
   b. $1,000,000 in the Common Stock in Growth Co. Subsidiary, Inc. ("GCS") (a new subsidiary established by GCC to manage and operate the assets being acquired)
   c. $1,300,000 (as a target—it could be more, it could be less) in the form of a contingent earn-out based upon the financial performance (such as a percentage of sales or net profits) of GCS over the next three years
   d. $200,000 in the form of a two-year consulting agreement at $100,000 per annum for the founding shareholders of TCI.

(Note that when part of the overall consideration to the seller will be a consulting agreement, there are often certain fiduciary issues which must be addressed in terms of a majority shareholder being favored over the minority shareholders. There are also certain tax advantages to the buyer when structuring the deal in this fashion.)

4. $500,000 of TCI debt, which will be assumed by GCC.

In structuring this deal, notice that GCC has created a new subsidiary to receive, manage and operate the assets being acquired from TCI which will help to insulate GCC assets in the event of a subsequent dispute and make the accounting for the earn-out component easier to calculate. GCC has also managed to shift the allocation of risk back to the seller by negotiating roughly 40 percent of the purchase price as being either contingent or deferred. From a liquidity and timing perspective, this deal is also favorable to GCC since it must use only 20 percent of its own funds to make the acquisition and has several years to repay the lion's share of its obligations to BBC and TCI. The officers of GCC have also managed to convince the shareholders of TCI to "buy in" to the future business plan of GCS, since they have agreed to take 25 percent of their consideration stock, in a consulting agreement and in the form of a contingent earn-out. Notwithstanding these attractive features to GCC/GCS, the TCI shareholders are not exactly in terrible shape either—they receive 50 percent of their selling price in cash at closing, get $500,000 of their accounts payable assumed by GCS/GCC, and are second in line (behind BBC) with a security interest in the assets sold.

The transaction discussed above raises a wide variety of legal documents which must be prepared and negotiated in order to consummate the transaction, such as:

- Asset Purchase Agreement (among GCC, GCS, and TCI)
- Intercreditor Agreement (between BBC and TCI)
- Loan Agreement (among BBC, GCC, and GCS)
- Promissory Note, Security Agreement, and Financing Statements (for BBC loan)
- Promissory Note, Security Agreement, and Financing Statements (for TCI takeback financing)

- Board of Directors's and Shareholders's Resolutions of TCI approving the transaction
- Board of Directors's Resolutions of GCC and GCS approving the transaction
- Certificates for the GCS Common Stock (for TCI shareholders)
- Assumption of Liabilities Agreement (also known as a "Liabilities Undertaking" by GCS to TCI, subject to the consent of the TCI creditors. In addition, TCI may want to obtain estoppel certificates or novation agreements from creditors covered by this agreement)
- Bill of Sale (for TCI assets sold to GCC and GCS)
- Bulk Sales Affidavits (if applicable under Article 6 of the state commercial code) (from TCI to its creditors)
- Disclosure Documents to TCI shareholders for issuance of GCS Warrants (if required by federal or state securities laws)
- Non-Competition and Non-Disclosure Agreements (for TCI management team to GCC and GCS)
- Consulting Agreements (which serve as part of the deferred compensation to certain TCI shareholders)
- Employment Agreements (to the extent that any of TCI's employees will be hired)
- Assignment of Key Contracts and Third-Party Consent Agreements (e.g., Leases, Loan Agreements) (from TCI to GCS)
- Opinion of TCI Counsel (to GCC and GCS)
- Lien Search Reports on TCI Assets
- Certificates of Compliance with Representations, Warranties, and Conditions Precedent by TCI President and Secretary
- Earn-Out Agreement (may be included in main body of Asset Purchase Agreement or be separate)
- Indemnification Agreement (may be included in main body of Asset Purchase Agreement or be separate)
- Escrow Agreement (if negotiated) (proceeds of sale price to be placed in escrow until certain post-closing conditions are met and post-closing adjustments are made by TCI, or as a contingency reserve fund in the event that representations and warranties are subsequently found to be untrue)

- Resignation and Release Agreements (from TCC employees who will not be retained after the transaction)
- Personal Guarantees (by key shareholders of GCC if demanded by BBC or TCI to secure the Promissory Notes)
- License Agreements (if any, to the extent that intellectual property rights are being retained by TCI and exclusively licensed by GCS)
- Allocation Certificates for federal, state and local tax filings (as well as UCC filings where applicable)
- List of Schedules and Exhibits to the Asset Purchase Agreement (to be compiled and prepared by TCI and its counsel)

Note: Had the transaction been structured as a stock purchase rather than an asset transaction, then TCI shareholders would also have to produce duly endorsed stock certificates, current corporate financial statements, certified copies of the corporate financial statements, certified copies of the corporate articles and by-laws, certificates of good standing, officer and director releases, termination and resignation agreements, termination of personnel and retirement plans (where applicable) and all other material corporate documentation at the closing.

Now, let's take a look at a few of these agreements in more detail.

The Asset Purchase (or Acquisition Agreement)

This document includes a statement of the parties to the transaction, the specific tangible and intangible assets that are being sold and liabilities that are being assumed/assigned, the manner in which the assets and liabilities will be sold, the terms and conditions of the transaction, the amount and terms of payment of the consideration to be paid by the purchaser, the assurances of the seller as to the status and performance of the assets being sold, the rights of each party if another party fails to perform as contemplated by the agreement or otherwise breaches its representations and warranties, and the timetable for the closing of the transaction.

The Asset Purchase Agreement should be balanced to protect the interests of both parties. From the buyer's perspective, the Asset Purchase Agreement should provide as much detail as possible concerning the status and performance of the business to be acquired; shift risk to the seller by establishing grounds for the buyer to terminate the transaction if the representations and warranties prove untrue and a basis for renegotiation if facts develop indicating that the transaction, as structured, is not what the buyer had bargained for; and provide a basis after closing for the buyer to seek monetary damages from the seller should the representations, warranties and covenants of the agreement prove untrue.

The Asset Purchase Agreement should provide a means for updating the information delivered to the purchaser by the seller and, if the transfer of the business is to occur on a date subsequent to the date on which the Asset Purchase Agreement is signed, the Asset Purchase Agreement should include covenants of the seller regarding its conduct of the business from the date of the Asset Purchase Agreement through the closing or termination of the Asset Purchase Agreement.

The initial draft of the Asset Purchase Agreement is prepared by GCC's counsel, as purchaser who is responsible for ensuring that the purchaser acquires the assets and liabilities bargained for without assuming responsibility for any undisclosed obligations of the business or the seller.

An outline of the GCC/TCI Asset Purchase Agreement is set forth below:

- Recitals identifying TCI and GCC, stating their relative roles, and the assets being sold
- Clauses which provide for the transfer of the assets being sold, the price to be paid and the manner in which the price will be paid (in the event securities are being issued in payment of the purchase price, methods of valuing those securities might be appropriate in this section) and, in connection with transfer of assets, provision for the buyer's assumption of liabilities
- Representations and warranties of TCI
- Representations and warranties of GCC
- A statement of the manner in which TCI will conduct the business (including restrictions on certain types of operations or merger purchases) prior to the closing

- Those conditions which are to precede the obligations of GCC to be performed at the closing
- Those conditions which are to precede the obligations of TCI to be performed at the closing
- A summary of the closing itself, the mechanics thereof, and the documents to be delivered at the closing
- Agreements and commitments relating to the relationship of the parties and the activities of the business sold after the closing
- Agreements relating to the survival of the representations and warranties of the parties and, importantly, the indemnification provisions to be provided by TCI and GCC
- For an asset transfer, provisions relating to bulk sales laws
- For a stock transfer, provisions relating to the securities laws and rights to resell securities issued pursuant to registration statements or otherwise
- A provision relating to brokers
- Provisions related to employee benefits
- Miscellaneous provisions including notices, the completeness of the agreement, the law governing the interpretation of the agreement, whether or not the provisions of the agreement will be severable and other general provisions desired by the parties

Legal counsel to GCC should also specify all conditions precedent to the obligations of the parties to close the transaction in the Asset Purchase Agreement. Conditions are generally factors beyond either party's control, such as regulatory approval or consents, the existence or nonexistence of which will excuse one or both parties from their obligation to close the transaction. The Asset Purchase Agreement should include remedies for losses, liabilities, damages or expenses arising out of a party's breach either before or after the acquisition.

Playing with the Buzz Words

Any veteran transactional lawyer knows that there are certain key "buzz words" that can be inserted into sections of the Purchase Agreement which will detract or enhance or even shift liability by and among the buyer and seller. Depending on which side of the fence you are on, look out for words or phrases like:

1. "materially"
2. "to the best of our knowledge"
3. "could possibly"
4. "without any independent investigation"
5. "except for . . ."
6. "subject to . . ."
7. "reasonably believes . . ."
8. "ordinary course of business"
9. "to which we are aware . . ."
10. "would not have a material adverse affect on . . ."
11. "primarily relating to . . ."
12. "substantially all . . ."
13. "might" (instead of "would")
14. "exclusively"
15. "other than claims which may be less than $———"
16. "have received no written notice of . . ."
17. "have used our best efforts (or commercially reasonable efforts) to . . .
18. endeavor to . . .

There is a wide variety of issues in the Asset Purchase Agreement that will be hotly negotiated between TCI and GCC, such as:

Indemnification

One of the most contested areas is the indemnification provisions, usually because GCC/GCS will want to be reimbursed for any transaction or occurrence which took place before closing that subsequently gives rise to some claim or liability. TCI shareholders, on the other hand, will want to make a "clean break" from liability attached to the assets being conveyed, including any responsibility for events which arose even before closing.

As discussed earlier in this book, one of the key aspects of an acquisition is the *negotiation and allocation of the risks* to each party both before and after closing. The goal is to allocate risk in a balanced and economically appropriate manner. The buyer is concerned with "core risks," such as those raised by a misrepresentation or breach of covenant by the seller and "collateral risks," such as those raised by facts and circumstances which were not necessarily anticipated by the parties at the time of the negotiation. Buyers and their counsel will often seek a full indemnity from the seller against any specific liabilities which have not been assumed by the buyer as part of the transaction and any damages or loss (including costs and expenses) which were incurred due to inaccuracy of representations, warranties or agreements. The party claiming indemnity is required to provide specific written notice of those claims to the other party and permit the other party to contest the claim. The indemnity provisions should provide for mutual access to all personnel and material which may be relevant to the claim and that no claim would be settled without the written consent of the injured party.

Indemnity provisions, along with opinions of counsel, are usually among the most contested negotiated items in a Purchase Agreement. The key variables to be negotiated, as set forth below, include: time (length of the post-closing obligations to indemnify), the deductibles/baskets, the "caps" or ceilings on liability, the measure of damages, and the possible offsets to seller obligation to indemnify. The seller will usually be unwilling to provide a comprehensive set of indemnity provisions. Counsel for the seller may also try to negotiate a "basket" or a trigger as part of the trade-off for cash adjustments and no personal liability for the buyer's stockholders. In our example, if the aggregate claims for which GCC demanded to be indemnified did not exceed $250,000, and a basket of $250,000 had been agreed to, no indemnity could be sought and GCC would only be entitled to indemnification for amounts in excess of $250,000. If TCI's counsel suggests that a "trigger of $250,000" rather than a "basket" should be built into the indemnity, then the "trigger" would provide that GCC could not seek indemnity unless the aggregate amount for which it was to be indemnified exceeded the triggering amount, in the case of GCC, $250,000. However, once the amount for which the indemnity was sought did exceed $250,000, GCC/GCS would have the right under the indemnity provision to recover from TCI all monies from the first dollar involved. In such case, the indemnity section could be drafted to state that any remedies available to either party were cumulative, so that they could be exercised one on top of another, and that they could be exercised at any time.

TCI and its advisors will seek a wide variety of additional limitations on the indemnification provisions. In addition to the "basket" negotiations, TCI could seek to establish a ceiling on overall liability, a limitation on the types of claims for which seller can be held liable, a limitation claims only to those for which the seller had actual knowledge (which make the buyer's burden of proof much higher in the event of a subsequent dispute), a limitation on the types of assets which would be available to repay GCC in the event of a claim, an exclusion of certain parties who will be held liable for certain types of claims, and a limitation on the time after closing (survival) after which GCC/GCS may no longer proceed against the seller for a breach or misrepresentation. It is not uncommon for GCS as seller to attempt to negotiate some staged step down in the amount of the overall indemnification ceilings over time following the closing. The seller may also want to investigate insurance from a third-party provider for inadvertent or negligent violations of the covenants leading to an indemnification claim. Those types of insurance policies have become relatively commonplace, but will not typically cover international or grossly negligent violations of the representations, warranties, or covenants. Sellers should also be aware of "double dipping"—which is when a breach triggers *both* a purchase price adjustment *and* a claim for indemnification, which is an obvious overenrichment of the buyer.

A sample negotiated indemnification provision (with a trigger) might look like this:

• *Indemnification by the Seller*. The Seller, TCI, and its shareholders, jointly and severally, covenants and agrees to indemnify, defend, protect and hold harmless GCC and GCS and their respective officers, directors, employees, stockholders, assigns, successors and affiliates (individually, an "Indemnified Party" and collectively, "Indemnified Parties") from, against and in respect of:

(a) all liabilities, losses, claims, damages, punitive damages, causes of action, lawsuits, administrative proceedings (including formal proceedings), investigations, audits, demands, assessments, adjustments, judgments, settlement payments, deficiencies, penalties, fines, interest (including interest from the date of such damages) and costs and expenses (including without limitation reasonable attorneys' fees and disbursements of every kind, nature and description) collectively, "Damages") suffered, sustained, incurred or paid by the GCC Indemnified Parties in connection with, resulting from or arising out of, directly or indirectly

(i) any misrepresentation or breach of any warranty of the Sellers, set forth in this Agreement or any schedule or certificate, delivered by or on behalf of the Seller in connection herewith; or

(ii) any nonfulfillment of any covenant or agreement on the part of any of the Sellers set forth in this Agreement; or

(iii) the business, operations or assets of the Sellers prior to the Closing Date or the actions or omissions of the Sellers' directors, officers, shareholders, employees or agents prior to the Closing Date (except as to the Assumed Liabilities); or

(iv) failure to comply with country of origin marking requirements imposed by the Federal Trade Commission or the U.S. Customs Service, including without limitation damages arising out of breaches of any contract relating to failure to deliver product as required under any contract or delivery of nonconforming goods pursuant to any contract, fines, or other penalties for violations of such requirements; or

(v) the Excluded Liabilities.

(b) any and all damages incident to any of the foregoing or to the enforcement of this Section 7.1.

- *Limitation and Expiration.* Notwithstanding the above:
  (a) there shall be no liability for indemnification under Section 7.1 unless, and solely to the extent that, the ag-

gregate amount of damages exceeds $250,000 (the "Indemnification Threshold"); *provided, however,* that the Indemnification Threshold shall not apply to:

(i) adjustments to the Purchase Price,

(ii) damages arising out of any breaches of the covenants of the Seller set forth in this Agreement or representations made in Sections 3.13 (environmental matters), 3.16 (inventory), 3.19 (employee benefit plans), 3.20 (conformity with law; litigation), 3.21 (taxes) or 3.26 (intellectual property), or

(iii) the Excluded Liabilities.

(b) the indemnification obligations under this Section 7 or in any certificate or writing furnished in connection herewith shall terminate on the later of clause (i) or (ii) of this Section 7.2(b):

(i) (1) third anniversary of the Closing Date, or

(2) with respect to representations and warranties contained in Sections 3.14 (real and personal property), 3.19 (employee benefit plans), 3.21 (taxes), and the Excluded Liabilities, on (A) the date that is six (6) months after the expiration of the longest applicable federal or state statute of limitation (including extensions thereof), or (B) if there is no applicable statute of limitation, ten (10) years after the Closing Date; or

(ii) the final resolution of a claim or demand (a "Claim") pending as of the relevant dates described in clause (i) of this Section 7.2(b) (such claim referred to as a "Pending Claim");

(c) for purposes of the indemnity in this Section 7, all representations contained in Section 3 are made without any limitations as to materiality; and

(d) for purposes of the Indemnification Threshold, all damages incurred by GCC or any of its affiliates under any of the related Acquisition Agreements shall be included within the Indemnification Threshold under this Agreement.

Note: The indemnification provision would then go on to address the procedures for making an indemnification claim.

• *Representations and Warranties ("R&Ws").* TCI will be expected to make a wide range of written and binding representations and warranties to GCS. These provisions are designed to articulate a wide range of information about the transaction as well as create recourse against TCI in the event of inaccurate disclosures. The R&Ws will include that the sale is not in breach of any other agreement or obligation of TCI, that the assets are free and clear of all clouds on title to the assets, that the assets are in good operating condition, that all material facts have been disclosed and so forth. Naturally, GCC/GCS will want the scope of the R&Ws to be as broad and comprehensive as possible, primarily because these clauses serve as a form of an insurance policy for GCS. GCS will also want to have as many parties as possible be *making* the R&Ws (e.g., not just TCI, but also key shareholders).

GCS will also want protection if it turns out that any representation or warranty has been breached, especially in an asset deal where the selling entity is likely to be an empty shell on a post-closing basis (this is another reason that GCS may insist on key TCI shareholders being a party to the representations). It will be incumbent on TCI and its counsel to negotiate limitations on the scope of these provisions where necessary.

The scope of the representations and warranties contained in the definitive purchase agreement are among the most difficult aspects of closing a transaction. This is the section where the TCI shareholders must "represent and warrant" everything about the company that has been told or implied to GCC/GCS. Representations and warranties set forth the financial responsibility for existing problems that may arise in the future, but which may not exist or be known to the parties at closing. The buyer typically views post-closing events that reduce assets or increase liabilities as being the responsibility of the seller.

These provisions set forth the financial responsibility of each party if certain unknown or unforeseen problems arise in the future due to an existing situation. In many of the representations and warranties, GCC may be willing to accept the phrase "to the best of the seller's knowledge" as a qualifier to certain provisions. In addition, some matters lend themselves to outside testing or evaluation by experts. Relying on the reports of outside experts may significantly reduce or even eliminate the need for certain areas to be addressed. In other cases, a time and/or dollar limit on a particular representation or warranty will be sufficient to allow the seller to provide assurances in situations where it would otherwise be unwilling to do so. For example, a dollar limit is often attached to environmental and product liability representations and warranties.

Sellers should make certain that their advisors are familiar with the types of representations and warranties they are likely to face and that the advisors are skilled in finding mutually acceptable positions. During actual negotiations, sellers should make a sincere attempt to understand the buyer's underlying motivation in requesting each warranty and representation and point out any facts or circumstances which may be inconsistent with a given request. In our example, TCI and their counsel should expect that GCC will insist on the following types of representations and warranties:

- The transaction is not in breach of any license or other agreement or violation of any order or decree of any court or other governmental body.
- TCI's business entity is properly organized under state corporate law, in good standing, and qualified to do the business it is doing in the states where it is doing business.
- TCI has clear title to all assets made part of the sale, and that these assets are not subject to any undisclosed restrictions or claims and are in good operating condition.
- TCI has no knowledge or reason to know that business relationship has changed with any customer or group of customers whose purchases constitute more than stated percent (usually 5 percent) of business's sales for the previous year.
- TCI represents that all required tax returns have been filed and required payments have been made.
- Licenses, zoning and other permission necessary to conduct TCI's business as it is being conducted have been obtained, and benefits may be transferred to GCC/GCS.

• TCI will need to represent and warrant the following facts regarding the accuracy of its financial statements (as presented to GCC):

1. Fairly present financial condition of business as of date of statements.
2. TCI is not subject to any material liability, including contingent liability, not reflected or noted in financial statements.
3. Statements prepared in accordance with generally accepted accounting principles.
4. Since date of statements, TCI has not transferred any assets to or on behalf of any owner or employee other than in payment of customary salaries:

• TCI is not in default on any material contract or loan nor is it aware of any claims pending or threatened against it.

• TCI owns specified patents, trademarks, trade names, and copyrights, and there is no knowledge of any claims of infringement pending or threatened.

• TCI is in compliance with all applicable local, state and federal laws and no notice of any claimed violations.

• TCI has not engaged or authorized to act as broker or finder in connection with sale.

• *Conditions Precedent to Closing.* This section is essentially a checklist of events which must occur as a condition to closing the transaction. Both GCS and TCI will have its share of items which must be accomplished and documents or consents which must be signed. The nature and scope of these conditions must be carefully considered since failure to satisfy then will give the opposing party the right to walk away from the transaction.

• *Conduct of Business Prior to Closing.* TCI must have a contractual obligation to preserve the goodwill of the business and condition of the assets during the time period between execution of the purchase agreement and closing of the transaction. The parties should negotiate all affirmative and negative covenants that will be imposed on the conduct of TCI during this time period, as well as the penalties for noncompliance (e.g., reduction of purchase price, ability to walk away from deal by GCS).

Common Mistakes in Preparing and Negotiating the Purchase Agreement

1. *Lack of attention or customization of the R&Ws.* The R&Ws are a key component of the Purchase Agreement that drive risk allocation issues. Yet, sellers often ignore the details and do not give careful thought to what they consider to be boilerplate and legal jargon. A post-closing dispute is *not* a great time for sellers to be reading these clauses for the first time. Similarly, lazy buyers will often plug in standard R&W clauses, failing to customize their specific concerns that they have about the seller's business and/or specific issues and problems that were identified in the due diligence process.
2. *The inadvertent assumption of liabilities.* Smart buyers use the purchase agreement provisions to hold sellers accountable for certain types of liabilities, but the failure to do so can result in the buyer stepping into the shoes of the seller inadvertently or unwittingly. A buyer inheriting liability that rightfully should have been retained by the seller can have a detrimental impact on the overall economics of the transaction. Be on the look out for employment discrimination claims, pre-closing tax liabilities, product liability claims and related issues that are often easily overlooked.
3. *Right deal, wrong structure.* Just as the parties often overfocus on price and underfocus on terms, so too can be the case with deal structure. Mistakes can be made when the "deal looks good on paper" but the structure selected is creating a material (and avoidable) adverse tax impact for one or more of the parties. Experienced tax advisors should weigh-in and the proposed structure *before* the "cement" has dried.
4. *Sloppy indemnification clauses and procedures.* From the buyer's perspective, the indemnification language in the Purchase Agreement should be custom-tailored to the nature of the seller's business and to the specific risks and concerns identified in due diligence. The interplay be-

tween time and dollar limits must be carefully considered. Certain types of businesses may be better served by larger time periods even if with smaller dollar sizes, and vice-versa for other types of businesses or risks. It is also critical to consider *how* the buyer will collect on a specific indemnification claim once it has been triggered. The consideration may be spread among 100+ shareholders—ask *who* will be accountable and push for a larger holdback which will serve as protection until the indemnification period has expired.

Other Key Agreements in an Asset Purchase

Intercreditor Agreement

An intercreditor agreement is a contract among multiple lenders (in this case TCI and BBC) to a particular borrower (GCC and GCS). The document governs the priority rights of the various lenders in the collateral (the assets acquired by GCC and GCS), otherwise known as subordination. Subordination and standby provisions govern "who gets what proceeds when" in the event of a default by the borrower. In the GCC/TCI transaction, it is likely that BBC and its counsel will prepare this agreement and demand that BBC receive the senior priority rights.

Non-Competition Agreements

Covenants against competition and disclosure of confidential information are commonly a key part of any business acquisition. This is especially true in situations like the GCC/TCI transaction where the management team of the target may be left out of the transaction and are therefore likely candidates to be future competitors. Counsel to GCS will naturally want to include covenants that are broad in terms of the scope of subject matter, duration and geographic territory. Although these agreements will be carefully scrutinized by the courts as potential restraints of trade, agreements prohibiting sellers from competing against buyers in a business purchase transaction are given considerably more latitude than in other agreements such as employment or consulting agreements.

Earn-Out Agreements

When earn-out agreements are negotiated as part of the purchase price in an acquisition, part of the consideration payable to TCI essentially becomes contingent on the ability of GCS to meet its financial and growth projections. In the GCC/TCI transaction, TCI shareholders are betting on the ability of the GCS management team to manage and operate the assets being acquired in an efficient and profitable manner. If any other of the TCI shareholders will become members of the GCS management team, then the earn-out provides an incentive for performance from which both GCC and TCI can gain.

The key terms of the earn-out agreement to be negotiated are: the formula to be used (e.g., What is being measured? Will the earn-out be tied to gross sales, net earnings, the award of a major post-closing contract, numbers of units sold, etc.); the duration of the earn-out; the floor and ceiling on the payout to be provided to TCI shareholders; the controls that TCI shareholders will have, if any, over the budgets and expenditures made by GCS or GCC; the effect of business distress or bankruptcy of GCS on the earn-out; and the tax implications of the transaction. It is critical that the parties to come to an agreement about the accounting system to be used, especially if the numbers are subject to manipulation.

The typical earn-out provides *additional* consideration to the seller if certain financial and/or performance targets are met and is often used to bridge a valuation gap in the negotiation of the price. But buyers may also want to consider "*reverse earn-outs*" as an additional *penalty* if performance targets are *not* met. For example, if the seller accepts a combination of cash and promissory notes, the principal of the note or the interest rate could be reduced if minimal performance criteria are not met; representations or warranties are breached; or if sales fall below a given level.

Earn-outs can be used as incentives, as equalizers or as risk mitigators. As an incentive, the earn-out may be used as a sweetener to motivate the founding entrepreneur (as seller) to stay on-board to help build the business after closing or to ensure that a technical or engineering team remains in place after closing. As an equalizer, it can be used to resolve differing views over the valuation of the seller's business, particularly when the seller feels that its stock or assets are being undervalued. As a risk mitigator, the earn-out can be used to hold a seller's feet to the fire regarding its representations of the future value of the company and to help ensure against overpayment if a buyer is unsure or unclear of the future value of the business.

The key issues to be addressed in the negotiation and structuring of the earn-out provisions include:

- The financial formula to be used to determine the contingent payments payable to the seller (e.g., specified minimum sales levels, net income before taxes, EBIDTA).
- The limitations that the seller will request to ensure that financial targets are reached.
- The audit and inspection rights to be granted by the seller to ensure against underpayment by the buyer.
- The business plan and financial benchmarks which are fair and reasonable over the course of earn-out period. These performance-driven milestones may be better measuring sticks for the payment of the earn-out than a strict financial formula, especially for high-tech businesses.
- Term of the earn-out period, the method and frequency of payment and the form of consideration itself, such as cash, stock, notes, and warrants.
- The relationship of the earn-out to the other liability and risk allocation sections of the Acquisition Agreement.

Sample Schedule of Documents to Be Exchanged at a Typical Closing

1. Deeds, bills of sale, and any other documents and instruments buyer deems sufficient to transfer title to seller's assets.
2. Certificate by shareholders that representations are true as of closing date and that shareholders have met obligations under agreement.

3. Certificate by officers of acquired corporation that representations and warranties are true as of closing date and that corporation has met its obligations under agreement.
4. Duly endorsed stock certificates.
5. Written opinion of seller's attorney to effect that to best of attorney's knowledge all representations are true, agreement has been duly executed and constitutes valid obligation of seller, and non-competition agreement is valid and enforceable.
6. Employment agreements.
7. Certified copy of duly adopted resolutions by board of directors and shareholders authorizing sale.
8. Certified copy of articles of incorporation and bylaws.
9. Incumbency certificate of each person executing documents relating to sale.
10. Title insurance covering real estate.
11. Releases of any claims officers or directors may have against seller or buyer.
12. Written resignations of certain officers and directors.
13. Letter from accountant certifying financial statements and that, following inquiries, accountant has no knowledge of any material adverse change in business's financial position between date of financial statements and closing.
14. Certificate of good standing from each state where corporation to be acquired has been doing business.
15. Estoppel certificates from creditors whose debts have been assumed by buyer.
16. Copy of bulk sales notice (for asset acquisitions).

Scope of the Assets

The typical buyer will want to specify a virtual laundry list of categories of assets to be purchased but the classic seller will want to modify the list by using words like "exclusively" or "primarily." The seller may want to exclude all or most of the cash-on-hand from the schedule of assets to be transferred. In some cases, the seller may want to license some of the technology rights in lieu of an outright sale or, at the very least, obtain a license back of what has been sold.

Security for the Seller's Take-Back Note

When the seller is taking back a note from the buyer for all or part of the consideration, the issue of security for the note is always a problem. Naturally, the seller will want non-contingent personal and corporate guaranties from the buyer and anyone else that it can manage to get. The buyer will be reluctant to offer such broad security. Several "creative" compromises have been reached between the parties, including partial or limited guaranties; the acceleration of the note based on post-closing performance; the right to repurchase the assets in the event of a default; the issuance of warrants or preferred stock in the event of default; commercial-lender-like covenants to prevent the buyer from getting into a position where they are unable to pay the note (such as dividend restrictions or limitations on excessive salaries); or contingent consulting agreements in the event of a default.

Who's on the Hook for the Financial Statements

The financial statements provided by the seller to the buyer in connection with the due diligence and prior to closing are often a hotly-contested item. The timing and scope of the financial statements as well as the standard to which they will be held is at issue. The buyer and its team may prefer a "hot-off-the-press" and recently completed audited set of financials from a Big 4 accounting firm and the seller will want to serve up a "best-efforts" unaudited and uncertified guesstimate. Somewhere in between is where most deals wind up, with verbiage such as "of a nature customarily reflected" and "prepared in substantial accordance with GAAP" and "fairly present the financial condition" being bantered around. The scope of the liabilities included on the statements and who will bear responsibility for unknown or undisclosed liabilities will also be negotiated in the context of the overall discussion of the financial statements.

Specific Precautions When Buying a Subsidiary

It has become very common for larger companies to consider the spin-off of a non-performing or non-core operating division or subsidiary. From the buyer's perspective, this can be an interesting opportunity that is also fraught with problems if not executed properly. The buyer should conduct detailed due diligence and create a structure which ensures that it is acquiring all of the assets, rights and resources that it needs to generate the spin-off business. Other key issues to consider include:

- Key functions being provided by the parent company or by an affiliate (e.g., accounting, IT, human resources or even legal) that need be replaced or dealt with in a transition services agreement.
- The need for the subsidiary to get access to certain intellectual property on systems aimed by the parent and which may need to be licensed (if they cannot or will not be assigned for license-back transition if acquired).
- The financial performance of the subsidiary being affected (positively or adversely) by inter-company sales.
- The parent company must agree not to compete with the subsidiary or raid its staff.

The Existence and Scope of the Non-Compete Clause

It is only natural for the buyer to expect that the seller will agree to stay out of the business being sold for some reasonable amount of time. Depending on the seller's stage of life and post-closing plans, which may include actual retirement, the parties are likely to argue over the scope, duration and geographic focus of the covenant against non-competition. The more difficult issues often arise when a conglomerate is spinning off a particular division or line of business and the remaining divisions will continue to operate in similar or parallel industries to the business being sold to the buyer. The allocation of the purchase price to a non-compete covenant raises certain tax issues which must be analyzed and these covenants may have only limited enforceability under applicable state laws if their scope or duration is deemed unreasonable or excessive.

Allocation of Risk

As discussed earlier in this chapter, the heart and soul of the Purchase Agreement is, in many ways, merely a tool for *allocating risk.* The buyer will want to hold the seller accountable for any post-closing claim or liability which arose relating to a set of facts which occurred while the seller owned the company or which has occurred as a result of a misrepresentation or material omission by the seller. The seller, on the other hand, wants to bring as much finality to the transaction as possible to allow some degree of sleep at night. When both parties are represented by skilled negotiators, a middle ground is reached both in general as well as on specific issues of actual or potential liability. The buyer's counsel will want to draft changes, covenants, representations and warranties which are strong and absolute, and the seller's counsel will seek to insert phrases like ". . . except insignificant defaults or losses which have not, or are not likely to, at any time before or after the closing, result in a material loss or liability to or against the buyer . . ." leaving some wiggle room for insignificant or non-material claims. The battleground will be the indemnification provisions and any exceptions, carve-outs or baskets which are created to dilute these provisions. The weapons will be the buzz words referenced above.

I have included, as Exhibit 10-3, as a reference point an abbreviated version of the Asset Purchase Agreement for use in the GCC/TCI transaction. This sample agreement is included to give the reader a feel for what the starting point or first draft of the agreement will look like before the negotiation process begins.

Exhibit 10-3. Sample asset purchase agreement.

THIS ASSET PURCHASE AGREEMENT ("Agreement") is made and entered into this ________ day of ________, 2006, by and among Growth Co. Corp., a Maryland corporation (the "Buyer") and Target Co., Inc., a New York corporation (the "Seller"), and Jane C. Doe and John F. Doe individually (each a "Shareholder" and collectively, the "Shareholders").

WITNESSETH:

WHEREAS, the Seller is engaged in the equipment manufacturing business and activities related thereto (herein referred to as the "Business"); and

(continues)

Exhibit 10-3. Continued.

WHEREAS, Seller and the Shareholders (constituting all of the beneficial shareholders of the Seller), desire to sell, convey, transfer, assign and deliver to Buyer the Business and substantially all of the assets, properties and operations used in the Business, and Buyer desires to purchase the Business and such assets, properties and operations, on the terms and subject to conditions contained in this Agreement, and other agreements related hereto.

NOW, THEREFORE, in consideration of the mutual benefits to be derived from this Agreement, the receipt and sufficiency of which are hereby acknowledged, the parties hereto hereby agree as follows:

1. **SALE AND PURCHASE OF ASSETS**

1.1 *Sale of Assets to Buyer.* Upon the terms and subject to the conditions herein set forth, at the Closing referred to in Section 3, Seller shall sell, transfer, assign, convey and deliver to Buyer, and Buyer shall purchase and acquire from Seller, all of the properties, assets and goodwill that are used in the Business, of whatever kind and nature, real or personal, tangible or intangible (including all rights of the Seller arising from its operation of the Business) and excluding only those assets referred to in Section 1.2 of this Agreement (collectively, the "Assets"), as those Assets exist on the Closing Date (as defined in Section 3). The Assets include, but are not limited to, the following:

(a) all of Seller's machinery, equipment, equipment leases, chemicals, supplies, vehicles, furniture, fixtures, tools, computers and all other personal property, wherever located, which are used in the Business, including, but not limited to, the items listed on Schedule 1.1(a);

(b) all interests of Seller in real property, including leases, options, rights of way, zoning and development rights and easements) described on Schedule 1.1(b);

(c) all inventory of Seller used in the Business, wherever located, including, without limitation, the parts, chemicals and materials listed on Schedule 1.1(c);

(d) all of Seller's computer software used in the Business, and all rights, title and interest of Seller in, to and under all trademarks, trademark rights, trademark applications, patents, patent rights, patent applications, trade secrets, inventions, training and equipment manuals, technology, methods, manufacturing, engineering, technical and any other know-how, processes, projects in development, trade names, service marks, other intellectual property rights and other proprietary information of the Seller used in or relating to the Business. All material intellectual property, including all trade names and patents used or held by Seller, are listed on Schedule 1.1(d);

(e) all of Seller's rights under any written or oral contracts, unfilled service and/or purchase orders, agreements, leases, instruments, registrations, licenses, certificates, distribution agreements or other documents, commitments, arrangements or authorizations relating to the Business, including, but not limited to, the agreements and other instruments identified on Schedule 1.1(e) (the "Contracts"); provided, that nothing contained in this Agreement shall be construed as an attempt to agree to assign any contract which is by itself non-assignable without the consent of the other party or parties thereto, unless such consent shall be given;

(f) all rights in connection with all permits, certificates, licenses, approvals, registrations and authorizations of Seller which may be necessary or desirable in order to conduct the Business (the "Permits");

(g) all of Seller's rights under manufacturers' and vendors' warranties relating to those items included in the Assets and all of Seller's similar rights against third parties relating to items included in the Assets;

(h) all of Seller's accounts receivable, notes and other receivables, unbilled costs and fees, all prepaid items, amounts on deposit of Seller, and other current assets existing on the Closing Date, including, but not limited to, the receivables and other assets set forth on Schedule 1.1(h), but excluding cash and cash equivalents;

(i) all goodwill, customer and vendor lists, telephone numbers, and other intangible property, and all of Seller's rights to commence or maintain future and existing actions relating to the operation of the Business or the ownership of the Assets, for events occurring after the Closing Date, and the right to settle those actions and retain the proceeds therefrom;

(j) all shares of stock and partnership interests owned by Seller, if any;

(k) all of Seller's rights under the insurance or similar policies in effect on or prior to the Closing Date set forth on Schedule 1.1(k);

(l) all financial, operational, and any other files, logs, books and records and data of the Business of Seller, (collectively, "Books and Records") and including, without limitation, all correspondence, accounting records, personnel records, purchase orders and invoices, customer records, supplier records, advertising and promotional materials and files, and other business records which are owned by Seller relating to the Business.

1.2 *Excluded Assets*. The following assets (the "Excluded Assets") shall be retained by the Seller and shall not be sold or assigned to Buyer:

(a) all cash on hand and cash equivalents (excluding the prepaid proceeds from the Baxter Contract) and cash-value life and other split-life insurance policies of Seller;

(b) the corporate minute books and stock books of Seller; and

(c) any lease, commitment or other agreement listed on Sched-

(continues)

Exhibit 10-3. Continued.

ule 1.2(c) with respect to which the Buyer does not desire to acquire concurrent with its purchase of the Assets under this Agreement, including any employee advance.

1.3 *Method of Conveyance*. The sale, transfer, conveyance and assignment by the Seller of the Assets to the Buyer in accordance with Section 1.1 hereof shall be effected on the Closing Date by the Seller's execution and delivery to the Buyer of a general assignment and bill of sale, in substantially the form attached hereto as Exhibit A (the "General Assignment and Bill of Sale"). At the Closing, all of the Assets shall be transferred by the Seller to the Buyer free and clear of any and all liens, encumbrances, mortgages, security interests, pledges, claims, equities and other restrictions or charges of any kind or nature whatsoever (collectively, "Liens") except for a lessor's interest in any leased assets or as otherwise listed in Schedule 4.5(a).

2. **PURCHASE PRICE**

The purchase price to be paid by the Buyer for the Assets to be sold, transferred and conveyed by the Seller pursuant to this Agreement shall be:

(a) cash in the amount of Three Million Dollars ($3,000,000), paid by cashier's check or wire transfer, subject to adjustment as described in Section 2.2; and

(b) two promissory notes, one for the principal amount of Five Hundred Thousand Dollars ($500,000) (the "Short-Term Note"); and the second for the principal amount of Eight Hundred Thousand Dollars ($800,000) (the "Long-Term Note" and, together with the Short-Term Note (the "Notes"), each Note subject to adjustment as described in Sections 2.3(a) and 2.3(b), in the forms attached hereto as Exhibits B-1 and B-2, with the Short-Term Note secured by a pledge of marketable securities pursuant to a Pledge Agreement and a Stock Power in the forms attached hereto as Exhibit C and Exhibit D.

3. **CLOSING**

3.1 *Date of Closing*. Subject to the terms and conditions set forth herein, the closing of the transactions contemplated hereby (the "Closing") shall be held at 10:00 a.m. at the offices of counsel for the Seller on or before ________, 2007, provided that all conditions to the Closing have been satisfied, or at such other time, date and place as shall be fixed by agreement among the parties hereto. The date on which the Closing shall occur is referred to herein as the "Closing Date." At the Closing, the parties shall execute and deliver the documents referred to in Section 3.2.

3.2 *Items to be Delivered at Closing*. At the Closing and subject to the terms and conditions herein contained:

(a) Seller shall deliver or cause to be delivered to Buyer the following:

(i) one or more Bills of Sale and such other good and sufficient instruments and documents of conveyance and transfer executed by Seller, in a form reasonably satisfactory to Buyer and its counsel, as shall be necessary and effective to transfer and assign to, and vest in, Buyer all of Seller's right, title and interest in and to the Assets, including without limitation, (A) good and valid title in and to all of the Assets owned by Seller, (B) good and valid leasehold interests in and to all of the Assets leased by Seller as lessee, and (C) all of the Seller's rights under all agreements, contracts, instruments and other documents included in the Assets to which Seller is a party or by which it has rights on the Closing Date;

(ii) all third-party consents required to be delivered as a condition to Closing as set forth in Section 8.2(d), which may be necessary or desirable in connection with the transfer of the Assets, including the Contracts and the Permits;

(iii) all of the agreements, contracts, commitments, leases, plans, computer programs and software, data bases whether in the form of computer tapes or otherwise, manuals and guidebooks, customer lists, supplier lists, and other documents, books, records, papers, files, office supplies and data belonging to the Seller which are part of the Assets;

(iv) one or more Assignment and Assumption Agreements executed by Seller;

(v) executed lease for the Seller's home offices (the "Darien Property"), attached hereto as Exhibit M and assignment of lease for the Seller's Wisconsin warehouse and office (the "Wisconsin Property"), transferring the leasehold and subleasehold interests in said properties to Buyer;

(vi) a written opinion of Joseph P. Doe, Esq., counsel for Seller, dated the Closing Date, in the form of Exhibit F hereto;

(vii) a certificate, signed by a duly authorized officer of the Seller and dated the Closing Date, representing that the conditions contained in Section 8.2(b) of this Agreement have been satisfied;

(viii) certified copies of resolutions of the Seller's Board of Directors and its Shareholders with respect to the approval of this Agreement and the transactions contemplated hereby (Exhibit O);

(ix) Employment Agreements, executed by Jane C. Doe and John F. Doe, respectively (Exhibits G and H, respectively); and

(x) any other opinions, certificates or other documents and instruments required herein to be delivered by the Seller or the Shareholders.

(continues)

Exhibit 10-3. Continued.

(b) Buyer shall deliver to the Seller the following:
   (i) the Purchase Price pursuant to Section 2 hereof;
   (ii) a certificate, signed by a duly authorized officer of the Buyer and dated the Closing Date, representing that the conditions contained in Section 8.1(a) of this Agreement have been satisfied;
   (iii) certified copies of resolutions of the Manager of the Buyer with respect to the approval of this Agreement and the transactions contemplated hereby;
   (iv) executed counterparts of the lease amendments with respect to the Darien and Wisconsin Properties;
   (v) the executed Promissory Notes;
   (vi) the Operating Agreement of the Buyer, providing for the Equity Interest in the Buyer to be issued to Seller, in accordance with Section 2.1(c) hereof;
   (vii) the Pledge Agreement and the Pledged Collateral Account Agreement executed by the Pledgor in accordance with Section 8.1(f) hereof;
   (viii) executed Employment Agreements as provided in Section 8.2(f); and
   (ix) any other certificates or other documents and instruments required herein to be delivered by Buyer.

4. **REPRESENTATIONS AND WARRANTIES OF THE SELLER**

In order to induce the Buyer to enter into this Agreement and to consummate the transactions contemplated hereby, the Seller and each of the Shareholders, jointly and severally, hereby represents and warrants to the Buyer as follows:

4.1 *Organization and Authority.* Seller is a corporation duly organized, validly existing and in good standing under the laws of the State of Illinois. Seller has the full power and authority to enter into and perform this Agreement, to own, operate and lease its properties and assets, to carry on its business as it is now being conducted, and to execute, deliver and perform its obligations under this Agreement and consummate the transactions contemplated hereby. Each Shareholder has the full power and authority to enter into and perform this Agreement. Seller has delivered to the Buyer complete and correct copies of its Articles of Incorporation and Bylaws, each as amended to date. Seller is duly qualified to do business as a foreign corporation and in good standing in Anytown.

4.2 *Authorization of Agreement.* The execution, delivery and performance by the Seller of this Agreement and of each and every document and instrument contemplated hereby and the consummation of the transactions contemplated hereby and thereby have been duly and validly authorized and approved by all necessary corporate action of the Seller. This Agreement has been duly executed and delivered by the Seller and each of the Shareholders and constitutes (and, when executed and delivered, each such other document and instrument will constitute) a valid and binding obligation of the Seller and each of the Shareholders, enforceable against the Seller and each of the Shareholders in accordance with its terms.

4.3 *Capitalization and Share Ownership of Seller.* The Seller's authorized capital stock consists of 1,000 shares of common stock, no par value. There are 1,000 shares of the Seller's common stock presently outstanding, all of which shares are owned by the Shareholders, free and clear of all Liens. All of the Shareholders' shares have been duly authorized and validly issued, are fully paid and nonassessable. No equity securities (or debt securities convertible into equity securities) of the Seller, other than the Shareholders' shares, are issued and outstanding. There are no existing contracts, subscriptions, options, warrants, calls, commitments or other rights of any character to purchase or otherwise acquire any common stock or other securities of the Seller.

4.4 *Non-Contravention; Consents and Approvals.*

(a) Neither the execution and delivery by the Seller of this Agreement nor the consummation by the Seller or the Shareholders of the transactions contemplated hereby, nor compliance by the Seller or the Shareholders with any of the provisions hereof, will (i) conflict with or result in a breach of any provision of the Articles of Incorporation or Bylaws of the Seller, (ii) result in the breach of, or conflict with, any of the terms and conditions of, or constitute a default (with or without the giving of notice or the lapse of time or both) with respect to, or result in the cancellation or termination of, or the acceleration of the performance of any obligations or of any indebtedness under, any contract, agreement, lease, commitment, indenture, mortgage, note, bond, license or other instrument or obligation to which the Seller or any Shareholder is a party or by which the Seller, the Shareholders or any of the Assets may be bound or affected, (other than such breaches, conflicts and defaults set forth in Schedule 4.4(a) hereto, which shall have been waived at or prior to the Closing) (iii) result in the creation of any Lien upon any of the Assets, or (iv) violate any law or any rule or regulation of any administrative agency or governmental body, or any order, writ, injunction or decree of any court, administrative agency or governmental body to which the Seller, the Shareholders or any of the Assets may be subject.

(b) Except as set forth in Schedule 4.4(b) hereto, no approval, authorization, consent or other order or action of, or filing with or notice to any court, administrative agency or other governmental authority or any other person is required for the execution and delivery by Seller or the Shareholders of this Agreement or the consummation by the Seller and the Shareholders of the transactions contemplated hereby.

(c) A description of all Permits held by Seller and necessary or desirable for the operation of the Business are set forth in

(continues)

Exhibit 10-3. Continued.

Schedule 4.4(c) hereto. All Permits listed in Schedule 4.4(c) are valid, and neither Seller nor any Shareholder has received any notice that any government authority intends to modify, cancel, terminate, or deny renewal of any Permit. No current or former stockholder, officer, director or employee of Seller or any affiliate of Seller owns or has any proprietary, financial or other interest in any Permit which Seller owns or uses. Seller has conducted the Business in compliance with the requirements, standards, criteria and conditions set forth in the Permits and other applicable orders, approvals, variances, rules and regulations and is not in violation of any of the foregoing. The transactions contemplated by this Agreement will not result in a default under or a breach of or violation of or adversely affect the rights and benefits afforded to the Seller by any Permits. Except as set forth in Schedule 4.4(c) hereto, no approval by a governmental authority is required for transfer to Buyer of such Permits.

4.5 *Ownership of Assets.*

(a) the Seller has and will have at the Closing good, valid and marketable title to each and every item of the tangible and intangible personal property and assets included in the Assets, and valid leasehold interests in all leases of tangible personal and real property included in the Assets, free and clear of any Liens except as set forth in Schedule 4.5(a). At the Closing, the Seller will transfer to Buyer good, valid and marketable title to the Assets, free and clear of any and all Liens, except as set forth in Schedule 4.5(a).

(b) No affiliate of the Seller has, or has indirectly acquired, any right, title or interest in or to any of the Assets.

(c) The Seller has not sold, transferred, assigned or conveyed any of its right, title and interest, or granted or entered into any option to purchase or acquire any of its right, title or interest, in and to any of the Assets or the Business. No third party has any option or right to acquire the Business or any of the Assets.

4.6 *Balance Sheet; Existing Condition; Ordinary Course.* Attached hereto as Schedule 4.6 are (i) the Seller's unaudited balance sheet (the "2006 Balance Sheet") as of December 31, 2006 (the "Balance Sheet Date"), together with the related unaudited statements of income, shareholders equity and cash flows for the year then ended, and (ii) the Seller's unaudited balance sheets as of December 2005 and 2004, together with the related unaudited statements of income, shareholders equity and cash flows for the years ended December 31, 2005 and 2004 (such unaudited financial statements for 2004, 2005 and 2006 being referred to herein collectively as the "Financial Statements"). The Financial Statements (i) are true, complete and correct, (ii) are in accordance with the books and records of the Seller, (iii) fairly, completely and accurately present the financial position of the Seller as of the respective dates thereof and the results of its operations for the periods presented and (iv) were prepared in conformity with generally accepted accounting principles consistently applied throughout the periods covered thereby. Since the Balance Sheet Date, except as set forth in Schedule 4.6 hereto, there has not been with respect to the Seller:

(a) any material adverse change in the Assets or the Business of the Seller from their condition as set forth on the 2006 Balance Sheet;

(b) any damage, destruction or loss, whether covered by insurance or not, materially and adversely affecting the Business or Assets of the Seller or any sale, transfer or other disposition of the Assets other than in the ordinary course of business;

(c) any declaration, setting aside or payment of any dividend, or any distribution with respect to the capital stock of the Seller or any direct or indirect redemption, purchase or other acquisition by the Seller of shares of its capital stock, or any payment to any affiliate of any intercompany payable or any transfer of Assets to any affiliate; or

(d) except as set forth on Schedule 4.6(d), any increase in the compensation payable by the Seller to any Shareholder or any of the Seller's officers, employees or agents, or in the payment of any bonus, or in any insurance, payment or arrangement made to, for or with any such officers, employees or agents.

Since the Balance Sheet Date, Seller has conducted its Business in the ordinary course and has made no material change to its marketing, purchasing, collections or accounting procedures.

4.7 *Litigation*. There is no litigation, suit, proceeding, action, claim or investigation, at law or in equity, pending or, to the best knowledge of the Seller or any Shareholder, threatened against, or affecting in any way the Assets, the Seller or any Shareholder's ability to own or operate the Business, or which questions the validity of this Agreement or challenges any of the transactions contemplated hereby or the use of the Assets after the Closing by the Buyer. Neither the Seller, nor any of the Shareholders, nor any of the Assets is subject to any judgment, order, writ, injunction or decree of any court or any federal, state, municipal or other governmental authority, department, commission, board, bureau, agency or other instrumentality.

4.8 *Compliance with Laws*. Except as set forth in Schedule 4.8, the Seller's Business has at all times been conducted in compliance with all applicable laws, regulations, ordinances and other requirements of governmental authorities (including applicable federal, state and local laws, rules and regulations respecting oc-

(continues)

Exhibit 10-3. Continued.

cupational safety and health standards). Except as set forth in Schedule 4.8, neither the Seller nor any Shareholder has received any notice, advice, claim or complaint from any employee or governmental authority that the Seller has not conducted, or is not presently conducting, its business and operations in accordance with all applicable laws and other requirements of governmental authorities.

4.9 *Permits and Licenses*. The Seller has all permits, certificates, licenses, approvals, registrations and authorizations required in connection with the conduct of the Business. The Seller is not in violation of, and has not violated, any applicable provisions of any such permits, certificates, licenses, approvals, registrations or authorizations. Except as set forth on Schedule 4.9, all permits, certificates, licenses, approvals, registrations and authorizations of the Seller which are necessary for the operation of the Seller's Business are freely transferable.

4.10 *Contracts*

(a) Schedule 4.10(a) contains a true and complete list of all material contracts and agreements related to or involving the Business or the Assets or by which any of the Assets is subject or bound in any material respect, including, without limiting the generality of the foregoing, any and all: contracts and agreements for the purchase, sale or lease of inventory, goods, materials, equipment, hardware, supplies or other personal property; contracts for the purchase, sale or lease of real property; contracts and agreements for the performance or furnishing of services; joint venture, partnership or other contracts, agreements or arrangements involving the sharing of profits; employment agreements; and agreements containing any covenant or covenants which purport to limit the ability or right of the Seller or any other person or entity to engage in any aspects of the business related to the Assets or compete in any aspect of such business with any person or entity (collectively, the "Scheduled Contracts"). As used herein, the terms "contract" and "agreement" mean and include every material contract, agreement, commitment, arrangement, understanding and promise whether written or oral. A complete and accurate copy of each written Scheduled Contract has been delivered or made available to the Buyer or, if oral, a complete and accurate summary thereof has been delivered to the Buyer.

Except as set forth on Schedule 4.10(a), the Scheduled Contracts are valid, binding and enforceable in accordance with their respective terms, are in full force and effect and were entered into in the ordinary course of business on an "arms-length" basis and consistent with past practices. The Seller is not in breach or default of any of the Scheduled Contracts and, except as set forth on Schedule 4.10(a), no occurrence or circumstance exists which constitutes (with or without the giving of notice or the lapse of time or both) a breach or default by the other party thereto. Neither the Seller nor any Shareholder has been notified or advised by any party to a Scheduled Contract of such party's intention or desire to terminate or modify any such contract or agreement. Neither the Seller nor any Shareholder has granted any Lien on any Scheduled Contract included in the Assets.

(b) Except as set forth on Schedule 4.10(b) and this Agreement, neither the Seller nor any Shareholder is a party to, and neither the Seller nor any Shareholder nor any of the Assets is subject or bound in any respect by, any written or oral contract and agreement related to or involving the Business which will affect in any manner the Buyer's ownership, use or operation of the Assets, including, without limitation any contracts or agreements (i) for the purchase, sale or lease of inventory, goods, equipment or for the performance or furnishing of services; (ii) for the furnishing of services for which the Seller has received payment in advance of furnishing such services and has not yet furnished such services; and (iii) containing any covenant or covenants which purport to limit the ability or right of the Seller or any other person or entity to engage in any aspects of the business related to the Assets or compete in any aspect of such business with any person or entity.

(c) Except as set forth on Schedule 4.10(c), all Scheduled Contracts included in the Assets will be fully and validly assigned to the Buyer as of the Closing.

(d) Except as set forth in Schedule 4.10(d), there is no Scheduled Contract or any other Contract included in the Assets which cannot be terminated without any further obligation, payment or penalty upon thirty-days notice or more to the other party or parties to such Contract.

4.11 *Condition of Purchased Assets*. Each and every one of the tangible Assets to be purchased by Buyer pursuant to this Agreement is in good operating condition and repair, ordinary wear and tear excepted, and is fit and suitable for the purposes for which they are currently used by Seller. The Assets include all of the properties and assets of Seller required, necessary or desirable to enable Buyer to conduct the operation of the Business in the same manner in which the Business has been conducted prior to the date hereof by Seller.

4.12 *Customers*. Seller has delivered to Buyer a complete and accurate list of all customers which has been included in Schedule 4.12. Except as set forth in Schedule 4.12, no current customer (i) has cancelled, suspended or otherwise terminated its relationship with the Seller or (ii) has advised the Seller or either Shareholder of its intent to cancel, suspend or otherwise terminate such relationship, or to materially decrease its usage of the services provided by Seller.

(continues)

Exhibit 10-3. Continued.

4.13 *Employee Benefit Plans*. Except as set forth in Schedule 4.13, there are not currently, nor have there ever been, any Benefit Plans (defined below) in place or established by Seller. "Benefit Plan" means any bonus, incentive compensation, deferred compensation, pension, profit sharing, retirement, stock purchase, stock option, stock ownership, stock appreciation rights, phantom stock, leave of absence, layoff, vacation, day or dependent care, legal services, cafeteria, life, health, accident, disability, workmen's compensation or other insurance, severance, separation or other employee benefit plan, practice, policy or arrangement of any kind, whether written or oral, including, but not limited to, any "employee benefit plan" within the meaning of Section 3(3) of ERISA. All group health plans of the Seller and have been operated in compliance with all applicable federal and state laws and regulations.

4.14 *Warranties*. Schedule 4.14 sets forth a complete and correct copy of all of the Seller's standard warranties (collectively, the "Warranties" or individually a "Warranty") currently extended by the Seller to the customers of the Seller. There are no warranty claims outstanding against the Seller.

4.15 *Trademarks, Patents, etc*. Except as set forth in Schedule 4.15, the Seller does not own or have any rights to any patents, trademarks, trade names, brand names, service marks, service names, copyrights, inventions or licenses and rights and applications with respect to the foregoing (collectively, the "Marks and Patents"). All the Marks and Patents are valid and have not been abandoned, and there are no prior claims, controversies, lawsuits or judgments which affect the validity of the Seller's rights to the Marks and Patents nor are there any legal proceedings, claims or controversies instituted, pending or, to the best knowledge of the Seller or the Shareholders, threatened with respect to any of the Marks and Patents, or which challenge the Seller's rights, title or interest in respect thereto. Except as set forth on Schedule 4.15, none of the Marks and Patents is the subject of any outstanding assignments, grants, licenses, Liens, obligations or agreements, whether written, oral, or implied. All required renewal fees, maintenance fees, amendments and/or other filings or payments which are necessary to preserve and maintain the Marks and Patents have been filed and/or made. The Seller owns or has the right to use all Marks and Patents and the like necessary to conduct its Business as presently conducted and without conflict with any patent, trade name, trademark or the like of any other person or entity.

4.16 *Insurance*. Set forth in Schedule 4.16 is a complete and accurate list of all insurance policies which the Seller maintains with respect to its Business or the Assets. Such policies are in full force and effect. Such policies, with respect to their amounts and types of coverage, are adequate to insure fully against risks to which the Seller, the Business or the Assets are normally exposed in the operation of the Business. There has not been any material adverse change in the Seller's relationship with its insurers or in the premiums payable pursuant to such policies. The insurance coverage provided by the Seller's insurance policies shall not be affected by, and shall not lapse or otherwise be terminated by reason of, the execution of this Agreement. Neither the Seller has or either Shareholder received any notice respecting the cancellation of such insurance policies.

4.17 *Environmental Matters.*

(a) Except as set forth on Schedule 4.17(a) attached hereto, Seller has obtained all permits, licenses, and other authorizations (collectively, the "Licenses") which are required in connection with the conduct of the Business under all applicable Environmental Laws (as defined below) and regulations relating to pollution or protection of the environment, including Environmental Laws and regulations relating to emissions, discharges, releases or threatened releases of pollutants, contaminants, chemicals, or industrial, toxic or hazardous substances or wastes into the environment (including without limitation, ambient air, surface water, groundwater, or land) or otherwise relating to the manufacture, processing, distribution, use, treatment, storage, disposal, transport, or handling of pollutants, contaminants, chemicals, or industrial, toxic or hazardous substances or wastes.

(b) Except as set forth in Schedule 4.17(b), Seller is in substantial compliance in the conduct of the Business with all terms and conditions of the Licenses and is in substantial compliance with all other limitations, restrictions, conditions, standards, prohibitions, requirements, obligations, schedules and timetables contained in the Environmental Laws or contained in any regulation, code, plan, order, decree, judgment, injunction, notice (written or verbal) or demand letter issued, entered, promulgated or approved thereunder.

(c) Except as set forth on Schedule 4.17(c), neither Seller nor any Shareholder is aware of, nor has Seller received any written or verbal notice of, any past, present or future events, conditions, circumstances, activities, practices, incidents, actions or plans which may interfere with or prevent compliance or continued compliance with any Environmental Laws or any regulations, code, order, decree, judgment, injunction, notice (written or verbal) or demand letter issued, entered, promulgated or approved thereunder, or which may give rise to any common law or legal liability, or otherwise form the basis of any claim, action, demand, suit, proceeding, hearing, study or investigation, based on or related to the Seller's, processing, storage, distribution, use, treatment, disposal, transport, or handling, or the emission, discharge, release or threatened release into the environment, of any

(continues)

Exhibit 10-3. Continued.

pollutant, contaminant, chemical, or industrial, toxic or hazardous substance or waste.

(d) There is no civil, criminal or administrative action, suit, demand, claim, hearing, notice or demand letter, notice of violation, investigation, or proceeding pending or threatened against Seller or the Shareholders in connection with the conduct of the Business relating in any way to any Environmental Laws or regulation, injunction, notice or demand letter issued, entered, promulgated or approved thereunder.

(e) For purposes of this Agreement, "Environmental Laws" means collectively, all federal, state and local environmental laws, common law, statutes, rules and regulations including, without limitation, the Comprehensive Environmental Response, Compensation and Liability Act (42 U.S.C. Sec. 9061 et seq.), as amended, the Hazardous Materials Transportation Act (49 U.S.C. Sec. 1801 et seq.), as amended, the Resource Conservation and Recovery Act (42 U.S.C. Sec. 6901 et seq.), as amended, the Federal Water Pollution Control Act (33 U.S.C. Sec. 1251 et seq.), as amended, the Safe Drinking Water Act (42 U.S.C. Sec. 300f et seq.), as amended, the Clean Air Act (42 U.S.C. Sec. 7401 et seq.), as amended, the Toxic Substances Control Act (15 U.S.C. Sec. 2601 et seq.), as amended, the Federal Emergency Planning and Community Right-to-Know Act (42 U.S.C. Sec. 11001 et seq.), as amended, any "superfund" or "super-lien" law and such statutes and ordinances as may be enacted by state and local governments with jurisdiction over any real property now owned or leased by the Seller or any real property upon which the Seller now conducts its Business and any permits, licenses, authorizations, variances, consents, approvals, directives or requirements of, and any agreements with, any governments, departments, commissions, boards, courts, authorities, agencies, officials and officers applicable to such real property or the use thereof and regulating, relating to, or imposing liability or standards of conduct concerning any pollutant, contaminant, chemical, or industrial, toxic or hazardous substance or waste.

4.18 *Notes, Accounts or Other Receivables.* Set forth on Schedule 1.1(h) is a complete list of Seller's notes, accounts or other receivables included in the Assets as existing on the Closing Date and included in the Estimated Accounts Receivable valuation pursuant to Section 2.2. All of the Seller's notes, accounts or other receivables included on Schedule 1.1(h) are properly reflected on the books and records of the Seller, and are in their entirety valid accounts receivable arising from bona fide transactions in the ordinary course of business.

4.19 *Real Estate.*

(a) The Seller does not own any real property.

(b) The Seller has valid leasehold interests in all of the real property which it leases or purports to lease, free and clear of any Liens, other than the interests of the lessors, including the Darien Property and the Wisconsin Property.

(c) The Seller enjoys peaceful and undisturbed possession under all of the leases pursuant to which Seller leases real property (the "Real Property Leases"). All of the Real Property Leases are valid, subsisting and in full force and effect and there are no existing defaults, or events which with the passage of time or the giving of notice, or both, would constitute defaults by the Seller or, by any other party thereto.

(d) Neither Seller nor any Shareholder received notice of any pending condemnation, expropriation, eminent domain or similar proceedings affecting all or any portion of any real property leased by the Seller and no such proceedings are contemplated.

(e) The Shareholders enjoy peaceful and undisturbed possession of the Darien Property and have the right to lease and collect all rents on the Darien Property and clear of any Liens.

4.20 *No Guarantees.* The Seller has not guaranteed or pledged any Assets with respect to any obligation or indebtedness of any person or entity and no person or entity has guaranteed any obligation or indebtedness of the Seller.

4.21 *Taxes.*

(a) The Seller has timely filed or will timely file all requisite federal, state and other Tax (defined below) returns, reports and forms ("Returns") for all periods ended on or before the Closing Date, and all such Tax Returns are true, correct and complete in all respects. Neither the Seller nor any Shareholder has any knowledge of any basis for the assertion of any claim relating or attributable to Taxes which, if adversely determined, would result in any Lien on the assets of such Seller or any Shareholder or otherwise have an adverse effect on the Seller, the Assets or the Business.

(b) For purposes of this Agreement, the term "Tax" shall include any tax or similar governmental charge, impost, or levy (including, without limitation, income taxes, franchise taxes, transfer taxes or fees, sales taxes, use taxes, gross receipts taxes, value added taxes, employment taxes, excise taxes, ad valorem taxes, property taxes, withholding taxes, payroll taxes, minimum taxes or windfall profits taxes) together with any related penalties, fines, additions to tax or interest imposed by the United States or any state, county, local or foreign government or subdivision or agency thereof.

4.22 *Labor Matters.* Schedule 4.22 sets forth a true and complete list of all employees of Seller together with a brief summary of their titles, duties, terms of employment and compensation arrangements, including the salary and any bonus, commission or other

(continues)

Exhibit 10-3. Continued.

compensation paid to each employee during the twelve (12) month period prior to the date hereof and the current employment and compensation arrangements with respect to each such employee. Further, with respect to employees of and service provided to Seller:

(a) Seller is not a party to any collective bargaining or similar labor agreements, no such agreement determines the terms and conditions of employment of any employee of Seller, no collective bargaining or other labor agent has been certified as a representative of any of the employees of the Seller, and no representation campaign or election is now in progress with respect to any of the employees of the Seller;

(b) Seller is and has been in compliance in all material respects with all applicable laws respecting employment and employment practices, terms and conditions of employment and wages and hours, including without limitation, any such laws respecting employment discrimination and harassment, workers' compensation, family and medical leave, the Immigration Reform and Control Act, and occupational safety and heath requirements, and has not and is not engaged in any unfair labor practice;

(c) there is not now, nor within the past three years, has there been, any unfair labor practice complaint against Seller, pending or to Seller's best knowledge, threatened before the National Labor Relations Board or any other comparable authority; nor any labor strike, slowdown or stoppage actually ending or, to Seller's best knowledge, threatened against or directly affecting Seller; there exist no other labor disputes with regard to Seller's employees or relative to Seller's Employee Technician Manual ("Manual"), including, without limitation, any reports of harassment, substance abuse, disciplinary, safety or punctuality problems in contravention of Seller's Manual, or other acts or omissions filed or recorded by or against any employee of Seller. Seller's cessation of operations will not violate any laws, rules, regulations or employment policies applicable to its employees.

(d) As of the Closing Date, each employee of the Seller have received any pay owed him or her with respect to vacation, compensatory or sick time and any other employee benefits due employee, except as otherwise set forth in Schedule 4.22(d).

4.23 *Absence of Undisclosed Liabilities*. Neither the Seller nor any Shareholder has any material liabilities or obligations with respect to the Business, either direct or indirect, matured or unmatured or absolute, contingent or otherwise, other than (a) those reflected in the 1996 Balance Sheet and (b) those liabilities or obligations incurred, consistently with past business practice, in or as a result of the normal and ordinary course of business since the Balance Sheet Date.

4.24 *Liabilities*. The liabilities to be assumed by Buyer pursuant to this Agreement consist solely of liabilities of Seller under Contracts included in the Assets which relate solely to the operation of the Business and the Assumed Liabilities in Schedule 1.2.

4.25 *Accuracy of Documents and Information*. The information provided to the Buyer by the Seller and the Shareholders with respect to the Seller, the Assets and the Business, including the representations and warranties made in this Agreement and in the Schedules attached hereto, and all other information provided to the Buyer in connection with their investigation of the Seller, does not (and will not at the Closing Date) contain any untrue statement of a material fact and does not omit (and will not omit at the Closing Date) to state any material fact necessary to make the statements or facts contained herein or therein not misleading.

4.26 *Brokers and Agents*. Neither Seller nor any Shareholder has employed or dealt with any business broker, agent or finder in respect of the transactions contemplated hereby.

5. **NON-COMPETITION**

Each of the Shareholders agrees that for a period of six (6) years from the date of this Agreement, he or she shall not, directly or indirectly: (a) engage in competition with the Buyer in any manner or capacity (e.g., as an advisor, consultant, independent contractor, principal, agent, partner, officer, director, stockholder, employee, member of any association, or otherwise) or in any phase of the business conducted by the Buyer during the term of this Agreement in any area where the Buyer is conducting or initiating operations during the period described above; provided, however, that ownership by a Shareholder as a passive investment, of less than one (1) percent of the outstanding shares of capital stock of any corporation listed on a national securities exchange or publicly traded in the over-the-counter market shall not constitute a breach of this provision; (b) hire or engage or attempt to hire or employ any individual who shall have been an employee of the Buyer at any time during within one (1) year prior to such action taken by a Shareholder, whether for or on behalf of such Shareholder or for any entity in which such Shareholder shall have a direct or indirect interest (or any subsidiary or affiliate of any such entity), whether as a proprietor, partner, co-venturer, financier, investor or stockholder, director, officer, employer, employee, agent, representative or otherwise; or (c) assist or encourage any other person in carrying out, directly or indirectly, any activity that would be prohibited by the above provisions of this Section if such activity were carried out by Shareholder, either directly or indirectly; and in particular each Shareholder agrees that he or she will not, directly or indirectly, induce any employee of the Buyer to carry out, directly or indirectly, any such activity. In the event of any conflict between this provision and the terms of an Employment Agreement in full force and effect, the Employment Agreement will govern.

6. **REPRESENTATIONS AND WARRANTIES OF THE BUYER**

In order to induce the Seller to enter into this Agreement and to con-

(continues)

Exhibit 10-3. Continued.

summate the transactions contemplated hereby, each of the Buyer, jointly and severally, hereby represents and warrants to the Seller as follows:

6.1 *Buyer's Organization*. The Buyer is a limited liability company duly organized, validly existing and in good standing under the laws of the State of Maryland. The Buyer has all requisite power and authority to own and operate and lease its properties and assets, to carry on its business as it is now being conducted and to execute, deliver and perform its obligations under this Agreement and consummate the transactions contemplated hereby.

6.2 *Authorization of Agreement*. The execution, delivery and performance by the Buyer of this Agreement and of each and every agreement and document contemplated hereby and the consummation of the transactions contemplated hereby and thereby have been duly authorized by all necessary corporate action of the Buyer. This Agreement has been duly and validly executed and delivered by Buyer and constitutes (and, when executed and delivered, each such other agreement and document will constitute) a valid and binding obligation of the Buyer, enforceable against the Buyer in accordance with its terms.

6.3 *Non-Contravention; Consents*. Neither the execution and delivery by the Buyer of this Agreement nor the consummation by the Buyer of the transactions contemplated hereby, nor compliance by the Buyer with any of the provisions hereof, will (i) conflict with or result in a breach of any provision of the Articles of Organization or Operating Agreement of the Buyer, (ii) result in the breach of, or conflict with, any of the terms and conditions of, or constitute a default (with or without the giving of notice or the lapse of time or both) with respect to, or result in the cancellation or termination of, or the acceleration of the performance of any obligations or of any indebtedness under any contract, agreement, commitment, indenture, mortgage, note, bond, license or other instrument or obligation to which the Buyer is now a party or by which the Buyer or its respective properties or assets may be bound or affected (other than such breaches, conflicts and defaults as shall have been waived at or prior to the Closing) or (iii) violate any law or any rule or regulation of any administrative agency or governmental body, or any order, writ, injunction or decree of any court, administrative agency or governmental body to which the Buyer may be subject. No approval, authorization, consent or other order or action of, or filing with or notice to any court, administrative agency or other governmental authority or any other person is required for the execution and delivery by the Buyer of this Agreement or consummation by the Buyer of the transactions contemplated hereby (other than such consents as shall have obtained at or prior to the Closing).

6.4 *Litigation*. There is no litigation, suit, proceeding, action, claim or investigation, at law or in equity, pending, or to the best knowledge of the Buyer, threatened against, or affecting in any way, the Buyer's ability to perform its obligations as contemplated by this Agreement.

6.5 *The Equity Interest*. The Equity Interest has been duly authorized and issued in accordance with the terms hereof and the Operating Agreement.

6.6 *Accuracy of Financial Statements*. The Financial Statement for the Seller set forth in Schedule 6.6, is true and correct in all material respects.

7. **FURTHER AGREEMENTS OF THE PARTIES**

7.1 *Operation of the Business*. From and after the Balance Sheet Date until the Closing Date, except to the extent contemplated by this Agreement or otherwise consented to in writing by the Buyer, the Seller shall have continued to operate its Business in substantially the same manner as presently conducted and only in the ordinary and usual course and substantially consistent with past practice and in substantial compliance with (i) all laws and (ii) all leases, contracts, commitments and other agreements, and all licenses, permits, and other instruments, relating to the operation of the Business, and will use reasonable efforts to preserve intact its present business organization and to keep available the services of all employees, representatives and agents. The Seller and each of the Shareholders shall have continued to use its, his or her reasonable efforts, consistent with past practices, to promote the Business and to maintain the goodwill and reputation associated with the Business, and shall not take or omit to take any action which causes, or which is likely to cause, any material deterioration of the Business or the Seller's relationships with material suppliers or customers. Without limiting the generality of the foregoing, (a) the Seller will have maintained all of its equipment in substantially the same condition and repair as such equipment was maintained prior to the Balance Sheet Date, ordinary wear and tear excepted; (b) the Seller shall not have sold, transferred, pledged, leased or otherwise disposed of any of the Assets, other than in the ordinary course of business; (c) the Seller shall not have amended, terminated or waived any material right in respect of the Assets or the Business, or do any act, or omit to do any act, which will cause a breach of any material contract, agreement, commitment or obligation by it; (d) the Seller shall have maintained its books, accounts and records in accordance with good business practice and generally accepted accounting principles consistently applied; (e) the Seller shall not have engaged in any activities or transactions outside the ordinary course of business; (f) the Seller shall not have declared or paid any dividend or make any other distribution or payment of any kind in cash or property to the Shareholder or other affiliates; and (g) the Seller shall not have increased any existing employee benefits, established any new employee benefits plan or amended or modified any existing Employee Plans, or otherwise incurred any obliga-

(continues)

Exhibit 10-3. Continued.

tion or liability under any employee plan materially different in nature or amount from obligations or liabilities incurred in connection with the Employee Plans.

7.2 *Consents; Assignment of Agreements*. Seller shall obtain, at the earliest practicable date, all consents and approvals of third parties (whether or not listed on Schedule 4.4) which are necessary or desirable for the consummation of the transactions contemplated hereby (including, without limitation, the valid and binding transfer of the Assets to Buyer) (the "Consents"). The Consents shall be written instruments whose form and substance are reasonably satisfactory to Buyer. The Consents shall not, without Buyer's express consent, impose any obligations on Buyer or create any conditions adverse to Buyer, other than the conditions or obligations specified in this Agreement.

7.3 *No Discussions*. The Seller shall not enter into any substantive negotiations or discussions with any third party with respect to the sale or lease of the Assets or the Business, or the sale of any capital stock of the Seller, or any other merger, acquisition, partnership, joint venture or other business combination until the earlier to occur of the (a) Closing Date or (b) the termination of this Agreement.

7.4 *Employee Matters*. The Seller shall permit the Buyer to contact and make arrangements with the Seller's employees for the purpose of assuring their employment by the Buyer after the Closing and for the purpose of ensuring the continuity of the Business, and the Seller agrees not to discourage any such employees from being employed by or consulting with the Buyer. Nothing herein shall obligate the Buyer to employ or otherwise be responsible for any of the Seller's employees, (other than the persons with whom the Buyer has entered or will enter into an employee agreement in accordance with Section 8.2 hereof) or pay any employee any compensation or confer any benefit earned or accrued prior to the Closing Date, except as set forth in Schedule 4.22(d).

7.5 *Notice Regarding Changes*. The Seller shall promptly notify the Buyer in writing of any change in facts and circumstances that could render any of the representations and warranties made herein by the Seller materially inaccurate or misleading.

7.6 *Furnishing of Information*. The Seller will allow Buyer to make a complete examination and analysis of the Business, Assets and records, financial or otherwise, of the Seller. In connection with the foregoing review, Seller agrees that it shall furnish to the Buyer and Buyer's representatives all such information concerning the Seller's Business, Assets, operations, properties or affairs as may be reasonably requested.

7.7 *Notification to Customers*. At the Buyer's request and in a form approved by the Buyer, the Seller agrees to notify all customers of the Business identified by Buyer and all customers of the Business during the year preceding the Closing as identified by Buyer, either separately or jointly with the Buyer, of the Buyer's purchase of the Business and Assets hereunder and that all further communications or requests by such customers with respect to the Business and Assets shall be directed to the Buyer. Without limiting the foregoing, promptly following the Closing, the Seller shall send a letter, in a form approved by the Buyer, to each debtor with respect to the notes, accounts or other receivables included in the Assets directing that all payments on account of such receivables made after the Closing shall be made to the Buyer.

7.8 *Collection of Receivables*. The Seller agrees that it will reasonably cooperate with the Buyer in collecting the notes, accounts and other receivables included in the Assets from any customers and will immediately deliver to the Buyer the amount paid on any and all receivables it collects after the Closing Date in connection with the Business, less out-of-pocket expenses incurred by Seller at the request of Buyer.

7.9 *Brokers and Agents*. Buyer, on the one hand, and the Seller, on the other hand, agree to indemnify and hold the other harmless from and against all fees, expenses, commissions and costs due and owing to any other broker, agent or finder on account of or in any way resulting from any contract or understanding existing between the indemnifying party and such person.

8. **CONDITIONS PRECEDENT TO CLOSING**

8.1 *Conditions Precedent to the Obligations of Seller*. Seller's and Shareholders' obligations to consummate the transactions contemplated by this Agreement shall be subject to the fulfillment, at or prior to Closing, of each of the following conditions (any or all of which may be waived in writing, in whole or in part, by the Seller and the Shareholders):

(a) The Buyer shall have performed and complied in all material respects with each obligation and covenant required by this Agreement to be performed or complied with by them prior to or at the Closing.

(b) The representations and warranties of the Buyer contained herein shall be true and correct in all material respects at and as of the Closing Date as if made at and as of such time.

(c) Buyer shall have delivered to the Seller the items set forth in Section 3.2(b) of this Agreement.

(d) No action, suit or proceeding by any person shall have been commenced and still be pending, no investigation by any governmental or regulatory authority shall have been commenced and still be pending, and no action, suit or proceeding by any person shall have been threatened against the Buyer, the Seller or the Shareholders, (a) seeking to restrain, prevent or change the transactions contemplated hereby or questioning the validity or legality of any such transactions or (b) which if resolved adversely to any party, would materially and adversely affect the business or condition, financial or otherwise, of the Buyer, or the Seller.

(continues)

Exhibit 10-3. Continued.

(e) All proceedings to be taken by the Buyer in connection with the transactions contemplated hereby and all documents incident thereto shall be reasonably satisfactory in form and substance to the Seller and its counsel, and the Seller and said counsel shall have received all such counterpart originals or certified or other copies of such documents as it or they may reasonably request.

(f) Buyer shall have delivered to the Seller the Pledge Agreement together with the marketable securities and other collateral securing the Note.

(g) Buyer shall have delivered to the Seller all such other certificates and documents as the Seller and its counsel shall have reasonably requested.

8.2 *Conditions Precedent to the Obligations of the Buyer*. The obligation of the Buyer to consummate the transactions contemplated by this Agreement shall be subject to the fulfillment, at or prior to Closing, of each of the following conditions precedent (any or all of which may be waived in writing, in whole or in part, by the Buyer):

(a) The Seller shall have performed and complied in all material respects with each obligation and covenant required by this Agreement to be performed or to be complied with by it on or prior to the Closing Date.

(b) The representations and warranties of the Seller and the Shareholders contained herein or in any Schedule attached hereto shall be true and correct in all material respects at and as of the Closing Date as if made at and as of such time.

(c) The Seller and the Shareholders shall have delivered or caused delivery of the items set forth in Section 3.2(a) hereof.

(d) Except as otherwise set forth in this Agreement, the Buyer shall have received written evidence, in form and substance satisfactory to it, that all material consents, waivers, authorizations and approvals of, or filing with or notices to, governmental entities and third parties required in order that the transactions contemplated hereby be consummated have been obtained or made.

(e) There shall not have occurred since the Balance Sheet Date any material damage or loss by theft, casualty or otherwise, whether or not insured against by the Seller or the Shareholders, of all or any material portion of the Assets, or any material adverse change in or interference with the Business or the properties, assets, condition (financial or otherwise) or prospects of the Seller.

(f) Buyer shall have entered into an employment agreement with Jane C. Doe and John F. Doe, in substantially the forms attached hereto as Exhibit G and Exhibit H, respectively.

(g) No action, suit or proceeding by any person shall have been commenced and still be pending, no investigations by any governmental or regulatory authority shall have been commenced and still be pending, and no action, suit or proceeding by any person shall have been threatened against the Buyer, the Seller or the Shareholders, (a) seeking to restrain, prevent or change the transactions contemplated hereby or questioning the validity or legality of any such transactions or (b) which if resolved adversely to any party, would materially and adversely affect the business or condition, financial or otherwise, of the Buyer, or the Seller.

(h) All proceedings to be taken by the Seller and the Shareholders in connection with the transactions contemplated hereby and all documents incident thereto shall be reasonably satisfactory in form and substance to the Buyer and its counsel, and the Buyer and said counsel shall have received all such counterpart originals or certified or other copies of such documents as it or they may reasonably request.

(i) Seller shall have delivered to the Buyer all such other certificates and documents as the Buyer or its counsel shall have reasonably requested.

9. **INDEMNIFICATION, SURVIVAL OF REPRESENTATIONS, AND WARRANTIES**

9.1 *Indemnification by Seller and Shareholders*. Each of the Sellers and the Shareholders, jointly and severally, covenants and agrees to indemnify, defend, protect and hold harmless the Buyer and any of the Buyer's officers, directors, stockholders, representatives, affiliates, assigns, successors in interest, and current and former employees, each only in their respective capacities as such (collectively, the "Buyer Indemnified Parties"), from, against, and in respect of:

(a) any and all liabilities, claims, losses, damages, punitive damages, causes of action, lawsuits, administrative proceedings, demands, judgments, settlement payments, penalties, and costs and expenses (including, without limitation, reasonable attorneys' fees, travel expenses, expert witness fees and disbursements of every kind, nature and description) (collectively, "Damages"), suffered, sustained, incurred, or paid by Buyer or any other Buyer Indemnified Party in connection with, resulting from or arising out of, either directly or indirectly:

(i) any misrepresentation or breach of any warranty of the Seller or any Shareholder set forth in this Agreement or any Schedule or certificate delivered by or on behalf of the Seller or any Shareholder in connection herewith; or

(ii) any nonfulfillment of any covenant or agreement on the part of the Seller or any Shareholder set forth in this Agreement; or

(iii) the Business, operations or Assets of the Seller prior to the Closing Date or the actions or omissions of the

(continues)

Exhibit 10-3. Continued.

Seller's directors, officers, shareholders, employees, or agents prior to the Closing Date (except with respect to the Assumed Liabilities); or

(iv) the Excluded Liabilities.

(b) any and all Damages incident to any of the foregoing or to the enforcement of this Section 9.1.

9.2 *Limitation and Expiration.* The indemnification obligations under this Section 9 or in any other certificate or writing furnished in connection with the transactions contemplated hereby shall terminate on the later of (i) the date that is six (6) months after the expiration of the longest applicable federal or state statute of limitation (including extensions thereof), or (b) if there is no applicable statute of limitation, four years after the Closing Date, or (c) the final resolution of a claim or demand (a "Claim") as of the relevant dates described above in this Section.

9.3 *Indemnification by Buyer.* The Buyer covenants and agrees to indemnify, defend, protect and hold harmless the Shareholders, the Seller and any of the Seller's officers, directors, stockholders, representatives, affiliates, assigns, successors in interest, and current and former employees, each only in their respective capacities as such (collectively, the "Seller Indemnified Parties"), from, against and in respect of:

(a) any and all Damages sustained, incurred or paid by Seller or any other Seller Indemnified Party in connection with, resulting from or arising out of, either directly or indirectly:

(i) any breach of any warranty of the Buyer set forth in this Agreement or any Schedule or certificate delivered by or on behalf of the Buyer in connection herewith; or

(ii) any nonfulfillment of any covenant or agreement on the part of the Buyer set forth in this Agreement; or

(iii) the ownership of the purchased Assets or the operation of the Business by the Buyer following the Closing Date.

(b) any and all Damages incident to any of the foregoing or to the enforcement of this Section 9.3.

9.4 *Notice Procedures; Claims.* The obligations and liabilities of the parties under this Section with respect to, relating to, caused (in whole or in part) by or arising out of claims of third parties (individually, a "Third Party Claim" and collectively, "Third Party Claims") shall be subject to the following conditions:

(a) The party entitled to be indemnified hereunder (the "Indemnified Party") shall give the party obligated to provide the indemnity (the "Indemnifying Party") prompt notice of any Third Party Claim (the "Claim Notice"); provided that the failure to give such Claim Notice shall not affect the liability of the Indemnifying Party under this Agreement unless the failure materially and adversely affects the ability of the Indemnifying Party to defend the Third Party Claim. If the Indemnifying Party promptly acknowledges in writing its obligation to indemnify in accordance with the terms and subject to the limitations of such party's obligation to indemnify contained in this Agreement with respect to that claim, the Indemnifying Party shall have a reasonable time to assume the defense of the Third Party Claim at its expense and with counsel of its choosing, which counsel shall be reasonably satisfactory to the Indemnified Party. Any Claim Notice shall identify, to the extent known to the Indemnified Party, the basis for the Third Party Claim, the facts giving rise to the Third Party Claim, and the estimated amount of the Third Party Claim (which estimate shall not be conclusive of the final amount of such claim or demand). The Indemnified Party shall make available to the Indemnifying Party copies of all relevant documents and records in its possession.

(b) If the Indemnifying Party, within a reasonable time after receipt of such Claim Notice, fails to assume the defense of any Third Party Claim in accordance with Section 9.4(a), the Indemnified Party shall (upon further notice to the Indemnifying Party) have the right to undertake the defense, compromise or settlement of the Third Party Claim, at the expense and for the account and risk of the Indemnifying Party.

(c) Anything in this Section 9.4 to the contrary notwithstanding, (i) the Indemnifying Party shall not without the written consent of the Indemnified Party, settle or compromise any Third Party Claim or consent to the entry of judgment which does not include as an unconditional term thereof the giving by the claimant or the plaintiff to the Indemnified Party of an unconditional release from all liability in respect of the Third Party Claim; (ii) if such Third Party Claim involves an issue or matter which the Indemnified Party believes could have a materially adverse effect on the Indemnified Party's business, operations, assets, properties or prospects of its business, the Indemnified Party shall have the right to control the defense or settlement of any such claim or demand, at the expense of the Indemnified Party without contribution from the Indemnifying Party; and (iii) the Indemnified Party shall have the right to employ its own counsel to defend any claim at the Indemnifying Party's expense if (x) the employment of such counsel by the Indemnified Party has been authorized by the Indemnifying Party, or (y) counsel selected by the Indemnifying Party shall have reasonably concluded that there may be a conflict of interest between the Indemnifying Party and the Indemnified Party in the conduct of the defense of such action or (z) the Indemnifying Party shall not have employed counsel to assume the defense of such claim in accordance with Section 9.4(a).

(d) In the event that the Indemnified Party should have a claim against the Indemnifying Party hereunder which does not in-

(continues)

Exhibit 10-3. Continued.

volve a claim or demand being asserted against or sought to be collected from it by a third party, the Indemnified Party shall promptly send a Claim Notice with respect to such claim to the Indemnifying Party. If the Indemnifying Party does not notify the Indemnified Party within thirty (30) calendar days that it disputes such claim, the amount of such claim shall be conclusively deemed a liability of the Indemnifying Party hereunder.

(e) Nothing herein shall be deemed to prevent any Indemnified Party from making a claim hereunder for potential or contingent claims or demands, provided that (i) the Claim Notice sets forth (A) the specific basis for any such potential or contingent claim or demand and (B) the estimated amount thereof (to the extent then feasible) and (ii) the Indemnified Party has reasonable grounds to believe that such a claim or demand will be made.

9.5 *Survival of Representations, Warranties, and Covenants*. All representations, warranties, and covenants made by the Seller, the Shareholders, and the Buyer in or pursuant to this Agreement or in any document delivered pursuant hereto shall be deemed to have been made on the date of this Agreement (except as otherwise provided herein) and, if a Closing occurs, as of the Closing Date. The representations of the Seller and the Shareholders will survive and the Closing and remain in effect until, and will expire upon, the termination of the relevant indemnification obligation as provided in Section 9.2. The representations of Buyer will survive and remain in effect until and will expire upon, the later of the third anniversary of the Closing Date or the satisfaction in full of any payment obligation pursuant to the Promissory Note.

9.6 *Indemnification Trigger*. Notwithstanding the provisions of Section 9.1 or 9.3 above, neither Seller nor Buyer shall be liable to the other to the other for any indemnification under this Section 9 unless and until the aggregate amount of Damages due to an Indemnified Party exceeds Two Hundred Thousand Dollars ($200,000) (the "Trigger Amount"). Once the Trigger Amount has been exceeded, the Indemnified Party shall be entitled to indemnification for all Damages, including the amount up to the Trigger Amount and any amount in excess thereof. The foregoing trigger provision shall not apply, however, with respect to any Damages suffered, sustained, incurred or paid by an Indemnified Party related to Taxes or assessments by any governmental authority, or with respect to any claim of actual fraud or intentional misrepresentation relating to a breach of any representation or warranty in this Agreement.

9.7 *Remedies Cumulative*. The remedies set forth in this Section 9 are cumulative and shall not be construed to restrict or otherwise affect any other remedies that may be available to the Indemnified Parties under any other agreement or pursuant to statutory or common law.

10. **POST-CLOSING MATTERS**

10.1 *Transition Services*. The Seller agrees to provide reasonable assistance to the Buyer in connection with the transition of the Business to the Buyer. The Shareholders will provide assistance to Buyer in accordance with their respective Employment Agreement.

10.2 *Further Assurances*. The Seller and each of the Shareholders hereby covenants and agrees to (a) make, execute and deliver to the Buyer any and all powers of attorney and other authority which the Seller may lawfully make, execute and deliver, in addition to any such powers and authorities as are contained herein, which may reasonably be or become necessary, proper or convenient to enable the Buyer to reduce to possession, collect, enforce, own or enjoy any and all rights and benefits in, to, with respect to, or in connection with, the Assets, or any part or portion thereof, and (b) upon the Buyer's request, to take, in the Seller's name, any and all steps and to do any and all things which may be or become lawful and reasonably necessary, proper, convenient or desirable to enable the Buyer to reduce to possession, collect, enforce, own and enjoy any and all rights and benefits in, to, with respect to, or in connection with, the Assets, and each and every part and portion thereof. The Seller and each of the Shareholders also covenants and agrees with the Buyer, its successors and assigns, that the Seller and each of the Shareholders will do, execute, acknowledge and deliver, or cause to be done, executed, acknowledged and delivered, any and all such further reasonable acts, instruments, papers and documents as may be necessary to carry out and effectuate the intent and purposes of this Agreement. From and after the Closing Date, Seller will promptly refer all inquiries with respect to ownership of the Assets or the Business to Buyer.

10.3 *Payment of Liabilities; Discharge of Liens*. The Seller shall satisfy and discharge as the same shall become due, all of Seller's liabilities, obligations, debts and commitments including but not limited to Tax Liabilities, in accordance with this Agreement, other than the Assumed Liabilities.

10.4 *Transfer of Permits; Additional Consents*. Subsequent to the Closing, Seller shall use its reasonable efforts to effectively transfer to Buyer all Permits which were not so transferred at or prior to the Closing and to obtain all approvals, consents and authorizations with respect to such transfers. In addition, subsequent to the Closing, to the extent requested by Buyer, Seller shall use its reasonable efforts to obtain any required consents of the other parties to the Scheduled Contracts included in the Assets to the assignment thereof to the Buyer which were not obtained at or prior to the Closing.

10.5 *Inspection of Documents, Books and Records; Financial Reports*. Subsequent to the Closing, Buyer shall make available for inspection by Seller or its authorized representatives during regular

(continues)

Exhibit 10-3. Continued.

business hours and upon reasonable notice, any original documents conveyed to Buyer under this Agreement. Upon reasonable notice to the Buyer, for five years from the Closing Date forward, Seller or its representatives shall be entitled, at Seller's expense, to audit, copy, review and inspect the Buyer's books and records at the Buyer's offices during reasonable business hours. For so long as any payment obligation is outstanding under this Agreement, Buyer shall make available to Seller and its representatives, copies of Buyer's annual corporate tax returns and any quarterly financial statements or reports prepared or compiled by or for Buyer.

10.6 *Acceleration of Notes.* In the event that Buyer shall subsequently sell, convey, transfer or assign assets of the Buyer, to a non-affiliated third party (other than as collateral under a lien or security arrangement), the value of which is greater than twenty-five percent of the total assets of the Buyer at the time of the transfer, all amounts of principal and interest then outstanding under both Notes shall become immediately due and payable.

11. **RISK OF LOSS**

Prior to the Closing, the risk of loss (including damage and/or destruction) of all of the Seller's property and assets, including without limitation the Assets, shall remain with the Seller, and the legal doctrine known as the "Doctrine of Equitable Conversion" shall not be applicable to this Agreement or to any of the transactions contemplated hereby.

12. **MISCELLANEOUS**

12.1 *Entire Agreement.* This Agreement, and the Exhibits and Schedules to this Agreement constitute the entire agreement between the parties hereto with respect to the subject matter hereof and supersede all prior negotiations, agreements, arrangements and understandings, whether oral or written, among the parties hereto with respect to such subject matter, (including, without limitation, the letter of intent dated January ____, 2006, as amended, between the Seller and the Buyer).

12.2 *No Third Party Beneficiary.* Nothing expressed or implied in this Agreement is intended, or shall be construed, to confer upon or give any person, firm, corporation, partnership, association or other entity, other than the parties hereto and their respective successors and assigns, any rights or remedies under or by reason of this Agreement.

12.3 *Amendment.* This Agreement may not be amended or modified in any respect, except by the mutual written agreement of the parties hereto.

12.4 *Waivers and Remedies.* The waiver by any of the parties hereto of any other party's prompt and complete performance, or breach or violation, of any provision of this Agreement shall not operate nor be construed as a waiver of any subsequent breach or violation, and the failure by any of the parties hereto to exercise any right or remedy which it may possess hereunder shall not operate nor be construed as a bar to the exercise of such right or remedy by such party upon the occurrence of any subsequent breach or violation.

12.5 *Severability*. If any term, provision, covenant or restriction of this Agreement (or the application thereof to any specific persons or circumstances) should be held by an administrative agency or court of competent jurisdiction to be invalid, void or unenforceable, such term, provision, covenant or restriction shall be modified to the minimum extent necessary in order to render it enforceable within such jurisdiction, consistent with the expressed objectives of the parties hereto. Further, the remainder of this Agreement (and the application of such term, provision, covenant or restriction to any other persons or circumstances) shall not be affected thereby, but rather shall be enforced to the greatest extent permitted by law.

12.6 *Descriptive Headings*. Descriptive headings contained herein are for convenience only and shall not control or affect the meaning or construction of any provision of this Agreement.

12.7 *Counterparts*. This Agreement may be executed in any number of counterparts and by the separate parties hereto in separate counterparts, each of which shall be deemed to be one and the same instrument.

12.8 *Notices*. All notices, consents, requests, instructions, approvals and other communications provided for herein and all legal process in regard hereto shall be in writing and shall be deemed to have been duly given (a) when delivered by hand, (b) when received by facsimile transmission, with printed confirmation of transmission and verbal (telephonic) confirmation of receipt, (c) one day after being sent by a nationally-recognized overnight express service or (d) five (5) days after being deposited in the United States mail, by registered or certified mail, return receipt requested, postage prepaid, as follows:

If to the Seller: Target Co., Inc.
16602 Side Avenue
Anytown, USA 01206
Attn: President

If to Buyer: Growth Co. Corp.
12345 Main Street
Anytown, USA 01234
Attn: Chief Executive Officer

or to such other address as any party hereto may from time to time designate in writing delivered in a like manner.

12.9 *Successors and Assigns*. This Agreement shall be binding upon and shall inure to the benefit of the parties hereto and their respective successors and assigns. None of the parties hereto shall assign any of its rights or obligations hereunder except with the express written consent of the other parties hereto.

12.10 *Applicable Law*. This Agreement shall be governed by, and shall be construed, interpreted and enforced in accordance with, the internal laws of the State of Maryland.

(continues)

Exhibit 10-3. Continued.

12.11 *Expenses*. Each of the parties hereto agrees to pay all of the respective expenses incurred by it in connection with the negotiation, preparation, execution, delivery, and performance of this Agreement and the consummation of the transactions contemplated hereby.

12.12 *Confidentiality*. Except to the extent required for any party to obtain any approvals or consents required pursuant to the terms hereof, no party hereto shall divulge the existence of the terms of this Agreement or the transactions contemplated hereby without the prior written approval of all of the parties hereto, except and as to the extent (i) obligated by law or (ii) necessary for such party to defend or prosecute any litigation in connection with the transactions contemplated hereby.

12.13 *Attorneys' Fees*. In the event any suit or other legal proceeding is brought for the enforcement of any of the provisions of this Agreement, the parties hereto agree that the prevailing party or parties shall be entitled to recover from the other party or parties upon final judgment on the merits reasonable attorneys' fees and expenses, including attorneys' fees and expenses for any appeal, and costs incurred in bringing such suit or proceeding.

IN WITNESS WHEREOF, the parties have executed and delivered this Agreement on the date first above written.

GROWTH CO. CORP.
By: ____________________
____________, Chief Executive Officer

TARGET CO., INC.
By: ____________________
____________, President

CHAPTER 11

Keeping M&A Transactions on Track

Managing the Deal Killers

Deal killers. We have all seen them and had to manage through them. They come in all shapes, sizes, and varieties with different reasons, justifications, and rationalizations. They can emanate from the buyer, the seller or any number of third parties, such as lenders, investors, key customers or suppliers, professional advisors . . . or all of the above. Some deal killers are legitimate for deals that deserve to die and some are emotional, financial or strategic in nature. They can be very costly to all parties to the transaction, especially when significant costs have already been incurred and for certain advisors and investment bankers, it means not getting paid. Clearly, deal killers inflict a lot of pain along their path of destruction of a transaction.

Most "deal killers" can be put into one of the following major categories:

- Price and valuation
- Terms and conditions
- Allocation of risk
- Third-party challenges

Communication and Leadership

The first step in keeping a transaction on track (and greatly increasing the chance of deal killer avoidance) is to have strong communication and leadership by and among all parties and key players to the transaction. As in football, each team (e.g., buyer, seller, source of capital) should appoint a quarterback, who will be the point person for communication and coordination. Too many lines of communication, like too many chefs in one kitchen, will create confusion and misunderstanding—which are fertile conditions that allow a deal killer to pollinate. The more that the quarterbacks coordinate, communicate, and anticipate problems with the various members of their team and promptly discuss key issues with the quarterbacks of the other teams, the greater the chances that the transaction can and will close.

Some of the key tasks of the transactional quarterback and each team to keep the transaction on track towards closing include:

- Putting a master strategic plan in place (with realistic expectations re: financial and post-closing objectives)
- Building the right team
- Communication and teamwork
- Orchestration and leadership
- Momentum and timetable accord
- Avoiding emotion: Sellers must avoid the "Don't-call-my-baby-ugly" syndrome and buyers must avoid falling in love with a given transaction
- Early start on governmental and third-party appeals
- Creative problem solving
- Cooperation and support from financing sources
- Facilitating agreement on the key value drivers of the seller's business/intellectual capital issues

Diagnosing the Source of the Problem

When a potential deal killer does arise, each quarterback should first diagnose the source of the problem. Where is the issue coming from and what can be done to fix it? A deal killer for one party may not be a deal killer for another party. Take a look at Exhibit 11-1. The old adage "where you stand often depends on where you sit" clearly applies here. For example, a lender to a buyer coming at a higher lending rate than anticipated may significantly alter the attractiveness of the transaction from the buyer's perspective but may be viewed as a non-issue for the seller.

Exhibit 11-1. The source of the problem will dictate the solution.

Seller	Stakeholders ☐ Minority shareholders ☐ Key employees ☐ VC investors ☐ Family members	Third-Party Approaches ☐ Regulatory ☐ Lenders ☐ Lessors ☐ Unions	ALL PARTIES
Buyer	Sources of Capital ☐ Debt ☐ Equity ☐ Mezzanine	Professional Advisors ☐ Lawyers ☐ CPAs ☐ Investment Bankers ☐ Consultants	

Understanding the Types of Deal Killers

Once the *source* of the deal killer has been analyzed, the respective quarterbacks should focus on the specific *type* of deal killer. Most deal killers can and should be resolved—either with creative restructuring, effective counseling or precision document redrafting. Some deal killers *cannot* be resolved (they are just too big and hairy) and other deal killers *should not* be resolved (like trying to squeeze a square peg into a round hole).

Deal killers some in a wide variety of flavors, and include the following:

- Egos clashing
- Misalignment of objectives
- Inexperienced players
- Internal and external politics (board-level, executives, venture investors, etc.)
- Due diligence red flags/surprises

- Pricing and structural challenges (price versus terms)
- Valuation problems (tax/source of financing/in general)
- Third-party approval delays
- Seller's/buyer's source of capital remorse
- Employee and customer issues
- Overdependence on the founder/key employee/key customer or relationship
- Loss of trust/integrity during the transactional process
- Nepotism
- Failure to develop a mutually-agreeable post-closing integration plan
- Shareholder approvals
- Accounting/financial statement irregularities (post-WorldCom)
- Sarbanes-Oxley post-closing compliance concerns
- Breakdowns in leadership and coordination/too little or too many points of communication
- Too little or too much "principal to principal" communications
- Crowded auctions
- Impatience to get to closing versus loss of momentum (flow and timing issues)
- Incompatibility of culture and/or business systems (e.g., IT infrastructure, costs and budgeting policies, compensation and reward programs, accounting policies)
- Force-feeding deals that don't meet M&A objectives (square peg/round hole; bad deal avoidance/good deal capture, systems and filters)
- Who's driving the bus in this deal? (mergers versus acquisitions)
- Changes in seller performance during the transactional process (upside surprises versus unexpected downside surprises)
- Loss of a key customer or strategic relationship during the transactional process
- Failure to agree on post-closing obligations, roles and responsibilities
- Environmental problems (buyers less willing to rely on indemnification and insurance protections)
- Unexpected changes in the buyer's strategy or operations dur-

ing the transactional process (including a change in management or strategic direction)

Curing the Transactional Patient

Although a detailed discussion of the tools available to "kill a deal killer" is beyond the scope of the chapter—and is probably as broad as the number of tools available to the Orkin® man to kill the hundreds of different insects and rodents—some of the more common tools are listed below. The first step is for each quarterback to ensure that the transaction *can* and *should* be fixed. If so, these tools can be very valuable in mending a broken deal:

- Earn-outs/deferred and contingent post-closing consideration
- Representations, warranties, and indemnities (tools to adjust allocation and assumption of risk; weighting of priorities issues)
- Adjusting the post-closing survival period of R&Ws
- Holdbacks and security interests
- Closing date audits
- Third-party performance guaranties/performance bonds/escrows
- M&A insurance policies
- Restrictions on sale by seller of buyer's securities issued as part of the overall consideration
- Recasting of financial projections and retooling post-closing business plans

Conclusion

Bad deals deserve to die a peaceful death. Not all transactions are meant to be closed: (a) at this time; (b) at this valuation; (c) between these parties; or (d) under these terms and conditions. But if a transaction can be saved, then it should be saved. The quarterback on each team must have the transactional experience, the business acumen, and the communication skills to diagnose the source and nature of the problem and enough familiarity with all of the tools available to get the transaction back on track towards closing.

Post-Closing Challenges

The closing of a merger or acquisition usually brings a great sigh of relief to the buyer, seller, and their respective advisors. Everyone has worked hard to ensure that the process went smoothly and that all parties are happy with the end result. But the term *closing* can be misleading in that it suggests a sense of finality, when in truth the hard work, particularly for the buyer, has just begun.

Often one of the greatest challenges for the buyer is the post-closing integration of the two companies. The integration of human resources, the corporate cultures, the operating and management information systems, the accounting methods and financial practices, and related matters are often the most difficult part of completing a merger or acquisition. It is a time of fear, stress and frustration for most of the employees who were *not* on the deal team and may only have limited amounts of information regarding their roles in the post-closing organization. Estimates are as high as three out of every five M&A deals results in an ineffective plan for the external integration of the two companies. And even if there is a plan, well they don't always work out as anticipated. The consequences of a weak or ineffective transition plan are the buyer's inability to realize the transaction's true value, wasted time and resources devoted to solving post-closing problems, and in some cases, even litigation.

The focus of this chapter is on understanding and anticipating the nature and types of post-closing challenges faced by both buyer and seller *after* the deal is completed. The seller must facilitate a smooth transition of ownership and management to the buyer's team without ego, emotion, or politics. The buyer must have procedures in place to prevent the seller from undermining these transitional efforts and assume control of the company—also without ego, emotion, or politics. Post-closing challenges may arise in a wide variety of subject areas, which are addressed in this chapter—e.g., operations, finance, personnel, and information systems. As we will see, a series of emotional and psychological factors must be considered, and strong leadership is needed to guide affected employees through the process.

A Time of Transition

Post-closing challenges raise a wide variety of human fears and uncertainties that must be understood and addressed by both buyer and seller. The fear of the unknown experienced by the employees of the seller must be addressed and put to rest; otherwise, the employees' stress and distraction will affect the seller's performance and the viability of the transaction. The need to quickly integrate the two corporate cultures also raises personal and psychological issues that must be addressed. Once word of a deal leaks out to employees, the uncertainty associated with the change will likely lead to widespread insecurity and fear of job loss at all levels of the organization.

Many of the fears experienced by the employees of *both* buyer and seller result from expectations of downsizing to cut costs, avoid duplication, and achieve the economies of scale potential provided by the transaction.

Another common problem is the psychological consequences of "seller's remorse," particularly when the seller remains on-site in a consulting capacity or even as a minority owner. The seller can be so accustomed to managing the business that he/she may not be open to changes in strategies or policies implemented by the buyer.

The seller undermines the buyer's efforts or contradicts its authority. These sellers often want the *benefit* of the bargain but seem unwilling to accept the *burden* of the bargain and relinquish control of the company. These problems are particularly common in mergers where the management and flow of the deal may be one of shared objectives and values as opposed to an acquisition that more clearly has a designated quarterback.

In attempting to realize the true value of a merger or acquisition, the buyer must coordinate a smooth and efficient post-closing process. Important issues that need to be managed fall into three areas—people, places, and things. Some issues are addressed in the closing documents. Most require forethought in order to anticipate potential pitfalls. The bottom line is that if the buyer doesn't plan to address the following issues, the chances for failure or for not fully realizing success are greatly increased.

Staffing Levels and Other People Problems

One of the primary areas that an acquiring company looks to in order to realize the projected return on its investment is the new company's level of staffing. If a certain number of employees can be eliminated, it is more likely that earnings projections will be met or exceeded. The hard part is deciding who stays, and in what positions, and who goes. Much of this depends on the nature of the acquisition. On the one hand, if the terms dictate that the acquired firm is to maintain its independence, it is much more difficult to reduce staffing levels. On the other hand, if the acquired firm is absorbed into the acquirer, staff cutbacks are probably appropriate and healthy. This is the greatest source of employee fear and is the fuel that powers the rumor mill. But some of these fears are valid. An April 2005 report published by Challenger, Gray & Christmas recommended that job cuts following M&A deals in the first quarter of 2005 soared to nearly 77,000, over six times the rate of the last quarter of 2004 and three times the rate of the first quarter of 2004. The biggest cuts came in the telecom and high tech industries.

Strategic Post-Closing Issues

1. Who should lead the transition team?
2. Which changes should be made and how quickly?

3. How will the changes be presented and sold?
4. How can the seller's transition from owner to employee status be managed?
5. How can "turfmanship" be avoided?

The first step in determining staffing levels is to divide the workforce into management and staff/labor. These two groups must be distinguished because the terms of employment are often quite different. Management is often party to employment contracts, and receives deferred compensation, stock options, and other issues, while staff can be protected by union contracts and/or federal or state employment laws.

Management

In many ways, management staffing is a much easier problem to resolve. Most employment agreements and/or management benefits can be quantified to determine the cost of such decisions. This should have been examined during the due diligence process and worked into the pricing for the transaction.

The primary task of resolving the level of management staffing is to determine where there are redundancies and who are the most qualified candidates. Such a process is normally driven by the acquiring company, but it is not a bad idea to involve the acquired company as well. Only in this way can a true evaluation be made. Failure to consider all candidates fairly may result in a lower return on the investment.

All candidates must be evaluated objectively. It is often difficult to do so because emotions often cloud the judgment of the evaluators. For the acquiring company, choosing the incumbent management team is an easy decision. However, a formal evaluation of all candidates can lead to a stronger, more diverse team. While change can be difficult, it is necessary to embrace the change inherent in acquisitions to enhance your chances of success.

Labor

Labor is often protected by union contracts and labor laws. This limits the options available when deciding who should stay and who should go. However, it should not prevent the buyer from evaluating all employees. By evaluating first and then worrying about possible protections, the buyer gains a much better sense of the quality of the workforce that does ultimately remain.

The same rules apply to evaluating labor as to evaluating management. Be objective. Be balanced. Be honest. The buyer shortchanges itself by not doing so. Develop a selection methodology by targeting certain employees for layoff or retention based on performance and experience. Make sure that the applied criteria are documented and objective and are supported by a performance evaluation and that any review of personnel files and performance evaluations is confidential. This may require the formation of a review committee made up of representatives from each organization to ensure that the terminations occur according to agreed upon procedures.

Once the selections are made, they must be examined from a legal point of view. The following is a list of legal considerations to be examined:

- Employment agreements that may contain conditions that are unacceptable to the buyer or conditions that may be triggered in the event of a merger or acquisition.
- Employees on family leave, pregnancy leave, workers' compensation, or disability, who have certain rights to comparable positions upon their return to work, which may or may not be consistent with staffing plans after the acquisition.
- Whistle-blowers who could bring claims of wrongful discharge.
- WARN (Worker Adjustment and Retraining Notification) notices, which must be sent 60 days in advance by the seller to its employees if there is a plan to close facilities.
- Union contracts that could fall under the National Labor Relations Act (NLRA), which protects the rights of union, as well as nonunion, employees on matters of wages, hours, and working conditions.
- Race, religion, or sex discrimination for which the buyer may be held accountable under civil rights legislation, even if claims are filed based on events that occurred before the acquisition.

- Age discrimination under the Age Discrimination in Employment Act (ADEA) and/or Older Workers Benefit Protection Act (OWBPA), which protects workers against changes in the workforce or changes in benefit plans that would discriminate against workers over 40 or make age-based distinctions.
- Compliance with the Americans with Disabilities Act (ADA), which, among other things, requires a review of job descriptions to ensure that there is a distinction between essential and nonessential duties and a review of property leases to determine who is responsible (the lessee or the lessor) for renovations required under the ADA.
- Violations of the Fair Labor Standards Act (FLSA) or Equal Pay Act, especially concerning the determination of exempt versus nonexempt positions; a violation in this area could lead to substantial payments to current and former employees for overtime worked but not paid.
- Problems that could develop under the Occupational Health and Safety Act (OSHA) if current compliance is not verified and the cost of future compliance is not factored into operating results.
- To ensure that the employees being acquired are legally able to work in the United States, the burden of compliance is on the employer under the Immigration Reform and Control Act (IRCA).
- Lack of compliance with the Drug-Free Workplace Act and various government contract laws can lead to suspended payments or terminated contracts for a seller that is a federal government contractor.
- Whether state law counterparts to federal employment laws have precedence.

The bottom line is that the buyer needs to conduct a thorough labor and employment review. This entails all manner of documents related to such issues. Each transaction is unique in that the above issues will apply in differing degrees.

Customers

When a buyer acquires a business, one of the most valuable assets is the customer base. One of the post-closing challenges is to determine the profitability of the customers. Often the acquired company has legacy customers that they have been unwilling or unable to terminate if the customer is unprofitable or difficult to manage. The acquirer should review all customers for profitability and sustainability. It makes little sense to keep a customer if it is not possible to make a profit on the relationship, unless the customer enables the merged company to penetrate a new market or if the customer helps achieve scale economies, thereby enabling other customers to be profitable. However, even in these cases, there is a limit to the amount of losses that make financial sense. In addition, the customer may be a direct competitor of the buyer or of one of the buyer's customers. As a result, it is important to evaluate the seller's customer base. It may be necessary to discount the value of the acquisition to account for a customer base that is unprofitable or duplicative and that provides little additional strategic value.

Perhaps more important, however, is for the seller to transfer the goodwill of its customers to the buyer. A disgruntled employee can very quickly destroy this goodwill and perhaps jeopardize a significant income stream on which the value of the acquisition was based. The key steps to transferring this goodwill are:

- Personal introductions to customer contacts
- Social events to acquaint customers with the new owners
- Letters from both the seller and buyer that thank customers for their business and announce the new management and plans for the merged entity

Vendors

Suppliers are much more often overlooked than customers. After all, any vendor can easily be replaced. Since this is often true, it is necessary for the buyer to conduct a thorough review of the existing suppliers to ensure that the seller is getting the best prices and terms. However, there are certain suppliers whose replacement would cause significant disruption. This can occur in situations where there is only one supplier of a given product or service, or if the supplier is an integral part of a just-in-time inventory system. Essential vendors are a key component of the continued success and uninterrupted operations of a company.

Of special importance are suppliers that provide professional services—in particular, bankers, accountants, and lawyers. The standard assumption is that the combined company will use the buyer's professional suppliers, but this may not always be desirable or feasible. If a buyer is purchasing a business in a different industry, the bankers may not have the appropriate expertise. The legal counsel of the seller may be better suited to deal with certain local matters or be more cost-effective. The accountants of the seller may be providing outsourcing of certain tasks for which it may not be practical to change immediately. These factors should be considered carefully before any key relationships are terminated. Ultimately, it may be best to continue to use both firms for certain purposes, subject to any potential conflicts of interests being resolved.

Problems Involving Places

Often one of the larger expenses on the income statement, rent and/or lease payments are a natural place for a buyer to focus on when evaluating the efficiencies to be gained by a merger. It would seem to be an easy issue to resolve: In acquiring this company, we can reduce the staff by *x* percent, which means that we need *x* percent less of square footage in which to work. In addition, the staff has *x* percent more square footage per employee than our company. As a result, total square footage can be reduced by *x* percent, thereby saving $*x*. But very few decisions in a merger or acquisition can be resolved with a simple mathematical equation. There usually are people involved, and with people come emotions and unpredictability. This has to be accounted for when looking at space, just as much as when examining staffing levels.

When examining the space requirements of the combined entity, it is certainly helpful to consider the square footage. The space should be evaluated to determine if the rent is more or less expensive than other company space and if the amount of space is more than is needed. This will go a long way toward helping to cut expenses in order to reach the target return.

However, there must also be human considerations. How long have the employees been in this space? How does the commute compare to where they might be relocated? How much interaction is required between the staff being relocated and staff in a different location? How much reconfiguration of the office and facilities of each company will be required to accommodate additional staff or functions? How much productivity can be expected from these people during the course of the move?

Failure to explore these and other related questions can open up a can of worms. Location is a factor that can effect the overall integration of the buyer by the seller and can lead to significant turnover. It is taken very personally by many employees. Our suggestion is to take steps to maximize your efficiency of space and property but to do so considering the human elements of the changes.

Problems Involving Attitudes and Corporate Culture

The mating dance was fun. The due diligence was outright friendly. The negotiations were cordial. All has gone well. Now, let's get on with the business. And by the way, I think we'll do things our way. After all, we are the buyer.

This is a perfect example of how to ruin months of goodwill with the seller and its employees. It is a perfect example of how to cause problems on the level of corporate culture. Many of the problems associated with mergers and acquisitions are rooted in a lack of sensitivity to the cultures of the combining entities.

There are four keys steps to make sure that such issues don't cloud the success of an otherwise wonderful marriage:

1. Allow cultural differences to play a part when determining the value of the deal.
2. Realize that the cultures of both companies are important.
3. Admit that it is not in either company's interest to maintain both cultures (unless the organizations are going to remain autonomous, in which case the cultural differences may be immaterial to continued performance).
4. Figure out how to combine the two cultures in a way that will prevent the deal from exploding.

If cultural differences are not uncovered during the due diligence process and incorporated into the terms of the deal, there will usually be disappointment in the return on the investment. The primary reason this issue can affect the value of the deal is that cultural differences often spell decreased productivity, which leads to lower revenues and income, and hence the combined entity may be worth less than expected. As a result, it is often wise to place a conservative value on at least the first year's earnings and cash flow. After that, the value should depend on the experience the buyer has obtained as a result of prior acquisitions. If this is the first acquisition and there is no staff with experience in such matters, the buyer would be well served to be conservative in future years as well!

Because of the longevity of the companies that are now seeking to create a single operating entity, the culture of each is usually deeply ingrained. If this were not the case, the companies would probably not be successful and hence not be attractive merger candidates. In many cases, company employees are unaware of the strength of the culture and how it impacts daily activities.

Recognizing that it is not feasible to keep both cultures seems obvious. This would translate into having two different ways to perform each function. This is a clear recipe for chaos and lack of unity, factors that are normally noticed by outsiders even though efforts are made to hide them. The bottom line is that if the two companies don't act as one, the chances of success are greatly minimized. There will be internal problems—low morale, disparate goals, redundancy—and external ones—poor customer service, disenchanted investors, and negative press.

The most difficult part of merging two corporate cultures is to identify the common ground. Believe it or not, this usually exists. Look not at the operational level but at the philosophical level. Once a common primary goal can be agreed upon, and referenced back on many occasions, the true process of merging the cultures can begin. This primary goal must be agreed upon at the top and communicated to all levels. Only then can functional-level details be worked out.

Corporate culture is such a nebulous, personal concept that it can often be difficult to get your arms around it. This makes it even more difficult to plan for and incorporate into any merger planning. But if it is ignored, it is an issue that can linger for years and ultimately contribute to disappointment on many levels, not to mention return on investment!

Benefit and Compensation Plans

With the advent of the Employee Retirement Income Security Act (ERISA), and other legislation concerned with compensation and benefits, managing the merging of benefit and compensation plans has taken on added importance. All of the issues concerned with benefit and compensation plans should be worked out in the course of negotiations. Failure to do so, especially as concerns pension plans, can result in costly surprises that cannot be readily addressed afterwards.

As a result of the elaborate structure of such plans, the primary concern should be the ERISA-covered plans—in particular, defined benefit pension plans. The options available for ERISA-covered pension plans (defined benefit as well as defined contribution) include terminating the existing plan, freezing the benefits accrued up to the acquisition, merging the two companies' plans, maintaining two plans, or converting to an entirely different plan. Each of these options has benefits and pitfalls, but the primary issue is the potential costs. The costs include required contributions, the amount of unfunded liabilities (in the case of defined benefit plans), and cash flow requirements. Only after evaluating the magnitude of these costs can you make an educated decision as to the course to take.

Another issue to consider is the integration of other compensation and benefit components, such as medical, life, and disability insurance; severance policies; and reimbursement of medical and child care expenses. As with ERISA-covered plans, the options available are similar—maintain separate systems, choose one system over the other, or choose a combination of the two systems. The method of integration chosen is often driven by the costs involved, but it should also take into account the overall compensation and benefits philosophy.

Believe it or not, making the above choices is the easy part. The hard part comes with the closing of the transaction and the need to integrate the plans of the two companies. The first step is to set the objectives of the integration. The objectives should cover such factors as the cost, funding, adequacy, and competitive position of the plan.

Once the objectives have been set, the pre-merger plans of both organizations should be reviewed relative to the objectives outlined for the choice made. In addition, the option chosen should be compared to the general marketplace. Finally, the plan should be evaluated by a representative group of employees. Assuming the plan has passed all of the above tests, it is now time to implement. As with most post-closing issues, implementation spells the success or failure of the plan. The key function in a successful implementation of benefit and compensation plans is communication. Without good communication of the plan's objectives and details, implementation will be moderately successful, at best. The importance of benefit and compensation plans at every level of the workplace means that without successful implementation of such plans, no matter how well other aspects of the consolidation may be handled, the situation can spell disaster for employee morale and the ability of the combined entity to work as one.

Corporate Identity

Now that the two companies have become one, it only stands to reason that the merged entity is different from what existed before. Yet this is a point that can often be forgotten when it comes to corporate identity. Since there is essentially a *new* company, it may be important to consider a new corporate identity in the form of the company name and/or logo.

This may seem obvious, but the real issue goes much deeper. A corporate identity defines what makes a corporation unique. The company name and logo are merely manifestations of that identity. Before such issues can be decided, it must be determined what the corporation stands for, where it is going, and how it is different from other corporations. Only then does it make sense to put a name on it and identify an image with it.

There are several aspects of a corporation that go into its identity. These include market share, industry group identification, customer base, employees, and direction. Most, if not all, of these aspects are altered in some way as the result of a merger or acquisition. The key is to identify what changes have occurred and respond to them by shaping the image or identity that is communicated to the public.

Legal Issues

Following the closing of the transaction, there are many legal and administrative tasks that must be accomplished by the acquisition team to complete the transaction. The nature and extent of these tasks will vary, depending on the size and type of the financing method selected by the purchaser. The parties to any acquisition must be careful to ensure that the jubilation of closing does not cause any post-closing matters to be overlooked.

In an *asset acquisition,* these post-closing tasks typically include the following:

- Final verification that all assets acquired are free of liens and encumbrances
- Recording of financing statements and transfer tax returns
- Recording of any assignments of intellectual property with the Library of Congress or Patent and Trademark Office
- Notification of the sale to employees, customers, distributors, and suppliers
- Adjustments to bank accounts and insurance policies

In addition to the above, a *stock acquisition* may also include the following:

- Filing articles of amendment to the corporate charter or articles of merger
- Completion of the transfer of all stock certificates
- Amendments to the corporate bylaws
- Preparation of all appropriate post-closing minutes and resolutions

Such actions require legal counsel familiar with the issues of corporate governance and intellectual property. While the buyer's legal counsel attends to these matters, management can more readily focus on the other aspects of the business combination for which they are better qualified and more effective.

Minimizing the Barriers to Transition

No matter how hard you try and how well you anticipate the issues that need to be addressed, the natural response of most people is to avoid change. As a result, it is important to be aware of the various aspects of change management and address them as well. The primary emotion that will be encountered in dealings with various groups will be *fear*. There will be fear on the part of employees, as relates to such things as job security, workplace location, and reporting structure. But you may also have to deal with fear on the part of customers (the buyer may discontinue a product line) and suppliers (the buyer may already have someone to supply that good).

Communication

The primary tool for dealing with fear, and many of the other emotions that surface during the course of acquisition transition, is communication. If a merger is thought of as the beginning of a marriage, think of the amount of communication that is necessary in the first few weeks and months of such a relationship. As with any relationship, a lack of communication typically means a lack of success.

In a merger, the two keys to effective communication are to determine (1) the importance of the information and (2) who should communicate it. Information should be communicated in the order of its importance. This means that you want to first communicate that information that affects people directly, including changes in:

- The organization, especially who is staying and who is leaving
- Reporting structures
- Job descriptions and responsibilities
- Title, compensation, and benefits
- Job location and operating procedures

As a result of the importance of this information, the person doing the communicating is also important. A trusted person from the seller's side, along with an important person from the buyer's side, works best. This will assist in the transition and add credibility to the process.

The next most important information is the introduction of the new management team and the transition to new managers and employees. It is a bit disconcerting to walk the halls in an organization and not know people. Think of how it feels on the first day of a new job. Well, that's how it feels for all the employees of an acquired company. By making an effort to introduce the key players, people are more comfortable. They can place a name with a face and know who is being referred to in discussions. This can help overall efficiency because employees will be focusing on doing their job rather than wondering who someone is and how that person might affect their career. It also helps in the socialization process among the employees, which in turn contributes to efficiency! This, of course, is more difficult as organizations grow larger. You can, however, introduce those people that are most likely to run into each other.

Finally, communicate the new reporting structure and have individual managers introduce the two sides when there will be day-to-day interaction. If possible, have the prior manager make some kind of handover to the new. Some kind of group meeting or social gathering among the employees of various departments, especially those that interact regularly, can go a long way in making everyone more comfortable with the new faces, functions, and procedures.

Post-Merger Task Force

One of the tools through which communication can be made more effective is a *post-merger task force.* Such an entity should be composed of a representative group from both sides of the transaction and should be formed after the due diligence process. The role of such a group, which needs to be defined and communicated early, is to uncover, evaluate, and resolve post-merger problems.

The importance of effectively communicating the role of the task force cannot be emphasized enough. Failure to do so will limit its effectiveness and call into question the resolve of the new organization. In a very real sense this is the first operating decision to be seen by the seller's employees and thus it will greatly influence the new employees' perception of the acquiring organization.

The composition of the task force has a bearing on its effectiveness and the integrity of the buyer, as viewed by the seller's employees. As a result, the CEO should probably avoid making him or herself a member. An honest assessment of those being considered for the task force will go a long way toward establishing its credibility. If one of the members from the seller's side is an employee who is not respected by the majority of the workforce, people will not take the task force seriously.

The role of the task force is best kept simple. It can serve as a conduit from labor to management to resolve problems that arise during the course of the merger. In this way, a dialogue can be opened and people will get the impression that actions are being taken to address concerns. The task force can also be used to organize the information that needs to be communicated to the new employees. The amount of information to be communicated can be overwhelming, and the way it is communicated can also cause problems. The task force can serve to communicate the issues in order of importance and to address them accurately. This helps prevent the grapevine from disseminating erroneous information. Creating the dialogue and organizing the information serve to help reduce or eliminate the fear discussed earlier.

Once its work is completed, the task force must be dissolved. This is easier said than done, as it is much easier to say when the merger activity begins than to define when it is over. The first sign that the end of the task force's life is near is when all the information deemed to be important in relation to the merger has been disseminated. An additional indication is the amount of information flowing back from the employees to the task force has significantly waned. Nonetheless, it is often helpful to give the task force a set life at its beginning—60 or 90 days—and to evaluate the situation at that time. The final call will come from the CEO, when it is determined that the value of the task force has been expended and it is now time to get to work to realize the true value of the combination.

The importance of a well-planned and smooth post-closing transition cannot be emphasized enough. Without the proper attention to these matters, the value of the transaction may never be realized. This will require assembling a team with proven implementation skills and a desire to see the transaction work. The sheer number of issues that need to be addressed can seem overwhelming at first glance. But the importance of these issues in the success of a business combination cannot be overemphasized. By planning properly, paying attention to the details, and picking the right people for the job, a buyer will gain confidence in its ability to successfully integrate the seller into its operations. This will serve to encourage further growth through mergers and acquisitions.

Post-Merger Integration Key Lessons and Best Practices

Here are some key lessons learned for developing an effective post-closing integration plan:

1. *Pick your poison*. Many deals fail because a strategy for integrating (or not) the two cultures was never clearly defined. Will the seller's culture become dominant? Will the buyer's culture be absorbed by the seller's team and employees? Or will, if feasible, the cultures be allowed to "peacefully co-exist?" Or will it be a hybrid driven by compromise and merit (e.g. they do *that* better, but we do *this* better, so let's find ways to truly combine the best of the best in each area). Buyers should not lose sight of the value of the culture that they are buying, just because their ego or ignorance assumes that *their* culture must be dominant on a post-closing basis.
2. *Align cultural decisions with overall M&A goals and growth strategy*. Employees want to see a *fit* between the post-closing integration decisions made *and* the overall strategy which is driving the transaction. If the CEO of BuyerCo talks about the need to cut costs, but then nobody is fired, then employees are relieved (for now) but confused. If the BuyerCo CEO talks about the need for geographic expansion, but then closes offices and plants, the decisions *do not appear aligned* with the strategy which has been articulated.
3. *Compatibility does not always mean an exact match*. Post-closing executives and consultants will often "force feed" a quest for "sameness" that is unnecessary. Cultures can

be compatible and functional even if they are not an exact mirror image of each other. For example, both could be driven by merit-driven performance and rewards, even if the rewards are not exactly the same. Both could be driven by customer service excellence, even if that manifests itself in very different ways, especially if the two companies are in different types of businesses.

4. *Communicate early and communicate often*. The more that can be done to reduce or eliminate the stress and fear of the typical employee, the better. If the leadership is perceived as playing their cards too close to the vest or being fearful of making the hard decisions, both cultures will erode quickly, having a significant adverse effect on the value of the entity on a post-closing basis.
5. *Reach for the stars, but be realistic about post-closing objectives*. The excitement and optimism expressed during the transaction is wonderful and is energy which should be contagious but post-merger goals should be realistic and attainable. Goals that are neither believable nor achievable will only disappoint the investors, the employees, vendors and customers and reflect poorly on the management team of the recently-integrated company. I am sure that every CEO of BuyerCo believes in her "heart of hearts" that getting this deal done will increase the value of the company by tenfold or even twentyfold down the road—but is that realistic in the near-term? And if no, is it realistic to have employees believe that a tenfold increase in value in the near-term is the actual goal, only to be disappointed when it is nowhere even close?
6. *Meaningful systems need to be in place to set, measure and adjust the goals of the transaction.* A clear set of 12/24/36 month "goals and objectives" to be achieved as a result of *this* transaction should be articulated as part of the post-integration plans. Yes, some portion of the results will be intangible and difficult to measure (e.g., our customers just "feel better" about us now), but even goodwill should manifest itself in higher customer loyalty and increases in sales *that can be easily measured*. Repeat sales, upsales, renewals to commitments, lower turnover rates *can* all be measured and closely monitored.

7. *Treat both sets of customers as gold*. At the end of the day, you can write up all of the press releases in the world, but if customers are not convinced that this M&A deal is *good for them*, then the objectives of the deal will not be met. Take the time to *explain* the post-closing *value proposition* to both sets of customers. If the deal will result in lower costs or better pricing, then tell them and show them how and why. If the deal will result in higher prices but better service and support, then be ready to justify and explain the value of the trade-off. If the deal will result in broader and better product lines or service offerings, then have your cross-selling strategies and tools ready to go. Remember that your competitors will try to attack the deal and market to your customers if they see the opportunity, and you need to be ready to push back.
8. *Don't hide the poop under the rug*. In an attempt to paint a rosy post-closing picture, buyers and sellers may choose to defer problems and challenges identified pre-closing to some undefined time period after closing. This "we'll get to it later" approach is a time bomb just waiting to explode and the clean-up will not be pretty. The failure to either unearth lurking problems, or worse, the intentional decision to ignore them, is a recipe for disaster. Problems in the area of human resources, environmental liabilities, lack of clear ownership in intellectual property, poorly-drafted earn-outs, unpaid taxes, unclear major customer commitments, underfunded pension plans, etc. are not problems that will go away with the waiving of a post-closing magic wand. The parties may feel pressure from the marketplace or from their advisors or from their sources of capital to "just go ahead and get this deal closed and we'll figure out these problems later," which is bad advice and a bad strategy. The delays in closing that solving these problems would create are viewed as the evil, instead of the problems themselves. Yes, momentum is important and there may be minor problems which are not worth the derailing of a transaction, but material issues and challenges *must* be resolved prior to closing.

9. *Do your due diligence the right way the first time*. Improper or hasty due diligence often results in post-merger integration plans going awry. Key issues that *should* have been discovered and dealt with *pre-closing* wind up to be a source of tension and dispute post-closing because due diligence was piecemeal or improperly staffed. Due diligence staffing means the right *number* of people with the right skill sets who are prepared to invest the time and effort to ask the right questions and challenge the answers that don't make sense. Subject matter experts should be brought in when necessary, especially for high-tech or biotech/life science transactions. For example, if you are buying a government contractor and one of the key assets is a long-term supply contract with the Department of Defense for providing advanced technology and support, then those contracts had *better* be reviewed by someone more senior and more knowledgeable than a second-year general corporate practice associate of your local law firm.

Alternatives to Mergers and Acquisitions

You will recall from Chapter 1 that we established that mergers and acquisitions, at least from the buyer's perspective, was an inorganic growth strategy. The buyer's Acquisition Plan identifies one or more transactions which will enhance market share, create economies of scale, penetrate new geographic and categorical markets and provide a basis for raising additional capital. Hopefully at this point you feel comfortable with the logistics, challenges, and mechanics of this strategy as well as the legal, financial and strategic aspects of mergers and acquisitions.

However, there is a wide variety of alternative strategies that focus on the building of *external* relationships, which achieve these same objectives. The primary differences among these strategies is the *degree of control* which results between the parties after the consummation of the relationship. If you take a look at Exhibit 13-1, you will see that mergers and acquisitions appears to the far left as being a growth strategy which results in the strongest level of control, since it doesn't get much stronger than 100 percent ownership! As you move your way to the right, you will see strategies such as joint ventures, franchising, licensing, strategic alliances, and distributorships. These are alternatives to mergers and acquisitions in that all of these strategies and relationships envision a dynamic and syn-

Exhibit 13-1. Growth strategy horizon.

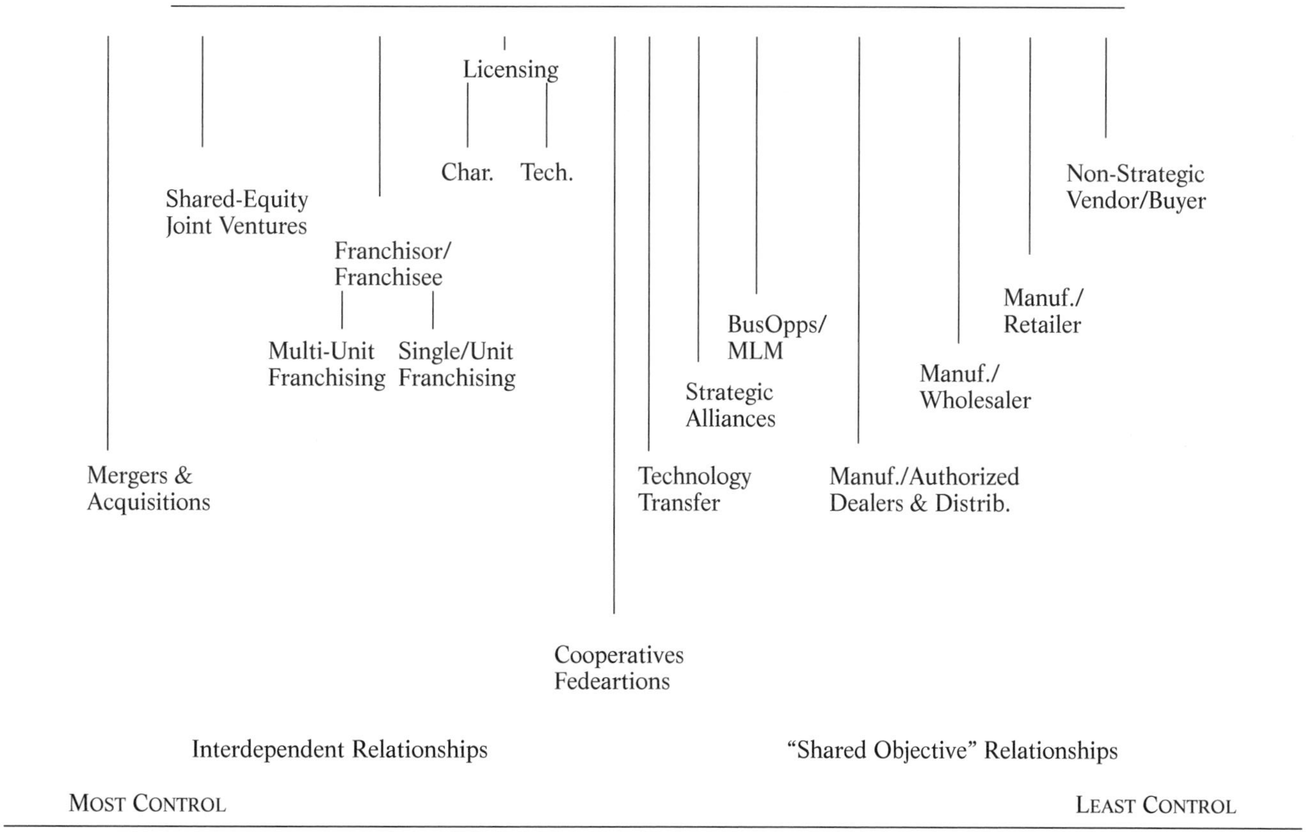

Licensing

Char.

Tech.

Shared-Equity
Joint Ventures

Non-Strategic
Vendor/Buyer

Franchisor/
Franchisee

Manuf./
Retailer

BusOpps/
MLM

Multi-Unit
Franchising

Single/Unit
Franchising

Manuf./
Wholesaler

Strategic
Alliances

Mergers &
Acquisitions

Technology
Transfer

Manuf./Authorized
Dealers & Distrib.

Cooperatives
Fedeartions

Interdependent Relationships

"Shared Objective" Relationships

MOST CONTROL

LEAST CONTROL

ergistic working relationship, but one that falls short of a metamorphosis. In some cases, these strategies and relationships are designed to be long-term and truly independent, and in other cases the relationships are slightly more non-committal and merely have "shared objectives." Let's take a look at a few of these alternatives.

Growth Strategy Alternative #1: Joint Ventures

Another strategic alternative to an acquisition which is available to today's small and growing companies is a legal structure known as a "joint venture." Joint ventures are typically structured as a partnership or as a newly formed, co-owned corporation where two or more parties are brought together to achieve a series of strategic and financial objectives on a short-term or a long-term basis. Emerging growth and middle-market companies that want to explore this strategy should give careful thought to the type of partner they are looking for and what resources they will be contributing to the newly formed entity. Like the raising of a child, each parent will be making their respective contribution of skills, abilities and resources.

Joint ventures, strategic partnering, cross-licensing, and technology transfer agreements are all strategies designed to obtain one or more of the following: (1) direct capital infusion in exchange for equity and/or intellectual property or distribution rights; (2) a "capital substitute" where the resources which would otherwise be obtained with the capital are obtained through joint venturing; or (3) a shift of the burden and cost of development (through licensing) in exchange for a potentially more limited upside.

Embarking on a search for a joint venture partner is a bit like the search for a spouse. Care should be taken to truly conduct a thorough review of prospective candidates and extensive due diligence should be done on the final few which are being considered. Develop a list of key objectives and goals to be achieved by the joint venture or licensing relationship and compare this list with those of your final candidates. Take the time to understand the corporate culture and decision making process within each company. Consider some of the following issues: (1) How does this fit with your own processes? (2) What about each prospective partner's previous experiences and track record with other joint venture relationships? (3) Why did these previous relationships succeed or fail?

In many cases, smaller companies looking for joint venture partners wind up selecting a much larger Goliath which offers a wide range of financial and non-financial resources which will allow the smaller company to achieve its growth plans. The motivating factor under these circumstances for the larger company is to get access and distribution rights to new technologies, products and services. In turn, the larger company offers access to pools of capital, research and development, personnel, distribution channels and general contacts that the small company desperately needs.

But proceed carefully. Be sensitive to the politics, red-tape and different management practices that may be in place at a larger company that will be foreign to many smaller firms. Try to distinguish between that which is being promised and that which will actually be delivered. If the primary motivating force for the small firm is really only capital, then consider whether alternative (and perhaps less costly) sources of money have been thoroughly explored. Ideally, the larger joint venture partner will offer a lot more than money. If the primary motivating force is access to technical personnel, then consider whether it might be a better decision to purchase these resources separately rather than entering into a partnership in which you give up a certain measure of control. Also, consider whether strategic relationships or extended payment terms with vendors and consultants can be arranged in lieu of the joint venture.

Why Consider a Joint Venture or Strategic Alliance?

- Develop a new market (domestic/international)
- Develop a new product
- Develop/share technology
- Combine complementary technology
- Pool resources to develop a production/distribution facility
- Acquire capital
- Execute a government contract
- Access a distribution network or sales/marketing capability

For example, suppose that an emerging company business named ProductCorp has the patents to protect the technology necessary to produce a wide range of new consumer products. They can commence a search for a "capital-rich" partner who will invest money into the construction of a manufacturing facility to be owned and operated by the newly-established entity. As an alternative, ProductCorp could enter into a joint venture with a larger competitor which already has the manufacturing capability to produce the products.

Each strategy has its respective advantages and disadvantages. The capital-rich joint venture partner brings the necessary financial resources to achieve company objectives, but cannot contribute experience in the industry. On the other hand, the larger competitor may offer certain operational and distribution synergies and economies of scale, but may seek greater control over ProductCorp's management decisions.

Understanding the Difference Between Joint Ventures and Strategic Alliances

	Joint Ventures	*Strategic Alliances*
Term	Usually medium- to long-term	Short-term
Strategic Objective	Often serves as the precursor to a merger	More flexible and non-committal
Legal Agreements and Structure	Actual legal entity formed	Contractually driven
Extent of Commitment	Shared equity	Shared objectives
Capital and Resources	Each party makes a capital contribution of cash or intangible assets	No specific capital contributions (may be shared budgeting on even cross-investment)

Tax Ramifications	Be on the lookout for double taxation unless pass-through entities utilized	No direct tax ramifications

Unlike franchising, distributorships, and licensing—which are almost always vertical in nature—joint ventures are structured at *either* horizontal or vertical levels of distribution. At the horizontal level, the joint venture is almost an alternative to a merger, in which two companies operating at the same level in the distribution channel join together (either by means of a partnership-type agreement or by joint ownership of a specially-created corporation) to achieve certain synergies or operating efficiencies. Consider the following key strategic issues before and during joint venture or strategic alliance negotiations:

- Exactly what types of tangible and intangible assets will be contributed to the joint venture by each party? Who will have ownership rights in the property contributed during the term of the joint venture and thereafter? Who will own property developed as a result of joint development efforts?
- What covenants of nondisclosure or noncompetition will be expected of each joint venturer during the term of the agreement and thereafter?
- What timetables or performance quotas for completion of the projects contemplated by the joint venture will be included in the agreement? What are the rights and remedies of each party if these performance standards are not met?
- How will issues of management and control be addressed in the agreement? What will be the respective voting rights of each party? What are the procedures in the event of a major disagreement or deadlock? What is the fallback plan?

Once all of the preliminary issues have been discussed by the joint venturer, a formal joint venture agreement or corporate shareholders' agreement should be prepared with the assistance of counsel. The precise terms of the agreement between the joint venturer and the company will naturally depend on the specific objectives of the parties. At a minimum, however, the following topics should be addressed in as much detail as possible:

- *Nature, Purpose and Trade Name for the Joint Venture.* The legal nature of the parties' relationship should be stated along with a clean statement of purpose to prevent future disputes. If a new trade name is established for the venture, provisions should be made as to the use of the name and any other trade or service marks should the project be terminated.
- *Status of the Respective Joint Venturers.* Clearly indicate whether each party is a partner, shareholder, agent, independent contractor, or any combination thereof.
- *Representations and Warranties of Each Joint Venturer.* Standard representations and warranties will include obligations of due care and due diligence as well as mutual covenants governing confidentiality and anti-competition restrictions.
- *Capital and Property Contributions of Each Joint Venturer.* A clear schedule should be established of all contributions whether in the form of cash, shares, real estate, or intellectual property. Detailed descriptions will be particularly important if the distribution of profits and losses are to be based on overall contribution. The specifics of allocation and distribution of profits and losses among the venturers should also be clearly defined.
- *Management, Control, and Voting Rights of Each Joint Venturer.* If the proposed venture envisions joint management, it will be necessary to specifically address the keeping of books, records and bank accounts, the nature and frequency of inspections and audits, insurance and cross-indemnification obligations, as well as responsibility for administrative and overhead expenses.
- *Rights in Joint Venture Property.* Each party must be mindful of intellectual property rights and the issues of ownership use and licensing entitlements should clearly be addressed not only for the venturers' presently existing property rights, but also for future use of rights (or products or services) developed in the name of the venture itself.

• *Default, Dissolution and Termination of the Joint Venture*. The obligations of the venturers and the distribution of assets should be clearly defined along with procedures in the event of bankruptcy and grounds for default.

Growth Strategy Alternative #2: Franchising

Over the last two decades, franchising has emerged as a popular expansion strategy for a variety of product and service companies, especially for those smaller businesses which cannot afford to finance internal growth. Recent International Franchise Association (IFA) statistics demonstrate that retail sales from franchised outlets comprise nearly 53 percent of all retail sales in the United States, estimated at over $11 trillion and employing over 11 million people in 2004. Notwithstanding these impressive figures, franchising as a method of marketing and distributing products and services is really only appropriate for certain kinds of companies. Despite the favorable media attention which franchising has received over the past few years, this strategy is not for everyone. This is because there is a host of legal and business prerequisites that must be satisfied before any company can seriously consider franchising as a method for rapid expansion.

Many companies prematurely select franchising as a growth alternative and then haphazardly assemble and launch the franchising program. Other companies are urged to franchise by unqualified consultants or advisors that may be more interested in professional fees than in the long-term success of the franchising program. This has caused financial distress and failure at both the growing company and franchisee level, usually resulting in litigation. Current and future members of the franchising community must be urged to take a responsible view towards the creation and development of their franchising programs.

Reasons for Franchising

There is a wide variety of reasons cited by successful growing companies as to why franchising has been selected as a method of growth and distribution. These reasons include:

- Obtain operating efficiencies and economies of scale.
- Achieve more rapid market penetration at a lower capital cost.
- Reach the targeted consumer more effectively through cooperative advertising and promotion.
- Sell products and services to a dedicated distributor network.
- Replace the need for internal personnel with motivated owner/operators.
- Shift the primary responsibility for site selection, employee training and personnel management, local advertising and other administrative concerns to the franchisee, licensee or joint venture partner with the guidance or assistance of the growing company.

In the typical franchising relationship, the franchisee shares the risk of expanding the market share of the growing company by committing its capital and resources to the development of satellite locations modeled after the proprietary business format of the growing company. The risk of business failure of the growing company is further reduced by the improvement in competitive position, reduced vulnerability to cyclical fluctuations, the existence of a captive market for the growing company's proprietary products and services (due to the network of franchisees) and the reduced administrative and overhead costs enjoyed by a growing company.

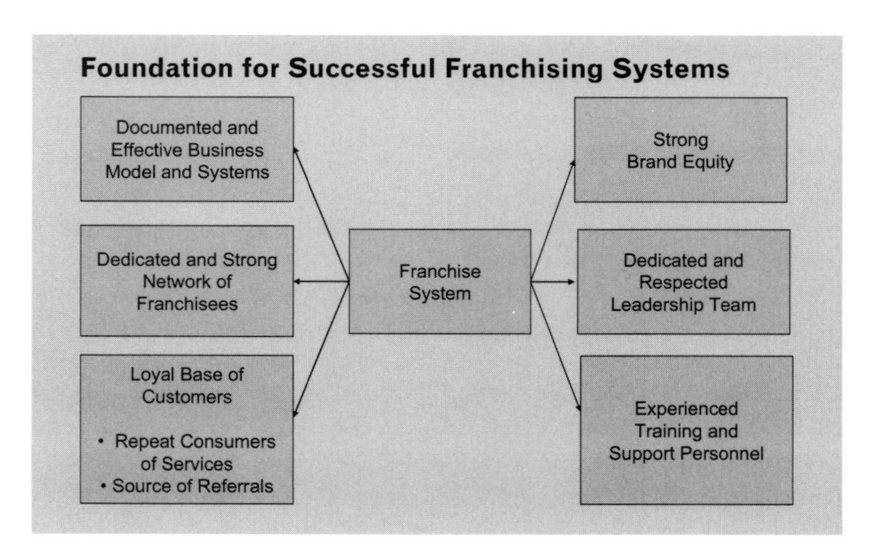

The Foundation for Franchising

Responsible franchising is the *only* way that growing companies and franchisees will be able to harmoniously co-exist in the 21st century. Responsible franchising means that there must be a secure foundation from which the franchising program is launched. Any company considering franchising as a method of growth and distribution, or any individual considering franchising as a method of getting into business, must understand the components of this foundation. The key components of this foundation are as follows:

- A *proven prototype location* (or chain of stores), which will serve as a basis for the franchising program. The store or stores must have been tested, refined and operated successfully and be consistently profitable. The success of the prototype should not be too dependent on the physical presence or specific expertise of the founders of the system.
- A *strong management team* made up of internal officers and directors (as well as qualified consultants) who understand both the particular industry in which the company operates as well as the legal and business aspects of franchising as a method of expansion.
- *Sufficient capitalization* to launch and sustain the franchising program to ensure that capital is available for the growing company to provide both initial as well as ongoing support and assistance to franchisees. A lack of a well-prepared business plan and adequate capital structure is often the principal cause of demise of many early-stage franchisors.
- A *distinctive and protected trade identity* which includes federal and state registered trademarks as well as a uniform trade appearance, signage, slogans, trade dress and overall image.
- *Proprietary and proven methods of operation and management* which can be reduced to writing in a comprehensive operations manual, not be too easily duplicated by competitors, be able to maintain its value to the franchisees over an extended period of time and be enforced through clearly drafted and objective quality control standards.
- *Comprehensive training program* for franchisees—both at the company's headquarters and on-site at the franchisee's proposed location at the outset of the relationship and on an ongoing basis.

• *Field support staff* who are skilled trainers and communicators who must be available to visit, inspect and periodically assist franchisees, as well as monitor quality control standards.

• A set of comprehensive *legal documents* that reflect the company's business strategies and operating policies. Offering documents must be prepared in accordance with applicable federal and state disclosure laws and franchise agreements should strike a delicate balance between the rights and obligations of growing company and franchisee.

• A demonstrated *market demand* for the products and services developed by the growing company that will be distributed through the franchisees. The growing company's products and services should meet certain minimum quality standards, not be subject to rapid shifts in consumer preferences (e.g., fads) and be proprietary in nature. Market research and analysis should be sensitive to trends in the economy and specific industry, the plans of direct and indirect competitors and shifts in consumer preferences.

• A set of carefully developed uniform *site selection criteria and architectural standards* that can be readily and affordably secured in today's competitive real estate market.

• *A genuine understanding of the competition* (both direct and indirect) that the growing company will face in marketing and selling franchises to prospective franchisees as well as that franchisee will face when marketing products and services.

• *Relationships with suppliers,* lenders, real estate, developers, and related key resources as part of the operations manual and system.

• Each growing company should develop a *franchisee profile and screening system* in order to identify the minimum financial qualifications, business acumen and understanding of the industry that will be required to be a successful franchisee.

• An effective system of *reporting and recordkeeping* to maintain the performance of the franchisees and ensure that royalties are reported accurately and paid promptly.

• *Research and development* capabilities for the introduction of new products and services on an ongoing basis to consumers through the franchised network.

• A *communication system* that facilitates a continuing and open dialogue with the franchisees, and as a result reduces the chances for conflict and litigation with the franchise network.

• National, regional and local *advertising, marketing, and public relations programs* designed to recruit prospective franchisees as well as consumers to the sites operated by franchisees.

Regulatory Issues

The offer and sale of a franchise is regulated at both the federal and state level. At the federal level, the Federal Trade Commission (FTC) in 1979 adopted its trade regulation rule 436 (the "FTC Rule") which specifies the minimum amount of disclosure that must be made to a prospective franchisee in any of the fifty states. In addition to the FTC Rule, over a dozen states have adopted their own rules and regulations for the offer and sale of franchises within their borders. Known as the "registration states," these states generally follow a more detailed disclosure format, known as the Uniform Franchise Offering Circular (UFOC).

Each of the registration states have slightly different procedures and requirements for the approval of a growing company prior to offers and sales being authorized. In all cases, however, the package of disclosure documents is assembled, consisting of a UFOC, franchise agreement, supplemental agreements, financial statements, franchise roster, an acknowledgement of receipt form and the special disclosures which are required by each state, such as corporation verification statements, salesperson disclosure forms and consent to service of process documents. The specific requirements of each state should be checked carefully by the growing company and its counsel.

Structuring and Preparing Franchise Agreements

The franchise agreement is the principal document that sets forth the binding rights and obligations of each party to the franchise relationship. The franchise agreement contains the various provisions which will be binding on the parties for the life of their relationship and therefore must maintain a delicate balance of power. On one hand, the franchisor must maintain enough control in the franchise agreement to enforce uniformity and consistency throughout the system, yet at the same time be flexible enough to anticipate changes in the marketplace, modifications to the franchise system and to meet the special considerations or demands caused by the franchisee's local market conditions.

The franchise agreement can and should reflect the business philosophy of the franchisor and set the tenor of the relationship. If well drafted, it will reflect the culmination of literally thousands of business decisions and hundreds of hours of market research and testing. The length, term and complexity will (and should) vary from franchisor to franchisor and from industry to industry. Many start-up franchisors make the critical mistake of "borrowing" terms of a competitor's franchise agreement. Such a practice can be detrimental to the franchisor and the franchisee since the agreement will not accurately reflect the actual dynamics of the relationship. Early-stage franchisors should resist the temptation to copy from a competitor or to accept the "standard form and boilerplate" from an inexperienced attorney or consultant. The relationship between the franchisor and franchisee is far too complex to accept such compromise in the preparation of such a critical document.

Regardless of the size, stage of growth, industry dynamics, or specific trends in the marketplace, all basic franchise agreements should address the following key topics:

- *Recitals.* The recitals or "introduction to the purpose of the agreement" essentially set the stage for the discussion of the contractual relationship. This section provides the background information regarding the development and ownership of the proprietary rights of the franchisor which are being licensed to the franchisee. The recitals should always contain at least one provision specifying the obligation of the franchisee to operate the business format in strict conformity with the operations manual and quality control standards provided by the franchisor.

- *Grant, Term, and Renewal.* The typical initial section of the franchise agreement is the grant of a franchise for a specified term. The length of the term is influenced by a number of factors including: market conditions; the franchisor's need to periodically change certain material terms of the agreement; cost of the franchise and franchisee's expectations in relation to start-up costs; length of related agreements necessary to the franchisee's operations such as leases and bank loans; and anticipated consumer demand for the franchised goods and services. The renewal rights granted to a franchisee, if included at all, will usually be conditioned upon the franchisee being in good standing (e.g., no material defaults by franchisee) under the agreement. Other issues that must be addressed in any provision regarding renewal include renewal fees, obligations to execute the "then-current" form of the franchise agreement, and any obligations of the franchisee to upgrade its facilities to the "latest" standards and design. The franchisor's right to relocate the franchisee, adjust the size of any exclusive territory granted, or change the fee structure should also be addressed.

• *Territory*. The size of the geographic area granted to the franchisee by the franchisor must be specifically discussed in conjunction with what exclusive rights, if any, will be granted to the franchisee with respect to this territory. These provisions address whether the size of the territory is a specific radius, city or county and whether the franchisor will have a right to either operate company-owned locations and/or grant additional franchises within the territory. After conducting market research, some franchisors will designate a specific territory that could be successful without market oversaturation, and then will sell that exact number of franchises, without regard to specific location selected within the geographic area. Any rights of first refusal for additional locations, advertising restrictions, performance quotas relating to territory, and policies of the franchisor with regard to territory are addressed in this part of the agreement.

• *Site Selection*. The responsibility for finding the specific site for the operation of the franchised business will rest either with the franchisor or franchisee. If the franchisee is free to choose its own site, then the franchise agreement will usually provide that the decision is subject to the approval of the franchisor. Some franchisors provide significant assistance in site selection in terms of marketing and demographic studies, lease negotiations and securing local permits and licenses, especially if a "turn-key" franchise is offered. Site selection, however, can be the most difficult aspect of being a successful franchisee, and as a result, most franchisors are reluctant to take on full responsibility for this task contractually. For additional protection and control, some franchisors will insist on becoming the landlord to the franchisee through a mandatory sublease arrangement once an acceptable site has been selected. A somewhat less burdensome method of securing similar protection is to provide for an automatic assignment of the lease to the franchisor upon termination of the franchise.

• *Services to Be Provided by the Franchisor.* The franchise agreement should clearly delineate which products and services will be provided to the franchisee by the franchisor or its affiliates, both in terms of the initial establishment of the franchised business ("pre-opening obligations") and any continuing assistance or support services provided throughout the term of the relationship ("post-opening services"). The pre-opening obligations will generally include a trade secret and copyright license for the use of the confidential operations manual, recruitment and training of personnel, standard accounting and bookkeeping systems, inventory and equipment specifications and volume discounts, standard construction, building and interior design plans, and grand opening promotion and advertising assistance. The quality and extent of the training program is clearly the most crucial pre-opening service provided by the franchisor, and should include classroom as well as on-site instruction. Post-opening services provided to the franchisee on a continuing basis generally include field support and troubleshooting, research and development for new products and services, development of national advertising and promotional campaigns and the arrangement of group purchasing programs and volume discounts.

• *Franchise, Royalty, and Related Fees Payable to the Franchisor: Reporting.* The franchise agreement should clearly set forth the nature and amount of fees that will be payable to the franchisor by the franchisee, both initially and on a continuing basis. The *initial franchise fee* is usually a non-refundable lump sum payment due upon execution of the franchise agreement. Essentially this fee is compensation for the grant of the franchise, the trademark and trade secret license, pre-opening training and assistance, and the initial opening supply of materials, if any, to be provided by the franchisor to the franchisee. A second category of fees is the *contin-*

uing fee, usually in the form of a specific royalty on gross sales. This percentage can be fixed or be based on a sliding scale for different ranges of sales achieved at a given location. Often minimum royalty payment will be required, regardless of the franchisee's actual performance. These fees should be payable either weekly or monthly and submitted to the franchisor together with some standardized reporting form for internal control and monitoring purposes. A weekly or monthly payment schedule will generally allow the franchisee to budget for this payment from a cash flow perspective, as well as provide the franchisor with an early warning system if there is a problem, and to react before the past due royalties accrue to a virtually uncollectible sum.

The third category of recurring fees is usually in the form of a *national cooperative advertising and promotion fund*. The promotional fund may be managed by the franchisor, an independent advertising agency or even a franchisee association. Either way, the franchisor must build a certain amount of control into the franchise agreement over the fund in order to protect the company's trademarks and ensure consistency in marketing efforts. Other categories of fees payable to the franchisor may include the sale of proprietary goods and services to the franchisee, consulting fees, audit and inspection fees, lease management fees (where franchisor is to serve as sublessor) and renewal or transfer fees. The obligations of the franchisee to provide periodic weekly, monthly, quarterly and annual financial and sales reports to the franchisor should also be addressed in the franchise agreement.

Quality Control. A well-drafted franchise agreement will always include a variety of provisions designed to ensure quality control and consistency throughout the franchise system. Such provisions often take the form of restrictions on the franchisee's sources of products, ingredients, supplies, and materials, as well as strict guidelines and specifications for operating procedures. These operating procedures will usually specify standards of service, trade dress and uniform requirements, condition and appearance of the facility, hours of business, minimum insurance requirements, guidelines for trademark usage, advertising and promotional materials, accounting systems and credit practices. Any restrictions on the ability of the franchisee to buy goods and services or requirements to purchase from a specific source should be carefully drafted within the perimeters of applicable antitrust laws. If the franchisor is to serve as the sole supplier or manufacturer of one or more products to be used by the franchisee in the day-to-day operation of the business, then such exclusivity must be justified by a product which is truly proprietary or unique, such as the eleven special herbs and spices which have been protected for many decades by KFC.

• *Insurance, Recordkeeping and Other Related Obligations of the Franchisee.* The minimum amounts and types of insurance which must be carried by the franchisee in connection with its operation of the franchised businesses should also be discussed. Typically the franchisor is named as an additional insured under these policies. Other related obligations of the franchisee which must be set forth in the franchise agreement include the obligation to:

- Keep proper financial records (which must be made available for inspection by the franchisor upon request).
- Maintain and enforce quality control standards with its employees and vendors.
- Comply with all applicable employment laws, health and safety standards and related local ordinances.
- Upgrade and maintain the franchisee's facilities and equipment.
- Continue to promote the products and services of the franchisor.
- Reasonably process requests by patrons for franchising information.
- Refrain from producing goods and services which do not meet the franchisor's quality control specifications or which may be unapproved for offer at the franchisee's premises (such as video games at a fast food restaurant or X-rated material at a bookstore).
- Not to solicit customers outside its designated territory.
- Personally participate in the day-to-day operation of the franchised business (required by many but not all franchisors).
- Refrain generally from any activity which may reflect adversely on the reputation of the franchise system.

• *Protection of Intellectual Property and Covenants Against Competition.* The franchise agreement should always contain a separate section on the obligations of the franchisee and its employees to protect the trademarks and trade secrets being licensed against misuse or disclosure. The franchisor should provide for a clause which clearly sets forth that the trademarks and trade names being licensed are the exclusive property of the franchisor and that any goodwill established is to inure to the sole benefit of the franchisor. It should also be made clear that the confidential operations manual is "on loan" to the franchisee under a limited use license, and that the franchisee or its agents are prohibited from the unauthorized use of the trade secrets both during and after the term of the agreement. To the extent that such provisions are enforceable in local jurisdictions, the franchise agreement should contain covenants against competition by a franchisee—both during the term of the agreement and following termination or cancellation.

- *Termination of the Franchise Agreement.* One of the most important sections is the section discussing how a franchisee may lose its rights to operate the franchised business. The various "events of default" should be carefully defined and tailored to meet the needs of the specific type of business being franchised. Grounds for termination can range anywhere from the bankruptcy of a franchisee to failure to meet specified performance quotas or strictly abide by quality control standards. Certain types of defaults will be grounds for immediate termination, while other types of default will provide the franchisee with an opportunity to fix its mistakes within a certain time period prior to termination. This section should address the procedures under which the franchisor will provide notice to the franchisee of the default(s) and clearly explain how much time it will have to rectify the problem, as well as the alternative actions that the franchisor may pursue to enforce its rights to terminate the franchise agreement. Such clauses must be drafted in light of certain state regulations which limit franchise terminations to "good cause" and have minimum procedural requirements that must be followed. The obligations of the franchisee upon default and notice of termination must also be clearly spelled out, such as the duty to return all copies of the operations manuals, pay all past due royalty fees and immediately cease the use of the franchisor's trademarks.

- *Miscellaneous Provisions.* As with any well-prepared business agreement, the franchise agreement should include a notice provision, a governing law clause, severability provisions, an integration clause and a provision discussing the relationship of the parties. Some franchisors may want to add an arbitration clause, a "hold harmless" and indemnification provision, a reservation of the right to injunctions and other forms of equitable relief, specific representations and warranties of the franchisee, attorney's fees for the prevailing party in the event of dispute and even a contractual provision acknowledging that the franchisee has reviewed the agreement with counsel and has conducted an independent investigation of the franchise and is not relying on any representations other than those expressly set forth in the agreement.

Growth Strategy Alternative #3: Technology and Merchandise Licensing

Licensing is a contractual method of developing and exploiting intellectual property by transferring rights of use to third parties *without* the transfer of ownership. Virtually any proprietary product or service may be the subject of a license agreement, ranging from the licensing of the Mickey Mouse character by Walt Disney Studios in the 1930s to modern day licensing of computer software and high technology. From a legal perspective, licensing involves complex issues of contract, tax, antitrust, international, tort and intellectual property law. From a business perspective, licensing involves a weighing of the economic and strategic advantages of licensing against other methods of bringing the product or service to the marketplace, such as direct sales, distributorships or franchises.

Many of the *benefits* of licensing to be enjoyed by a growing company closely parallel the advantages of franchising, namely to:

- Spread the risk and cost of development and distribution.
- Achieve more rapid market penetration.
- Earn initial license fees and ongoing royalty income.
- Enhance consumer loyalty and goodwill.
- Preserve the capital that would otherwise be required for internal growth and expansion.
- Test new applications for existing and proven technology.

- Avoid or settle litigation regarding a dispute over ownership of the technology.

The *disadvantages* of licensing are also similar in nature to the risks inherent in franchising, such as:

- A somewhat diminished ability to enforce quality control standards and specifications
- A greater risk of another party infringing upon the licensor's intellectual property
- A dependence on the skills, abilities and resources of the licensee as a source of revenue
- Difficulty in recruiting, motivating, and retaining qualified and competent licensees
- The risk that the licensor's entire reputation and goodwill may be damaged or destroyed by the act or omission of a single licensee
- The administrative burden of monitoring and supporting the operations of the network of licensees

Failure to consider all of the costs and benefits of licensing could easily result in a regretful strategic decision or being stuck with the terms of an unprofitable license agreement due to either an underestimation of the licensee's need for technical assistance and support or an overestimation of the market demand for the licensor's products and services. In order to avoid such problems, a certain amount of due diligence should be conducted by the licensor prior to engaging in any serious negotiations with a prospective licensee. This preliminary investigation will generally include market research, legal steps to fully protect intellectual property, and an internal financial analysis of the technology with respect to pricing, profit margins, and costs of production and distribution. It will also include a more specific analysis of the prospective licensee with respect to its financial strength, research and manufacturing capabilities, and reputation in the industry. Once the decision to enter into more formal negotiations has been made, the terms and conditions of the license agreement should be discussed. Naturally, these provisions will vary, depending on whether the license is for merchandising an entertainment property, exploiting a given technology or distributing a particular product to an original equipment manufacturer or value added reseller.

There are two principal types of licensing: (a) *Technology Licensing,* where the strategy is to find a licensee for exploitation of industrial and technological developments; and (b) *Merchandise and Character Licensing,* where the strategy is to license a recognized trademark or copyright to a manufacturer of consumer goods in markets not currently served by the licensor.

Technology Licensing

The principal purpose behind technology transfer and licensing agreements is to make a marriage between the technology proprietor, as licensor, and the organization that possesses the resources to properly develop and market the technology, as licensee. This marriage is made between companies and inventors of all shapes and sizes, but is often in the context of an entrepreneur that has the technology but lacks the resources to adequately penetrate the marketplace, as licensor, and the larger company, which has sufficient research and development, production, human resources, and marketing capability to make the best use of the technology.

The industrial and technological revolution has a history of very successful entrepreneurs who have relied on the resources of larger organizations to bring their products to market, such as Chester Carlson (xerography), Edwin Land (Polaroid cameras), Robert Goddard (rockets) and Willis Carrier (air conditioning). As the base for technological development becomes broader, large companies look not only to entrepreneurs and small businesses for new ideas and technologies, but also to each other, foreign countries, universities and federal and state governments to serve as licensors of technology.

In the typical licensing arrangement, the proprietor of intellectual property rights (patents, trade secrets, trademarks and know-how) permits a third party to make use of these rights pursuant to a set of specified conditions and circumstances which are set forth in a license agreement. Licensing agreements can be limited to a very narrow component of the proprietor's intellectual property rights, such as one specific application of a single patent, or be much broader in context, such as in a classic "technology transfer" agreement, where an entire bundle of intellectual property rights are transferred to the licensee in exchange for initial fees and royalties. The classic technology transfer arrangement is actually closer to a "sale" of the intellectual property rights, with a right by the licensor to get the intellectual property back if the licensee fails to meet its obligations under the agreement. An example of this type of transaction might be bundling a proprietary environmental clean-up system together with technical support and training services to a master overseas licensee with reversionary rights in the event of a breach of the agreement or the failure to meet a set of performance standards.

Merchandise and Character Licensing Agreements

The use of commonly recognized trademarks, brand names, sports teams, athletes, universities, television and film characters, musicians, and designers to foster the sales of specific products and services are at the heart of today's merchandise and character licensing environment. Manufacturers and distributors of a wide range of products and services license these words, images, and symbols to market clothing and housewares to toys and posters. Certain brand names and characters have withstood the test of time, while others fall prey to fads, consumer shifts and stiff competition.

The trademark and copyright owners of these properties and character images are motivated to license for a variety of reasons. Aside from the obvious desire to earn royalty fees and profits, many manufacturers view this licensing strategy as a form of merchandising to promote the underlying product or service. The licensing of a trademark for application on a line of clothing helps to establish and reinforce brand awareness at the consumer level. For example, when R.J. Reynolds Tobacco Company licenses a leisure apparel manufacturer to produce a line of Camel wear, the hope is to sell more cigarettes, appeal to the lifestyle of their targeted consumers, maintain consumer awareness *and* enjoy the royalty income from the sale of the clothing line. Similar strategies have been adopted by manufacturers in order to revive a mature brand or failing product. In certain instances, the spin-off product which has been licensed was almost as financially successful as the underlying product which it was intended to promote.

Brand name owners, celebrities, and academic institutions must be very careful not to grant too many licenses too quickly. The financial rewards of a flow of royalty income from hundreds of different manufacturers can be quite seductive, but must be weighed against the possible loss of quality control and dilution of the name, logo, or character. The loyalty of the licensee network is also threatened when too many licenses are granted in closely competing products. Retailers will also become cautious when purchasing licensed goods from a licensee if there is a fear that quality control has suffered or that the popularity of the licensed character, celebrity or image will be short-lived. This may result in smaller orders and an overall unwillingness to carry inventory.

This is especially true in the toy industry where purchasing decisions are being made by (or at least influenced by) the whims of a five-year-old child who may strongly identify with a character image one week and then turn his attention to a totally different character image the next week. It is incumbent on the manufacturers and licensees to develop advertising and media campaigns to hold the consumer's attention for an extended period of time. Only then will the retailer be convinced of the potential longevity of the product line. This will require a balancing of the risks and rewards between licensor and licensee in the character licensing agreement in the areas of compensation to the licensor, advertising expenditures by the licensee, scope of the exclusivity and quality control standards and specifications.

In the merchandise licensing community, the name, logo, symbol or character is typically referred to as the "Property" and the specific product or product line (e.g., the T-shirts, mugs, posters) is referred to as the "Licensed Product." This area of licensing offers opportunities and benefits to both the owners of the Properties and the manufacturers of the Licensed Products. For the owner of the Property, brand recognition, goodwill and royalty income are strengthened and expanded. For the manufacturer of the Licensed Products, there is an opportunity to leverage the goodwill of the Property to improve sales of the Licensed Products. The manufacturer has an opportunity to "hit the ground running" in the sale of merchandise by gaining access to and use of an already established brand name or character image.

Naturally, each party should conduct due diligence on the other.

From the perspective of the owner of the Property, the manufacturer of the Licensed Product should demonstrate an ability to meet and maintain quality control standards, possess financial stability and offer an aggressive and well-planned marketing and promotional strategy. From the perspective of the manufacturer of the Licensed Property, the owner of the Property should display a certain level of integrity and commitment to quality, disclose its future plans for the promotion of the Property and be willing to participate and assist in the overall marketing of the Licensed Products.

For example, if a star basketball player were to be unwilling to appear for promotional events designed to sell his own specially-licensed line of basketball shoes, this would present a major problem and is likely to lead to a premature termination of the licensing relationship. As a general rule, any well-drafted license agreement should address the following topics:

- *Scope of the Grant.* The exact scope and subject matter of the license must be initially addressed and carefully defined in the license agreement. Any restrictions on the geographic scope, rights of use, permissible channels of trade, restrictions on sublicensing, limitations on assignability, or exclusion of improvements to the technology covered by the agreement should be clearly set forth in this section.

- *Term and Renewal.* The commencement date, duration, renewals and extensions, conditions to renewal, procedures for providing notice of intent to renew, grounds for termination, obligations upon termination and licensor's reversionary rights in the technology should all be included in this section.

- *Performance Standards and Quotas.* To the extent that the licensor's consideration will be dependent on royalty income which will be calculated from the licensee's gross or net revenues, the licensor may want to impose certain minimum levels of performance in terms of sales, advertising and promotional expenditures and human resources to be devoted to the exploitation of the technology. Naturally, the licensee will argue for a "best efforts" provision that is free from performance standards and quotas. In such cases, the licensor may want to insist on a minimum royalty level that will be paid regardless of the licensee's actual performance.

• *Payments to the Licensor.* Virtually every type of license agreement will include some form of initial payment and ongoing royalty to the licensor. Royalty formulae vary widely, however, and may be based upon gross sales, net sales, net profits, fixed sum per product sold or a minimum payment to be made to the licensor over a given period of time) or may include a sliding scale in order to provide some incentive to the licensee as a reward for performance.

• *Quality Control Assurance and Protection.* Quality control standards and specifications for the production, marketing and distribution of the products and services covered by the license must be set forth by the licensor. In addition, procedures should be included in the agreement which allow the licensor an opportunity to *enforce* these standards and specifications, such as a right to inspect the licensee's premises, a right to review, approve or reject samples produced by the licensee and a right to review and approve any packaging, labeling or advertising materials to be used in connection with the exploitation of the products and services that are within the scope of the license.

• *Insurance and Indemnification.* The licensor should take all necessary and reasonable steps to ensure that the licensee has an obligation to protect and indemnify the licensor against any claims or liabilities resulting from the licensee's exploitation of the products and services covered by the license.

• *Accounting: Reports and Audits.* The licensor must impose certain reporting and recordkeeping procedures on the licensee in order to ensure an accurate accounting for periodic royalty payments. Further, the licensor should reserve the right to audit the records of the licensee in the event of a dispute or discrepancy, along with provisions as to who will be responsible for the cost of the audit in the event of an understatement.

• *Duties to Preserve and Protect Intellectual Property.* The obligations of the licensee, its agents and employees to preserve and protect the confidential nature and acknowledge the ownership of the intellectual property being disclosed in connection with the license agreement must be carefully defined. Any required notices or legends which must be included on products or materials distributed in connection with the license agreement (such as to the status of the relationship or actual owner of the intellectual property) are also described in this section.

• *Technical Assistance: Training and Support*. Any obligations of the licensor to assist the licensee in the development or exploitation of the subject matter being licensed are included in this section of the agreement. The assistance may take the form of personal services or documents and records. Either way, any fees due to the licensor for such support services, which are over and above the initial license and ongoing royalty fee, must also be addressed.

• *Warranties of the Licensor*. A prospective licensee may demand that the licensor provide certain representations and warranties in the license agreement. These may include warranties regarding the ownership of the technology, such as absence of any known infringements of the technology, or restrictions on the ability to license the technology, or that the technology has the features, capabilities, and characteristics previously represented in the negotiations.

• *Infringements*. The license agreement should contain procedures under which the licensee must notify the licensor of any known or suspected direct or indirect infringements of the subject matter being licensed. The responsibilities for the cost of protecting and defending the technology should also be specified in this section.

Growth Strategy Alternative #4: Distributorships and Dealerships

Many growing product-oriented companies choose to bring their wares to the marketplace through independent third-party distributors and dealerships. This type of arrangement is commonly used by manufacturers of electronic and stereo equipment, computer hardware and software, sporting goods, medical equipment, and automobile parts and accessories. These dealers are generally more difficult to control than a licensee or franchisee, and as a result the agreement between the manufacturer and the distributor will be much more informal than a franchise or license agreement.

In developing distributor and dealership agreements, growing companies must be careful to avoid being included within the broad definition of a "franchise" under the Federal Trade Commission Trade regulation rule 436, which would require the preparation of a disclosure document. To avoid such a classification, the agreement must impose minimal controls over the dealer, the sale of products must be at bona fide wholesale prices without any form of initiation fee and provide minimal assistance in the marketing or management of the dealer's business. A well-drafted distributorship agreement should, however, address the following key issues:

- What is the scope of the appointment? Which products is the dealer authorized to distribute and under what conditions? What is the scope, if any, of the exclusive territory to be granted to the distributor? To what extent will product, vendor, customer or geographic restrictions be applicable?
- What activities will the distributor be expected to perform in terms of manufacturing, sales, marketing, display, billing, market research, maintenance of books and records, storage, training, installation, support, and servicing?
- What obligations will the distributor have to preserve and protect the intellectual property of the manufacturer?
- What right, if any, will the distributor have to modify or enhance the manufacturer's warranties, terms of sale, credit policies, or refund procedures?
- What advertising literature, technical and marketing support, training seminars, or special promotions will be provided by the manufacturer to enhance the performance of the distributor?
- What sales or performance quotas will be imposed on the dealer as a condition to its right to continue to distribute the manufacturer's products or services? What are the rights and remedies of the manufacturer if the dealer fails to meet these performance standards?
- What is the term of the agreement and under what conditions can it be terminated? How will post-termination transactions be handled?

Differences Between Distributors and Sales Representatives

Distributors are often confused with sales representatives. There are many critical differences which must be understood. Typically, a distributor buys the product from the manufacturer, at wholesale prices, with the intent to resell to a retailer or directly to the customer. There is usually no actual fee paid by the distributor for the grant of the distributorship and the distributor will typically be permitted to carry competitive products. The distributor is expected to maintain some retail location or showroom where the manufacturer's products are displayed. The distributor must maintain its own inventory storage and warehousing capabilities. The distributor looks to the manufacturer for technical support, advertising contributions, supportive repair, maintenance and service policies, new product training, volume discounts, favorable payment and return policies and brand name recognition. The manufacturer looks to the distributor for in-store and local promotion, adequate inventory controls, financial stability, preferred display and stocking, prompt payment and qualified sales personnel.

Although the distributorship network offers a viable alternative to franchising, it is not a panacea. The management and control of the distributors may be even more difficult than that involved in franchising (especially without the benefit of a comprehensive franchise agreement) and the termination of these relationships is regulated by many state and anti-termination statutes.

The sales representative or sales agent, is an independent marketing resource for the manufacturer. The sales representative, unlike the distributor, does not typically actually purchase the merchandise for resale, nor are they typically required to maintain inventories or retail locations or engage in any special price promotions unless instigated by the manufacturer.

Index